The Teacher Team Leader Handbook

Simple Habits to Transform Collaboration in a PLC at Work®

CHAD M.V. **DUMAS**

Foreword by Ken Williams

Solution Tree | Press
a division of
Solution Tree

Copyright © 2025 by Chad M. V. Dumas

Materials appearing here are copyrighted. With one exception, all rights are reserved. Readers may reproduce only those pages marked "Reproducible." Otherwise, no part of this book may be reproduced or transmitted in any form or by any means (electronic, photocopying, recording, or otherwise) without prior written permission of the publisher.

555 North Morton Street
Bloomington, IN 47404
800.733.6786 (toll free) / 812.336.7700
FAX: 812.336.7790

email: info@SolutionTree.com
SolutionTree.com

Visit **go.SolutionTree.com/PLCbooks** to download the free reproducibles in this book.

Printed in the United States of America

Library of Congress Cataloging-in-Publication Data

Names: Dumas, Chad M. V., author.
Title: The teacher team leader handbook : simple habits to transform collaboration in a PLC at work / Chad M.V. Dumas.
Description: Bloomington, IN : Solution Tree Press, 2025. | Includes bibliographical references and index.
Identifiers: LCCN 2024013716 (print) | LCCN 2024013717 (ebook) | ISBN 9781960574985 (paperback) | ISBN 9781960574992 (ebook)
Subjects: LCSH: Professional learning communities. | Teachers--Professional relationships. | Educational leadership.
Classification: LCC LB1731 .D79 2025 (print) | LCC LB1731 (ebook) | DDC 371.1--dc23/eng/20240515
LC record available at https://lccn.loc.gov/2024013716
LC ebook record available at https://lccn.loc.gov/2024013717

Solution Tree
Jeffrey C. Jones, CEO
Edmund M. Ackerman, President

Solution Tree Press
Publisher: Kendra Slayton
Associate Publisher: Todd Brakke
Director of Acquisitions: Hilary Goff
Editorial Director: Laurel Hecker
Art Director: Rian Anderson
Managing Editor: Sarah Ludwig
Copy Chief: Jessi Finn
Production Editor: Gabriella Jones-Monserrate
Copy Editor: Charlotte Jones
Proofreader: Jessica Starr
Text and Cover Designer: Laura Cox
Content Development Specialist: Amy Rubenstein
Associate Editor: Elijah Oates
Editorial Assistant: Madison Chartier

To all those striving, day by day, to be and do better.

Acknowledgments

None of us are where we are because of our own volition. We all stand on the shoulders of giants. While the list of those to acknowledge is long, at the risk of inadvertently leaving some out, let me identify a few groups and individuals.

I have the blessing of serving with incredible educators almost every day of the week. As of this writing, you're in about half of the U.S. states, and even internationally. I hope you know who you are, and I learn from you every time I am with you (and some of your stories are included). Some of you pushed for me to write this book, and your encouragement and prompting is so very much appreciated.

Colleagues with whom I have worked over the years have and continue to push me. These include my time in Lincoln and work at the ESU in Kearney, the principalship in Gibbon and director of "CIA" in Hastings, the executive director role in Ames and teaching higher education courses at UNK, and of course all of the relationships and connections in between. The love, caring, and support that you continue to show–through phone calls, emails, social media, and even snail mail–means the world to me.

The Solution Tree family is unlike any organization that I've been part of. Jeff Jones, the humble and caring CEO, sets the tone for how everyone is treated. Of course, many thanks go to the entire author and editing team who helped get this book to fruition, including Claudia Wheatley, Kendra Slayton, Laurel Hecker, and the heavy lift of Gabi Jones-Monserrate, not to mention the PD team, including Alex Schwartz and Danielle McDonald. Fellow associates who push my thinking, share resources, and are just plain good people: thank you. You know who you are. And even with this, doesn't it seem ironic that I'm unable to express my gratitude for a publishing company using words?

Learning Forward provided an opportunity to craft a course with Kendall Zoller and Kathy Gross that helped me clarify (unknowingly at the time) my thinking for this book, pushing me to become better at my craft. Frankly, the learning, guiding, mentoring and, dare I say, friendship provided by Kendall (author of *The Choreography of Presenting: The 7 Essential Abilities of Presenters*; Zoller, 2024) forms the very foundation of this work. Without his support, I would be far less skilled in what I do, and unable to as coherently express the concepts laid out herein. And Elisa B. MacDonald (2023), author of *Intentional Moves: How Skillful*

v

Team Leaders Impact Learning, whose treatises on skillful team leadership and contributions to this manuscript are most assuredly appreciated.

Ken Williams' coaching helped me make sure that the work of teams stays focused on the main thing: ensuring that all students attain team-identified, grade-level essential outcomes. We are not here for ourselves, as adults, but are here to guarantee learning for each and every child in our classrooms. His guidance and gracious foreword make sure that this remains the priority of teams and the teacher team leader.

The journey to get this book in your hands has been far more rigorous than most. A small handful of people know the intensity of the challenges associated with it, and I would be remiss if I did not call out Allison Kerndt and Wendy Marsh by name for their role in getting it to you. It is not an understatement to say that this book simply would not be available without their expertise.

As the saying goes, behind every successful man is a strong woman. Dawn is the intellectual property design and development guru for our work. Her research, thoughtfulness, questioning, and insight make me better. And our two boys, Diel and Kalim, show genuine interest and support for this work. Finally, my family, starting with my parents, Ernie and Sandy, who were educators themselves, and continuing to Danelle and my brother, Jamie, looking down from above, who all continue to support me: Thank you.

Solution Tree Press would like to thank the following reviewers:

Kendra Bell
  Education Consultant
  Peoria, Arizona

Caitlin Fox
  Instructor and Practicum Facilitator
  Red Deer Polytechnic
  Red Deer, Alberta, Canada

Kristin Gellinck-Frye
  Director Special Programs
  Westside USD
  Quartz Hill, California

Benjamin J. Kitslaar
  Principal
  West Side Elementary School
  Elkhorn, Wisconsin

Jennifer Rasmussen
  Literacy Specialist and Instructional
    Service Director
  CESA 4
  West Salem, Wisconsin

Allison Zamarripa
  Literacy Instructional Specialist
  Pasadena Independent School District
  Pasadena, Texas

Visit **go.SolutionTree.com/PLCbooks** to download the free reproducibles in this book.

Table of Contents

About the Author xi

Foreword xiii

Introduction 1

    Professional Learning Community 2

    Teacher Teams as Engines of Improvement 3

        The Shift from Teacher to Teacher Team Leader 4

        Skills Needed to Collaborate and Inquire 5

    About This Book 6

        Part I: Teacher Team Leader Foundations 7

        Part II: Teacher Team Leader Actions 7

        How to Approach This Book 9

Part I: Teacher Team Leader Foundations 11

1 Defining Your Role 13

    Why Your Role Is Important 14

    What Your Role Is Not .15

    Major Characteristics of a Team 16

    Your Responsibilities .17

        Responsibility 1: Make It Safe 17

        Responsibility 2: Build Capacity 23

        Responsibility 3: Do the Work 26

    Conclusion 27

2 Understanding Your Approach 29

    Assumptions 29

        Assumption 1: People Do the Best That They Can 30

        Assumption 2: You Can Only Control You 31

        Assumption 3: Behavior Communicates 31

        Assumption 4: People Want to Get Stuff Done 31

        Assumption 5: Conflict Is Good 32

    Intentions 32

viii THE TEACHER TEAM LEADER HANDBOOK

Mindsets 34

Mindset 1: To See What Others Don't (Yet) See in Themselves 35

Mindset 2: To Be Humble With a Posture of Learning 36

Mindset 3: To Spread the Contagion of Joy 37

Role and Approach 37

What You Do: Moves and Techniques 38

What We Do Together: Strategies .39

Category Labels 40

Conclusion 41

Part II: Teacher Team Leader Actions 43

3 Getting Started 45

You Do It Yourself 46

Group Rapport 47

Breathing 50

Laughter and Humor 52

Pause 54

Third Point 57

We Do It Together 58

Physical Arrangement 59

Norms 60

Roles 62

Inclusion 65

Landing Page 66

Outcomes 69

Running Agenda Template 76

Putting It All Together 79

Possible Next Steps 81

Summary Reflective Questions 83

Conclusion 83

Chapter 3: You Do It Yourself Planning and Reflection Tool 84

Chapter 3: We Do It Together Planning and Reflection Tool 85

4 Gaining Momentum 87

You Do It Yourself 87

Paraphrase 88

Questions 92

Approachable and Credible Voice 96

Gestures and Words of Inclusion .98

And (Not But) 100

Break Eye Contact 102

We Do It Together 104

    Plan the Work, Then Work the Plan 105

    Celebrations 107

    Write It Down 110

    Others as Experts 111

    Sentence Stems 113

    Who Will Do What by When 114

Putting It All Together 115

    Possible Next Steps 118

    Summary Reflective Questions 119

Conclusion 119

Chapter 4: You Do It Yourself Planning and Reflection Tool 120

Chapter 4: We Do It Together Planning and Reflection Tool 121

5 Overcoming Obstacles 123

You Do It Yourself 123

    Specificity 124

    Decontaminate Space 126

    Attribution 129

    Individual Rapport 131

    Anonymize It 134

    Fourth Point 137

    Mode of Communication 138

We Do It Together 141

    Data Usage 141

    Self-Assessment 143

    Fist to Five 146

    Forced Choice 148

Putting It All Together 150

    Possible Next Steps 151

    Summary Reflective Questions 154

Conclusion 154

Chapter 5: You Do It Yourself Planning and Reflection Tool 155

Chapter 5: We Do It Together Planning and Reflection Tool 156

6 Refining Your Skills 159

You Do It Yourself 159

    Frozen Gesture 160

    Beat Gesture 162

    Hand Position 163

    Whisper 165

    I Interrupt Myself 167

Conclusion 168

Chapter 6: You Do It Yourself Planning and Reflection Tool 169

7 Addressing Challenges From the Field 171

Challenge: The Team Is Too Large or Too Small 172

Challenge: Members Fail to Follow Norms 173

1. Team Members Didn't Develop or Have Voice in Norm Creation, So They Don't Actually Reflect Team Members' Needs 173

2. The Team Does Not Regularly Revisit and Revise Norms 174

3. Individuals Do Not Hold Each Other Accountable to the Norms . . 174

Challenge: The Team Isn't Following the Agenda 176

1. Not Following Norms 177

2. Roles and Timekeeping to Keep Everyone on Task 177

3. Clarity of Why the Time as a Team Is Important 177

4. Clarity of the Work That Needs to Be Done 178

Challenge: The Team Fails to Follow Through on Decisions 178

1. Clarity of What the Decision Is 178

2. Clarity of Who Is Responsible for Implementation 179

3. Timelines for Implementation 179

4. Processes for Reporting Back 179

5. Memory 180

6. Lack of Trust in the Team 180

Challenge: One Member Dominates the Conversation 180

1. They Are a Verbal Processor 181

2. They Are Unsure of Their Own Knowledge or Skills 182

3. They Aren't Self-Aware of Their Own Domination of the Conversation 182

4. They Don't Feel Heard (or Even Valued) 182

Challenge: One Member Doesn't Engage in the Conversation 183

1. They Are an Internal Processor 183

2. They Are Unsure of Their Own Knowledge or Skills 183

3. They Aren't Self-Aware of Their Own Silence 184

4. They Don't Feel Heard or Even Valued Anyway 184

Challenge: The Work Meanders and Doesn't Gain Momentum 184

1. Clarify the Importance of the Team in Improving Each Other's Practice and Results for Students 185

2. Clarify What the Work of the Team Is 185

3. Establish an Overall Timeline for the Year 185

4. Align Agenda With the Overall Plan 186

5. Set Deadlines for Accomplishing the Work 186

Challenge: Colleagues Listen to Ideas, But Don't Change 186

If Issues Persist After Attempts to Solve Them 188

Conclusion 188

Epilogue 191

References and Resources 193

Index 199

About the Author

Chad M. V. Dumas is a Solution Tree Professional Learning Community at Work®, Priority Schools, RTI at Work®, and Assessment Collaborative associate and international consultant, presenter, and award-winning researcher. His focus is on building capacity for self, team, and system improvement. Having been a successful teacher, principal, central office administrator, professional developer, and consultant in a variety of school districts, he brings his passion, expertise, and skills to his writing and speaking as he engages participants in meaningful and practical learning. Chad offers readers and audiences educational research, engaging stories, hands-on tools, and useful knowledge and skills they can implement immediately.

The results of Chad's work speak for themselves. One district was identified as "Persistently Lowest Achieving" on his arrival, but within a few years, multiple schools were recognized as National PLC Models for improving student learning. Chad has served on and led accreditation visits for Cognia around the United States and world, presented nationally and internationally, collaborated with school boards, intermediate service agencies, state departments of education, and professional associations.

Dumas received a bachelor's degree in music education from the University of Nebraska, a master's degree in educational administration from Concordia University, and a doctorate in educational administration from the University of Nebraska.

To book Chad M. V. Dumas for professional development, contact pd@solutiontree.com.

Foreword

By Ken Williams

There is an elephant in the room. My ability to see elephants in a room is both a gift and a curse. The gift speaks to my level of awareness and insight provided by what I see. The curse is that I cannot unsee the elephant, and therefore am compelled to act. I didn't drag the elephant into the room; Chad Dumas did. The elephant of which I speak does not live in the title of Chad's book, *The Teacher Team Leader Handbook*. After all, collaborative teacher teams are embedded in the DNA of every school in North America and are the engine driving the right work in a professional learning community (PLC). Chad could've written a generic book full of tools, templates, tips, pithy anecdotes, and no elephants. But he chose a different path. The elephant in the room is in his book's subtitle, *Simple Habits to Transform Collaboration in a PLC at Work®*. The elephant is wearing an elephant-sized graphic T-shirt with the book's subtitle stretched across his side. There's no way to miss it. The subtitle has moved the honor of writing this foreword from an easy layup to a mission-driven endeavor that begins within the soul.

I met Chad in 2020 after reading his book *Let's Put the C in PLC: A Practical Guide for School Leaders*. A devoted missionary of the PLC at Work process, I felt an instant kinship and reached out to him. We met and talked about the book and our work as consultants, and as fate would have it, I was completing a book manuscript of my own, and Chad generously shared the details of his publishing journey. His guidance was instrumental in me getting my book *Ruthless Equity: Disrupt the Status Quo and Ensure Learning for All Students* published.

When you spend time with Chad, it won't be long before you conclude that he is one of the nicest people you've ever met. He is warm and thoughtful. He's one of those people who make you want to be better around them.

But don't let these descriptors fool you into believing that his warmth and thoughtfulness are any forms of weakness, because they are not.

Dr. Chad Dumas embraces hard things.

Let's get back to the elephant he dragged in . . .

In the book's introduction, Chad cites a study done by the Bill & Melinda Gates Foundation in 2014. The study noted that the most hated term in professional development is "professional learning community," or "PLC." In some contexts, an eleven-year-old study might appear dated. However, having worked with hundreds of schools and districts over a seventeen-year coaching and consulting career, it pains me to acknowledge that the term PLC may be hated even more now than it was in 2014.

Let's go back in time . . .

For over a decade, I got to sit at the feet of Dr. Rick DuFour, Dr. Bob Eaker, and Becky DuFour, the architects of the PLC at Work process. This journey, which led to transformative leadership and student learning results, began in 2000 with a professional learning workshop facilitated by Rick DuFour. At the end of that three-hour workshop, the picture he painted was so compelling that I wanted a ticket on the bus he was driving. I couldn't have told you five things about PLCs, because I was trying to manage the fire inside me around the why. Dr. DuFour was a man on a mission to teach anyone willing to submit how to build a learning-for-all culture, where not only the right kids (written with dripping sarcasm) win, but all kids win. I had little knowledge of the PLC process and lots of questions. I wasn't ready to run through a wall for professional learning communities; I was ready to run through a wall because of the mission to transform school results. PLCs were not the mission; they were the vehicle we drove to achieve the mission.

I was at a crossroads in my career because I was becoming discouraged hearing all the talk about why students can't learn. And then this man spoke only of why we can instead of why they can't. I was in, and immersed myself in the PLC at Work process! PLC remains the most effective vehicle to ensure equity, excellence, and achievement for all students, regardless of background. So how does a process like this devolve into the most hated term in all of education?

Here's how . . .

The System has betrayed us.

The power of professional learning communities is in how we lean into teachers' collective brilliance to ensure learning for students. Once essential learning outcomes have been identified, there are no more discussions of "Can they?" or "Can't they?" because essential means every student is required to master the standard to have success at the next grade level, in the next course, on the high-stakes assessment (where applicable), and in life beyond the K–12 system.

Since the end of the global COVID-19 pandemic, the System has made it its mission to excuse students from learning by focusing on perceived student ailments, so-called disadvantages, and a deficit mindset while overtly ignoring educator talents, skills, will, creativity, and training. The System is unhinged in its efforts to present students to teachers as damaged goods before the first day of school.

This organized offensive has eroded teacher efficacy and has reduced our profession to that of well-compensated victims, martyrs, and charity workers. School leaders constantly ask how they can get teachers to reflect more on their practice. My response to them is that if you tried to hold me accountable for the results of a box of goods you presented as damaged, I wouldn't be reflective about my practice either. No teacher comes to the field expecting the System to communicate that a student's background, the language they speak or don't speak, their parents, their parents' income, their neighborhood, or their race could have more impact than their collective expertise. For every message you read like this one, the System sends teachers twenty messages that say students arrive as damaged goods. The System is consumed with students' brokenness, not the collaborative brilliance of teachers. As a result, the work of PLCs in schools has moved from ensuring every student masters grade-level essential learning outcomes to having rudderless teams with no tangible outcomes and defining success not by results but by adult activity, effort, and intention.

And now, so-called PLC meetings have evolved into disheartening discussions about student ailments, why they can't, and little talk of the collective brilliance of teachers and why they can.

There's no denying that my relationship with Chad contributed to my agreeing to write this foreword. However, by far, the most important factor was that Chad is explicit about the mission of the collaborative team in a professional learning community. This book is about something other than managing a team of teachers who don't want to be at this meeting anyway. This book isn't about finding skills, tools, and tips to help team leaders manage meetings on the road to nowhere. This book isn't about trying to numb the pain of PLC meetings that result in no payoff. This book is about empowering team leaders to organize the team to ensure every student masters grade-level essential learning outcomes in every course and content area.

Without explicit discussion of the work of PLC teams, this book's content wouldn't matter, because it would be akin to rearranging the deck chairs on the *Titanic*.

Chad explicitly discusses the measurable outcomes of a professional learning community, and in this age of excusing learning based on student background, I'm proud of him and honored to write this foreword.

The Teacher Team Leader Handbook: Simple Habits to Transform Collaboration in a PLC at Work is a Swiss Army Knife for teacher team leaders! Aside from the standard blade, some versions of this multi-tooled pocketknife have a screwdriver, a nail file, tweezers, pliers, scissors, a fish scaler, a ballpoint pen, and more. You get the point. Swiss Army Knife owners don't use all the tools whenever they pull out theirs. Owners use what they need in a given situation, and all the other tools remain available, as needed.

Chad's book provides Swiss Army Knife–like tools for leaders. Barely experienced leaders and very experienced leaders will find value in this book. I recommend every teacher team leader read the first two chapters, as Chad lays a solid foundation for the role. For the new leader, these two chapters provide guidance. For experienced leaders, they provide an opportunity to calibrate and reset, and every leader benefits from his important tools and reminders. From there, the book is a practical resource full of tools, tips, protocols, and guidance.

One of my favorite quotes comes from *Jane Eyre* author Charlotte Brontë: "Let your performance do the thinking." The first critical question of a PLC at Work asks, "What do we want every student to know and be able to do?" Once you answer it, divide expected mastery into time frames. You can use six-week sprints, a nine-week quarter, or multiple fifteen-day cycles as in Maria Nielsen's (2024) book, *The 15-Day Challenge*. Once this is done, then the mission is set. The team's mission is to ensure every student masters grade-level essential learning outcomes. As the teacher team leader, everything you do serves that mission. Chad Dumas has provided every tool you need and then some to accomplish the task. He covers every base with the guidance of his expertise and his tools, templates, and protocols.

Emotional intelligence moves? Covered.

Logistic moves? Covered.

Techniques for facilitation? Covered.

Establishing protocols? Covered.

Facilitating? Covered.

Addressing concerns about teammates? Covered.

And so much more!

Without explicit clarity around the mission and work of a PLC, the teacher team leader role can feel like an unwanted burden—a sentence of sorts. Chad Dumas's explicit clarity around the mission of a PLC teacher team and his tools, tips, and expert guidance transform the role into a purposeful responsibility. The mission of the collaborative teacher team is to organize to ensure every student masters grade-level essential learning outcomes. *The Teacher Team Leader Handbook: Simple Habits to Transform Collaboration in a PLC at*

Work empowers team leaders to effectively guide their teams to deliver on the promise of equity, excellence, and achievement for all students, regardless of background. Chad Dumas's book will help make your PLC work meaningful.

-Ken Williams, Educator, Consultant, and Author of *Ruthless Equity*

To begin by always thinking of love as an action rather than a feeling is one way in which anyone using the word in this manner automatically assumes accountability and responsibility.

—bell hooks

Introduction

At the first staff meeting of the year, the building principal directs all staff to go to the teacher's lounge and sign up for a committee. A first-year teacher, fresh out of college and just over twenty-three years old, follows this directive. "School Improvement" looks interesting enough. So, he writes his name down with the other ten or twelve currently signed up. The meeting starts, and in short order, the committee needs to decide who will chair meetings moving forward. For some reason, this young man is selected to co-chair the work of the school improvement team. There's just one problem: He has no idea how to be a co-chair of the school improvement team, nor does he have any significant leadership experience.

That was me: completely and totally unprepared to lead learning for adult colleagues. Here I was, a non-core content area educator with no clue what school improvement actually was, and I was expected to be a teacher team leader. As a music teacher, my content area expertise in any other area was simply inadequate to advance the work of teams. Other members of the committee did know what school improvement meant, so I relied on their experience and input to make decisions. I had to learn quickly, so I worked to gain experience and climb through the ranks. Eventually, I became a high school principal and facilitated the transition from a dilapidated, century-old building to a new, $19 million facility. A couple of years later, I was leading the curriculum, instruction, and assessment processes for a mid-size, high-poverty, diverse district designated by the state as "Persistently Lowest Achieving." Within a few years, this district had five out of seven schools identified as national models.

While in some of my past positions, specifically principal and central office administrator, I may have had positional authority or power to make decisions, I always remembered that there was a time I didn't know anything at all about authority and had to rely on those around me. Indeed, even with positional authority, always relying on that authority isn't effective. Developing skills of influence, on the other hand, is.

As psychologist Julia DiGangi (2023) explains, commanding other people to behave in a way that aligns with your interests while denying theirs cannot create strong teams, precisely because it goes against the way human brains work. While certain situations require command energy (military exercises or stopping your kid from running into a busy street, for example), it rarely works in most realms of our lives (DiGangi, 2023). What team leaders need and what I have had to develop, over the course of the past quarter century, are skills of influence. Without the benefits of long-standing experience, positional authority, or content expertise, I have had to cultivate other ways to be able to increase the effectiveness of teams. Eventually, I came to understand that certain skills of influence are helpful in creating and sustaining an effective educational team. Thus, this book is a compilation of those simple, go-to moves, techniques, and strategies that will help teacher team leaders successfully navigate their roles to transform collaboration in a Professional Learning Community at Work®. These are actions that any person can take to improve a team's functioning.

> **These are actions that any person can take to improve a team's functioning.**

It would not be hyperbole to say that learning about and applying these habits have been revolutionary in my life. None of them are difficult, yet they will all have an incredible impact on you and your colleagues if you regularly practice and apply them. When you learn to see the right kind of potential in teacher teams and lead them accordingly, you will be able to transform collaboration for schoolwide change. The first step is to ensure that we have clarity about what a professional learning community is.

Professional Learning Community

At the foundation of this text is a term that is used frequently in the educational realm: professional learning community, or PLC. You are likely familiar with the definition (and, if not, please see p. 14 of DuFour et al, 2024) and implications of this term. Because it is foundational to the work of a teacher team leader, let's take a moment and examine the three words that comprise this concept.

Professional. Being a professional involves engaging in a career that involves some sort of prolonged training. Further, there is a knowledge base and language that is specific to a profession that is not part of another profession. Think of the jargon associated with lawyers or doctors. And think of our jargon, as well: objectives, learning targets, formative assessment, summative assessment, instructional framework, and more. The list could go on for pages, and that doesn't even include all of our alphabet soup acronyms! We, as a profession, have a knowledge base with terms and language that is specific to our work, and it is this knowledge base and language that partially keeps the work at a professional level.

Learning. Ours is the learning profession. We are focused on learning for students, and this also requires learning for adults. In a professional learning community, it is the adults who are focused on learning, because "when adults learn more, students learn more" (Owens, 2023). This concept is not called a student learning community. *We* are the professionals who are learning. The impact is on the students, but the work is on us. *We* are the ones who are engaging in learning together. Peter Senge (1990), organizational expert and author of *The Fifth Discipline*, notes that learning is at the heart of being a human. It is through learning that we are able to do that which we were previously unable to do, to recreate ourselves, and to reimagine the world around us and how we relate to it. And that, as human beings, we hunger for this deep learning that transforms our thinking, understanding, and action. Such is the learning of a professional learning community.

Peter Block (2008), author of *Community: The Structure of Belonging*, notes that one of the key challenges for our teams "is to transform the isolation and self-interest within our communities into connectedness and caring for the whole" (p. 1). Essentially, this means that when a group of people come together, they become more than just the sum of the parts. They become something that is greater than each individual, and this requires a new way of thinking, being, and doing in order to become a team. In order to build community.

Taken together, the term "professional learning community" is much more than a group of people meeting together on a regular basis. It is a group of professionals, those who have expertise in their field as educators. Their focus is on their own professional learning to guarantee student learning. And they do it together, in a community that transcends "isolation and self-interest" to become one where we recognize and leverage our "connectedness and caring" for each other (Block, 2008, p. 1). This is the vision of a PLC to which this book aspires.

> **As human beings, we hunger for this deep learning that transforms our thinking, understanding, and action.**

Teacher Teams as Engines of Improvement

While there is no single answer to the question of how to improve schools, the most promising strategy for improving teaching and learning is the implementation of PLC principles and processes (DuFour et al., 2021). Without a doubt, this approach has a solid track record with decades of experience improving student learning. And this path works for the long term, with teacher teams as the engine of this collaborative process (Kramer, n.d.).

The concept of professional learning communities is not new, finding its origins as early as the 1960s (allthingsplc, n.d.a.). The subsequent proliferation of the concept, due in large part to the work of Bob Eaker, Rick DuFour, Becky DuFour, and others, has made it so that groups of teachers working together have become more and more of a norm (DuFour et al., 2024).

As part of this expansion of the term and concept, efforts have focused on helping these groups move beyond simply collegial groups to become collaborative teams that improve their own practice and the results of students (allthingsplc, n.d.b.).

Yet teams struggle. A study conducted by the Bill & Melinda Gates Foundation in 2014 noted that the single most hated term in all of professional development is "professional learning community," or "PLC." Yikes! And while that dislike is usually based in misconceptions or poor implementation, my experience with educators all over the United States suggests that the dreaded connotation of the term persists. This negative perception is partly because teams have a variety of obstacles to effectiveness. These include a lack of focus, wasted time, inefficiency, lack of productivity, a reliance on outside directives, and more. All of these can, and many times do, lead to frustration, apathy, and even resentment. This is where the vital role of the team leader comes in advancing the concept and practice of becoming a PLC.

Now, please don't get me wrong: As noted earlier, there are decades of research and practice and solid evidence in schools and districts around the United States and the world that confirm the surest way to improve student learning is to become a PLC (DuFour et al., 2024). Without a doubt, when implemented *well*, it is a highly effective model. And because teacher teams are the engine of the process, teacher team leadership is foundational to doing PLC right.

The Shift from Teacher to Teacher Team Leader

The team leader is someone who is supposed to be empowered to maximize team effectiveness. It seems that designated school leaders (which I was for many years) make an assumption that if you are a quality teacher, or respected and liked by the staff, then you will make an excellent teacher team leader. With this assumption at play, we metaphorically throw teachers into teams and say, "Go be an effective team leader!" Unfortunately, this does not work all of the time. Most teachers are not prepared to lead adult learning. While many of the skills of an excellent teacher are similar to those of a team leader, they are not an exact match. Indeed, the most amazing teachers are sometimes ill-equipped to serve as a team leader.

The skills of relationship building, clarity around content, and the use of instructional and assessment strategies are deeply ingrained in the work of a teacher, yet the shift toward using these skills in working with adults is significant. For starters, relationship building, for the purpose of improving practice, is different with adults than with students. If one goes about building relationships with adults like a teacher does with students, the team leader could easily be perceived as condescending or manipulative. While well-intentioned by the team leader, this perception most certainly does not help with the interpersonal relationships needed to move the team forward.

A second area where amazing teachers may struggle in leading colleagues is with clarity around content. To be clear, the team leader is not expected to be an expert in the content being learned by the team itself. In a PLC, the content being learned is the actual work of the team. Further, this is typically codeveloped as a team in the moment. If the team leader is lucky, they are generally just one step ahead of their colleagues. This one step ahead only happens *if* they have been part of a training prior to leading their team. For example, the team leader may have learned about how to unpack standards in a one hour meeting only the week before leading their own team in doing this work. And if they are unlucky, they may not have had the opportunity to engage in the process in advance while still being expected to lead the work. The team leader is by no means an expert in this content like they are with the content they teach their students.

Finally, the individual classroom teacher is typically solely responsible for selecting, planning, implementing, and modifying daily instructional practices and day-to-day assessment strategies. In a learning team, the team makes decisions about essential unit outcomes, specific learning targets, and how the team will commonly assess those learning targets leading up to the commonly held end-of-unit assessment. A team leader who does all this work for the team will not build the team's capacity, which is one of the leader's primary responsibilities. In other words, in a classroom, the individual teacher is doing all of the daily decision making, and on a team, the work of the team leader is more at a macro level. These skills may not match. So while a teacher team leader may be absolutely amazing in the classroom, and many of the concepts transfer between classroom and team, the team leader likely needs to add to their skillset to be effective.

Skills Needed to Collaborate and Inquire

Unfortunately, no one ever taught us how to collaborate or even that we need to collaborate. In our education preparation programs, we learned content to teach and skills to teach it. We prepared really well for our independence in a classroom. Many of us are truly masters at our craft but are unaware of how we should function when working alongside other independent masters of their craft. Among other factors, success in teams comes from learning social, emotional, and interpersonal communication skills, such as the following.

- How to work with others in meaningful ways to challenge our practice

- How to develop strong, meaningful, interdependent relationships with adult colleagues based on sound communication science and brain-based research

- How to maximize our own and each others' effectiveness and efficiency when we come together as a group

In order to accomplish the above, team members and team leaders need certain knowledge, skills, and dispositions. These habits allow teams to access each other's expertise. And because the role of the teacher team leader is paramount in this endeavor, this text will focus on what the teacher team leader needs to know and be able to do in order to draw out from each other their best.

As you engage in this text, you will learn about lots of specific skills that will lead to successful collaboration and inquiry. However, your skills are not enough to transform collaboration; the work of improving the effectiveness of a team begins with who you are as a person. Success as a teacher team leader begins with clarity around concepts like the following.

- What's the job of the teacher team leader?
- How should you approach your own assumptions about the work of the team and your intentions?
- What are effective mindsets to employ in leading the team?

With this clarity in mind, then, the skills needed for collaboration can be used to maximize team effectiveness. It requires both clarity around who you are in leading the work, your being, and the skillful implementation of skills, your doing.

About This Book

This book is an attempt to demystify and make more widely known and used some simple ways to increase team leader effectiveness, and, thus, team effectiveness, by developing interpersonal communication skills for a healthy and thriving learning team. Teacher team leaders, this book is for you. The purpose is to build the knowledge and skills of teacher team leaders to be a catalyst for helping teams get more done in less time with greater joy; to truly become the engine that drives the most promising strategy for improving teaching and, more to the point, student learning; and to transform collaboration.

One lens through which you can approach this text is by actionably going about building and strengthening positive relationships and community in your team. The work herein is largely influenced by a handful of people and their work: authors Kendall Zoller (2019, 2021, 2022, 2024), Bob Garmston and Bruce Wellman (2016), Elisa B. MacDonald (2023), Bob Garmston and Carolyn McKanders (2022), Michael Grinder (2018), Richard and Rebecca DuFour and colleagues (2024), and consultants Toni Prickett, Sue Presler, Michael Dolcemascolo, and Art Costa. They laid the foundation, and I have built on their work to apply it directly and easily to teacher team leaders. Some of the moves, techniques, and strategies are original to my own experience and thinking. Most come from their masterful expositions and modeling, and I have organized them in such a way as to make implementation easier for the teacher team leader. Additionally, I have created simple descriptions, together with tools, reflective questions, and next level tips, to assist in that implementation. The book is divided into two parts: (1) Teacher Team Leader Foundations and (2) Teacher Team Leader Actions. They are organized as follows.

Part I: Teacher Team Leader Foundations

Part I of this book lays the groundwork for your internal state by defining your role, your key responsibilities, helpful assumptions to employ, and required mindsets for collaborative success.

Chapter 1 starts by outlining what the role is and why it's important, then clarifies the three key responsibilities of a teacher team leader (two of which are rarely, if ever, talked about, although they are implied in the work of the team leader) so that the team can ensure that students learn the small handful of grade-level essential outcomes identified by the team.

Chapter 2 homes in on the assumptions and mindsets that must be cultivated in ourselves to become more effective. This chapter also provides a brief description of the differences between moves, techniques, and strategies, as I see them. While it's not necessary to memorize these, it may be helpful to distinguish between them as you gain clarity about your work as a teacher team leader.

Part II: Teacher Team Leader Actions

Part II (chapters 3 through 7) lays out the specific moves, techniques, and strategies that will help you refine your approach to being a teacher team leader. Each action is divided into two types: (1) those that you do individually and (2) those that the team does together. Because you can only control you, the chapters begin with the actions that you take as the teacher team leader. These are largely individual interpersonal communication skills necessary to build a PLC with your colleagues. While those that the team does together may, in some ways, be easier to implement, these are shared second in order to reinforce the assumption that you can only control you.

Each of the moves, techniques, and strategies includes the following.

1. **Description:** A brief description of what it is (including the impact on others when implementing this action) and why it's important.

2. **Tool:** One or more tools for implementation.

3. **Reflective questions:** Considerations for you, the team leader, to self-assess and reflect on action.

4. **Next level tips:** Next steps for those who may already use the move, technique, or strategy to take their implementation to the next level (as needed).

At the end of chapters 3 through 6, you will find reproducible tools to help you think through the application of your learning from the sections titled You Do It Yourself and We Do It Together. The tools include a list of the moves, techniques, or strategies, as well as space for you to identify which ones you will implement immediately, which ones you need to practice (and when and how you will do that), and which ones you will save for later. At the end of these chapters, under Putting It All Together, you will also find a brief vignette of a teacher team leader, questions for you to reflect on and apply the learning from the chapter, and suggestions for how several of the moves, techniques, and strategies might be used to improve the team leader's practice and the work of the team.

Chapter 3 focuses on those steps that you and the team can take to get started in improving your effectiveness. These are actions that you or the team may already take, and some small refinements might make a significant impact in improving the work of the team. Even the highest-performing teams will gain insights from these getting-started steps.

Chapter 4 contains those actions that will help build a rhythm for improving effectiveness when your team is gaining momentum. While it's not necessary to have A+ implementation of the chapter 3 approaches to get into these processes, they will most definitely help the team refine its practice and your craft as you are gaining momentum.

Chapter 5 is the place to turn when obstacles arise. Of course, you don't have to wait for those challenges to appear. You can jump right to this chapter, if you want, and start preparing yourself (and practicing!) for when those roadblocks rear their heads.

Chapter 6 is completely about you, and these are all very subtle, nonverbal actions to refine your skills in influencing others for the purpose of increasing student learning. There is no need for you to wait until all other practices are mastered before delving into this chapter, as these will help with all of the other practices when combined effectively. So jump into chapter 6 and start refining your skills!

Chapter 7 pulls much of the learning from the book together with "stories from the field" to help you when you are navigating challenges. These are real-life, challenging scenarios from teacher team leaders like you. The chapter also presents ideas for which moves, techniques, and strategies might be helpful as that particular team moves forward.

How to Approach This Book

Please know that there is no one "right" way to read this book. Some will read it front to back, and others will jump around. My suggestion is that you read chapters 1 and 2 to frame your work as a team leader. This will ground you and lay the foundation for effective use of what you find in the rest of the book. After reading chapter 1 and chapter 2, feel free to jump around as it meets your needs, or read cover to cover, implementing your learning as you go.

While the focus of this book is on teacher team leaders, these simple, go-to actions are almost universally applicable to any team. Any leader at any level (such as principals, assistant principals, district office leaders, state department of education staff, higher education faculty, and others) will become more effective by using them. Even if you are not a teacher team leader but do engage with adults, you will find utility in studying and applying the contents of this text to your setting.

You may find that many of the moves, techniques, and strategies feel clumsy when you first give them a go. Remember that teaching also felt that way back when you were in school and learning how to do it. Quite frankly, it might have felt contrived. You had to write down what you intended to do, and you had to practice it with others observing you—first with fellow students, then with a professor, and finally with students. Then you continued to learn in your daily practice until it felt and became natural.

The practices in this book are the same, and this text gives you a framework to make it work. No doubt you will derive great joy in studying this text with other teacher team leaders in a book study of some sort. Together, you can practice the actions described herein, give each other feedback, laugh at your (likely) clumsy initial attempts, and refine your practice.

My hope is that, with the application of the contents of this book, you will increase your ability to influence others for the benefit of students. Maybe the mistakes that I made through the years can be avoided as you work to improve your own and your team's effectiveness, regardless of your age and experience, positional power, or content expertise. In other words, by applying the habits shared here, you will be able to truly transform collaboration.

> **By applying the habits shared here, you will be able to truly transform collaboration.**

PART I

Teacher Team Leader Foundations

In this part of the book, you're learning about yourself, because supporting the team starts with understanding yourself. In the next two chapters, you will clarify your role as a teacher team leader. As part of this clarity, we will identify and expound on your three responsibilities, as well as offer five assumptions and three mindsets to assist with the successful execution of those responsibilities.

A team of people is not a group of people who work together. A team is a group of people who trust each other.

—Simon Sinek

CHAPTER 1

Defining Your Role

No teacher can meet the needs of every student in their classroom. Even if they could dedicate every single moment of every single day, they can't do it. It's just not possible. As educational leaders, Richard DuFour and Robert Marzano say, *"No single person* has all the knowledge, skills, and talent to lead a district, improve a school, or meet all the needs of every student in his or her classroom" (*emphasis added*, DuFour & Marzano, 2011, p. 2). None of us know enough by ourselves. Through no fault of our own, none of us can do enough when we are alone. There just isn't enough of any one person to meet the needs of every student. We need each other, and our students need all of us in different ways and at different times.

Michael Fullan (1993), an influential educational leader, reinforces this notion and takes this idea a step further: We should also ensure that we're clarifying our identities as collaborators and inquirers in our school improvement endeavors. Otherwise, he says, we're essentially tinkering with the good work happening in schools and not getting to the crux of what it takes to improve learning for students.

All of the extraordinary measures that individually amazing teachers take each and every day is "just tinkering," according to Fullan (1993), unless we get to who we are as people, as collaborators and inquirers. It's not until we get to our personal identities as *collaborators improving our practice* and *inquirers into our own and each other's* work and perspectives that we can have substantive school improvement. And your role, as a teacher team leader, in ensuring this depth of reflection on practice cannot be overstated.

In this chapter, I will help you avoid "just tinkering" by clearly articulating what your responsibilities, as a teacher team leader, are and are not. In so doing, you will explore what it takes to avoid dysfunction and instead build purposeful community. You will learn about the two most important attributes of effective teamwork, how these relate to your responsibilities, and how the rest of this text supports those conditions. Finally, we will consider the relationship of efficacy and capacity, and how you can go about building both simultaneously.

Why Your Role Is Important

> Creating a collaborative environment doesn't just magically happen.

Creating a collaborative environment doesn't just magically happen. Key individuals throughout the school have to arise to make it happen. The need for someone in a designated position of leadership within any given team has been confirmed time and time again (Greer, 2019). While a strict hierarchy of individuals with a certain level of power is not necessary, and is actually significantly correlated with negative outcomes (Greer, de Jong, Schouten, & Dannals, 2018), individuals who are charged with moving the team forward are most definitely needed. And while, by itself, simply having someone in a designated leadership role doesn't necessarily improve effectiveness, that role is clearly vital. The considerations in this book will help you in this role to improve the team's effectiveness.

Typically, in addition to meeting with administrative staff on a regular basis, teacher team leaders serve as leaders, facilitators, or liaisons of their respective grade level, course, department, or other team. The specific title of the role isn't what matters—what's important is that these individuals have an added responsibility to ensure that their team functions effectively. In the words of Teresa Rensch (2020), team leaders use facilitation as a "superpower."

Combining Rensch's (2020) notion that facilitation is a "superpower" with the concept that hierarchical leadership is negatively correlated with effectiveness (Greer et al., 2018), we find that there is a certain duality in the importance of your role. In their meta-analysis, Lindred L. Greer and colleagues (2018) note that the more ambiguous the work, the more clearly a hierarchy must be established. And the more straightforward the tasks, the less that power structures are necessary to improve team effectiveness. As a team leader, you must navigate these concepts, shifting seamlessly between the facilitation of ideas and the direction of tasks. As we'll find out later in this chapter, the completion of tasks is less important than the facilitation of ideas or the creation of psychological safety (Duhigg, 2016).

The selection of the teacher team leader is not an accident. That person is a person who someone typically recognizes as having the knowledge and skills to *ensure* effectiveness. While not necessarily being stated outright, the task of ensuring effectiveness is certainly implied, and this is a tall order, indeed!

The improvement of student learning can be directly attributed to the quality of teamwork. Consider the following logical sequence that I have laid out so far.

1. The most promising approach to improving student learning is in becoming a PLC.

2. The team is the engine of that process.

3. Your role cannot be overemphasized in ensuring team effectiveness.

What's also true is that this role cannot be a burden for you. If you are to help the team be joyful in their work, you, yourself, must be joyful. People who help others maximize their effectiveness cannot be weighed down by an understanding of the importance of the task. Indeed, if the role is a burden for you, my hope is that this book will help to lift some of that burden.

Finally, fully internalizing the responsibilities, assumptions, and mindsets together with employing the moves, techniques, and strategies shared in this book does not guarantee you will be entirely successful with all people on your team. It's OK if you need backup at some point. To be effective, you cannot internalize tension that may very well come the way of the team (and possibly even be directed at you). Which leads to . . .

What Your Role Is Not

Just as concrete examples are helpful in understanding what something is, sometimes nonexamples are equally helpful in explaining and providing clarity. A teacher team leader is *not* an administrator in teacher's clothes. You are not a manager, a spy, or a snitch. You are not invested with power *over* your colleagues, but instead come into a situation of having power *with* your colleagues. Typically, this role is one where you do not evaluate your peers (though occasionally department chairs in large schools might have this responsibility as part of their work).

What you *are* is a member of a team of teachers trying to improve their effectiveness with a laser-like focus on improving student learning (Learning Forward, 2023). Many times, you will also serve as a liaison between the team and a school or district leadership team of some sort (such as a guiding coalition, school improvement team, building leadership team, and more). You will likely be asked to facilitate the team, bring new learning to your colleagues, and to share struggles with other leaders in the school. In short, the role of the teacher team leader is to ensure the effective functioning of the team in improving student learning.

While building a PLC is about working *together* to improve our practice and results, ironically, it starts with each of us. We can learn a lot from the

> **The role of the teacher team leader is to ensure the effective functioning of the team in improving student learning.**

1988 Michael Jackson hit, *Man in the Mirror*, in which he encourages listeners to improve their lives by improving themselves first. It starts with and within you.

Major Characteristics of a Team

You're no doubt familiar with the definition of a team from Richard DuFour and colleagues (2024) that has five criteria: (1) a group of people, (2) working together, (3) *interdependently*, (4) to achieve a *common goal*, (5) for which members hold each other *mutually accountable*. As a teacher team leader, by definition, this is what you are trying to accomplish—building a team, as opposed to just a group. As noted earlier, the concept of having teachers work in teams in schools has become commonplace. We form groups of people. Criteria one: check.

Those groups of people come together on a weekly basis, give or take. And they work together. Sometimes working together looks more like parallel performance than collaboration, but let's give the work the benefit of the doubt and assume that it's more collaborative than not. Criteria two: check.

With the third criteria, things get tricky. Interdependence means that I need *you* to be able to do *my* job, and *you* need *me* in order to do your job. Here comes part of your challenge as a team leader: to help create conditions where the individuals need each other. *Interdependence.*

Identifying common goals (criteria four) is a foundational element for creating interdependence on the team. SMART goals focused on student learning outcomes form this foundation, as the team works to co-craft what they will be working toward accomplishing. Without that common goal, we are still just a group of people.

Finally, criteria five—mutual accountability. In the following pages, you'll read about the three responsibilities of a teacher team leader. The second responsibility, building capacity, revolves significantly around this idea of mutual accountability. You, as the teacher team leader, cannot and should not be the hammer. Your role is not to be the boss of your colleagues or to be a snitch letting your superiors know about misbehavior or dysfunction. *Your job is to build capacity to do the work*, and part of that is by setting up systems of mutual accountability to ensure that everyone plays a part in holding each other accountable for doing the right work. While I have alluded to it a few times, and will continue to make note throughout this book, let me be absolutely explicitly clear: The purpose of the team is to guarantee that every student learns team-identified, essential, grade-level outcomes (Williams, 2023). Period. Everything in this book is centered on you, as the teacher team leader, ensuring that the team attains to this purpose. It is an undercurrent in everything the team does, and must be kept at the forefront of you and your colleagues' thinking. This is what is required for the team to be the engine of school improvement (Kramer, n.d.).

Your Responsibilities

Now that we have clarified what your role is and why it's important, together with articulating the characteristics of a team, let's now turn to the three major responsibilities of a teacher team leader. Of these three, most people think of only one as being a key responsibility. I contend that this third key responsibility, doing the work of a learning team, is actually the least important of your three responsibilities. The other two responsibilities that are rarely (if ever) discussed are even more vital than getting stuff done. Those more important responsibilities are:

1. Make it safe

2. Build capacity

The following sections will walk you through what it looks like to carry out these responsibilities effectively. These are natural actions derived from the principles of avoiding dysfunction and creating community and will result in the creation of a functional, meaningful teacher team.

Responsibility 1: Make It Safe

The technology behemoth Google conducted a study (Duhigg, 2016) to try to find out what makes the perfect team. Of the many factors that were identified as part of this Aristotle Project were two key points that rose above all other factors of team effectiveness: (1) social sensitivity and (2) equity of turn taking. Effective teams had a space where team members had the ability to express themselves, both their thinking and feeling, in a safe environment. Further, everyone spoke. Domination of one person, or the lack of input from another person, didn't happen.

This finding from the business world has plenty of applications to your work as a teacher team leader, specifically that your number one job is to make sure there is psychological safety. You need to make sure that members feel comfortable sharing their thoughts, and then that they *do* share their thoughts. More directly, psychological safety is "a belief that one will not be punished or humiliated for speaking up with ideas, questions, concerns, or mistakes, and that the team is safe for interpersonal risk-taking" (Edmondson, 2023). Without psychological safety, team effectiveness plummets.

Along these lines, Amy Edmondson (2023) developed a seven-item questionnaire to quantify psychological safety on a team.

> **Your number one job is to make sure there is psychological safety.**

1. If I make a mistake on this team, it is not held against me.
2. Members of this team are able to bring up problems and tough issues.
3. Members of this team sometimes accept others for being different.
4. It is safe to take a risk on this team.
5. It isn't difficult to ask other members of this team for help.
6. No one on this team would deliberately act in a way that undermines my efforts.
7. When working with members of this team, my unique skills and talents are valued and utilized.

(For a deeper dive into psychological safety, visit Amy Edmondson's website and resources found at https://amycedmondson.com.)

In a PLC, each of those seven items on Edmondson's (2023) questionnaire has application in a team setting. Translating to the role of the teacher team leader, to what extent do you personally not just tolerate, but encourage and celebrate.

> **There can't be trust without dialogue.**

1. Mistakes of yourself and colleagues?
2. The raising of problems and tough issues?
3. Differences of personality, preference, or style?
4. Risk-taking?
5. Requests for help?
6. Full-throttled support of team decisions and actions?
7. The unique skills and talents of each other?

In addition to the moves, techniques, and strategies elucidated in chapters 3–6, these are actions that you can take to fulfill your number one responsibility as a teacher team leader. And that is to create psychological safety.

Identifying Dysfunction

Paulo Freire (1970) wisely said that there can't be trust without dialogue. There are well-documented reasons why teams engage in dysfunctional behavior, and you have likely experienced these in one team or another. A simple search on Amazon for books on "team" brings up 50,000 results. There are so many because people recognize that teams need help in order to function optimally. One well-known resource that you have likely encountered is Patrick M. Lencioni's (2002) five documented reasons for dysfunction, listed and summarized here.

1. **Absence of trust:** An absence of trust manifests in team members being unwilling to be vulnerable with each other and showing their weaknesses. A willingness to admit mistakes and ask for help is absent.

2. **Fear of conflict:** An absence of trust turns into a fear of conflict. This, then, results in team members failing to voice their opinions. This avoidance of conflict results in inferior results.

3. **Lack of commitment:** A fear of conflict leads to a lack of commitment. Since team members don't take ownership of decisions—because they have failed to voice their opinions since they don't trust their colleagues—they don't feel committed to the work, the team, or the results.

4. **Avoidance of accountability:** That lack of commitment ensures that team members do not hold each other accountable.

5. **Inattention to results:** Without accountability, team members put their own desires ahead of team goals. This results in the team losing sight of their purpose, and in schools, student learning suffers.

As a teacher team leader, you want to be aware of these reasons for dysfunction while considering your role in building trust, engaging in productive conflict, ensuring commitment to the work and action, creating *shared* accountability, and using results.

What I would like to highlight here is that your team can completely avoid these dysfunctions. First, approach your role through the lens of a PLC, tied together with the responsibilities, assumptions, and mindsets shared later in this part of the book. Then, use the moves, techniques, and strategies described in the following chapters. You will find that, through the combination of the elements of being—who you are—with the application of the skills of doing, your team effectiveness will skyrocket. You will get more done, in way less time, and with greater group member joy. Collaboration will be transformed.

Creating Community

While avoiding dysfunction is a good starting point for your work as a teacher team leader, it's not the finish line. Frankly, simply avoiding dysfunction is a pretty low bar. What you want to aim for instead is a much higher aspiration, and that is community.

We tend to be really good at doing fun (and important) activities in our schools to make them enjoyable places for adults (and students!). I personally love donuts or granola in the lounge, candy bars in mailboxes, weekly shoutouts for a job well done, and more. These are great activities that are fun and bring us together.

As you know, many schools also have designated times in the day or week to gather with their colleagues. We have norms written down and may even remind ourselves of them and hold each other accountable to them. We have our laptops open and, if an administrator were to walk by, they would be impressed by our focus. This is still not enough to build *meaningful* community.

Each of these sets of conditions—a social environment; dedicated time, space, and resources; and a focus on the right work of the four critical questions—are necessary. But they are not enough. They are not enough to build a meaningful professional learning *community*.

Remember that Block (2008) notes that community involves "connectedness and caring for the whole" (p. 1). The responsibilities, assumptions, mindsets, moves, techniques, and strategies shared in this book are intended to help you, as a teacher team leader, do just that: connect and care for the whole. Applying the learning from this book will help to build a community that leverages each other's strengths to improve our practice and results for students. And by leveraging each other's strengths, your school will further its efforts toward becoming a PLC in the fullest sense of the term, a school where the team, the engine for driving improvement (Kramer, n.d.), is able to get more done, in less time, and with greater joy. You, as a teacher team leader, can be a significant catalyst for helping the team to do just that.

Being and Doing With Social Sensitivity

In order to create the psychological safety necessary for the team to flourish (Duhigg, 2016; Edmondson, 2023), you, as the team leader, must be aware of both your own inner state and the outward expression of that state, or both your being and doing; both who you are as a person and what you do as a leader.

Chapters 1 and 2 of this book focus on who you are as a leader—your being—because if you just go straight to doing without a firm foundation of who you are as a person and leader, the skills you implement may be seen as (or actually be) manipulative. As we dig into these three responsibilities of a leader, reflect on your own dispositions. Starting with chapter 3 (page 45), we will explore skills, the doing side of the equation. In Daniel Goleman and colleagues' (2017) research, the authors identify four parts to emotional and social intelligence.

1. **Self-awareness:** The ability to know your own self and your impact on others.

2. **Self-management:** The ability to manage your actions, thoughts, and feelings to achieve what you want.

3. **Social awareness:** A sense of social sensitivity and the ability to notice others' social cues and respond appropriately.

4. **Relationship management:** The ability to focus your interpersonal communication skills to effectively build relationships.

Figure 1.1 shows the relationship between Goleman and colleagues' (2017) emotional and social intelligence research and what you will learn in this book.

Goleman's Research	Resources in This Text
Self-awareness	Planning tools
Self-management	Reflection questions
	Self-assessment activities
Social awareness	Moves and techniques identified in chapters 3–6
Relationship management	

Source: Adapted from Goleman et. al (2017).

Figure 1.1: Resources in this book related to Goleman's research.

In order to be an effective team leader, and especially when ensuring social sensitivity of team members, you will want to build your emotional intelligence skills—no matter how strong you are in these already. Cultivating skills of self-awareness and self-management through reflection on action is a critical component of this (Goleman et al., 2017). The moves and techniques shared in chapters 3 through 6 will be particularly helpful in building social awareness and relationship management skills articulated by Goleman and colleagues (2017), as well. In other words, by engaging in the learning and activities shared in this text, you will build all four parts of emotional and social intelligence expounded on by Goleman and colleagues (2017).

One set of social sensitivity skills you will want to be aware of and manage are credibility versus approachability (see chapter 4, page 96, for a more in-depth examination of this topic and related strategies). Think of these two ideas on a continuum where high levels of credibility are on one end and high levels of approachability are on the other. Consider someone who is highly credible in their field—someone who can be intimidating to talk to because they are an expert and speak as such. On the other end, consider someone who is approachable and probably a good conversationalist and yet is a long way from instilling a credible sense of authority.

In your daily interactions with people, you emit differing levels of credibility and approachability depending on who you are interacting with. Be aware of this, and consider how this might impact your leadership on your team. As a colleague, you want to be sure that people see you as approachable. On the other hand, as a leader, you want to imbue a sense of credibility without being authoritarian. Know where you are on this continuum and work to balance the perceptions others have of you in order to maximize your effectiveness. See chapter 4, page 96, for a tool and reflective questions to assist you in developing this aspect of your emotional intelligence.

> **Work to balance the perceptions others have of you in order to maximize your effectiveness.**

Maintaining Equity of Voice Through Turn Taking and Protocols

The second element of psychological safety noted in the Duhigg (2016) study is where protocols come into play. In schools, we have lots of protocols: a protocol for arrival at school and a protocol for dismissal, protocols for going to lunch and cleaning up after lunch, protocols for walking down the hallway, turning in assignments, submitting leave requests, and many, many more. Yet, when we get in team meetings, protocols sometimes fly out the window, and we assume that since we are adults we can just "talk through" whatever we need to talk through. Protocols provide guardrails to assist with ensuring equity in turn taking and are therefore equal-opportunity challengers, meaning that, for most people, regardless of whether they speak up too much or too little, it will be a challenge to follow them. Be sure that you and your colleagues understand that the constraint of a protocol helps team members to exercise restraint in the conversation. The payoff of using protocols to create a safe space through equity of voice will be well worth the effort.

Many of the We Do It Together strategies shared in this book are examples of protocols in action. For example, the process of having and following an agenda is a protocol. Starting every meeting with an inclusion activity is a protocol. The way that you go about reviewing data with a specific tool is a protocol. These are all step-by-step procedures that will help your team to achieve equity of voice by ensuring turn taking.

In addition to the protocols shared here, there are other fantastic resources for teams to explore a variety of protocols that will assist with your functioning, from looking at data to examining student work, from navigating conflict to coming to a decision, and from identifying priorities to clarifying tasks. A few that may be helpful for your work include the following.

- School Reform Initiative. (2023). *Protocols.* www.school reforminitiative.org/protocols

- National School Reform Faculty. (2023). *NSRF Protocols and activities…from A to Z.* https://nsrfharmony.org/protocols

- Van Soelen, Thomas. (2021). *Meeting Goals: Protocols for Leading Effective, Purpose-Driven Discussions in Schools.* Bloomington, IN: Solution Tree Press.

To review this section: the number one responsibility of a teacher team leader is to make the environment psychologically safe for all members. This happens in two ways: (1) through working to develop social sensitivity, including aligning your own beliefs and actions, and (2) developing skills through the moves, techniques, and strategies shared later in this book. And if we want to transform collaboration, then protocols are a critical part of making this happen because of their ability to get everyone's voice in the room.

Responsibility 2: Build Capacity

You cannot do the work of a team, the third responsibility, by yourself. The work of improving your practice in ensuring that every student attains team-identified grade-level essential outcomes has to be done together. Therefore, building each others' capacity to do this work is the second responsibility of a teacher team leader.

The work of the team will evolve over time. Likely, it starts as you, the designated leader, creating agendas and assigning tasks. You are the one directly and overtly facilitating the conversations. You are the one reminding folks to bring certain artifacts to meetings. And you are the one who is sharing with the principal and others about the work of the team. This is all a great place to start. But it's not where you want to end. Building the capacity of the team means that you must be aware of and think about how to help others take on some of these tasks, to understand their purpose, to refine the work, and to further advance the functioning of the team. All of this, of course, is in service to the larger aim of improving student learning. The following sections explain just how to build capacity as a knowledge worker, and how to measure and enhance the efficacy of building capacity.

> **You cannot do the work of a team, the third responsibility, by yourself.**

How Knowledge Workers Build Capacity

It may be helpful to recognize that educators are *knowledge workers*, a term coined by Peter Drucker in *Landmarks of Tomorrow* way back in 1957. Knowledge workers are distinct from manual laborers, and they are further characterized by Thomas H. Davenport (2005) as follows:

> Knowledge workers . . . don't like to be told what to do. Thinking for a living engenders thinking for oneself. Knowledge workers are paid for their education, experience, and expertise, so it is not surprising that they often take offense when someone else rides roughshod over their intellectual territory. (p. 15)

As attested by a fitness tracker worn by any educator over the course of a day, we know well that physicality is most definitely a part of a teacher's daily work. Nonetheless, we mostly use our brains: We are in command of our content, instructional practices, assessment practices, classroom management techniques—the list goes on. And, ultimately, we are in charge of passing on knowledge to the next generation.

As knowledge workers, among other things, we desire challenges and continuous learning. While sometimes you'll hear an educator say something like, "Just tell me what to do," knowledge workers want to find meaning in their work, and such statements usually indicate that meaning has been lost at some point along the way. Hence, your job of building capacity.

For educators, building capacity means being involved in continuous learning so that we can innovate and get better together. And in order to continuously improve, we need to see that our efforts are paying off. The real motivator is student success and results in the classroom—students who can continue on their path of learning because of what happened in the classroom. The ultimate productivity in our field is improved student learning.

Linda Lambert (1998), in her landmark book *Building Leadership Capacity in Schools*, identified five principles for building capacity that I think lead to actionable tasks for you as a teacher team leader. In my own understanding (Dumas, 2020), these principles translate into the following. Figure 1.2 synthesizes Lambert's and my own work. It may be helpful in identifying look-fors in building capacity with your colleagues. After reading the list and observing the figure, what else might you add?

- **Leadership does *not* equal leader:** Even though you are the designated teacher team leader, all on the team have a role in leadership. The importance of rotating roles cannot be overemphasized in building the capacity of your colleagues.

- **Leadership equals learning:** All of us are in the same boat, working to improve our practice and results for students. The more that your language can reflect learning for both yourself and the team, the better.

- **All have the potential and right to work as leader:** Depending on the needs of the team at the time, different people may arise to take the lead. These shifts might happen based on roles, content

Characteristic	Description	What It Might Look Like . . .
Leadership does not equal leader.	Even though you are the designated teacher team leader, all on the team have a role in leadership.	• Rotating roles
Leadership equals learning.	All of us are in the same boat, working to improve our practice and student results.	• A language of learning • Openness to (and celebration of!) mistakes
All have the potential and right to work as leader.	Depending on the needs of the team at the time, different people may arise to take the lead.	• Roles rotating based on skills not position • Rotating leadership based on content, process, or other
Leading is a shared endeavor.	Just because you are the designated leader does not mean that you take on all responsibilities of the team.	• Who will do what by when
Upside-down triangle of power.	If you think that because you are the designated leader, you have power, you're wrong.	• Language of service • Decisions by consensus • Equity of turn taking

Source: Dumas, 2020; Lambert, 1998.

Figure 1.2: Identifying look-fors in building capacity.

(who has a greater grasp on topics throughout the year), processes (those that have experience engaging in certain protocols or planning processes), or other reasons.

- **Leading is a shared endeavor:** Just because you are the designated leader does not mean that you take on all responsibilities of the team. Who will do what by when (chapter 4, page 114) is a key tool in this regard.

- **Upside-down triangle of power:** If you think that because you are the designated leader, you have power, you're wrong. The team has the power, and you are the servant of the team.

The Relationship Between Building Capacity and Efficacy

One of the things I think about regarding building capacity is efficacy. When I have the capacity to do something, I also have a sense of efficacy—a feeling that I *can* do that something.

People don't typically say, "I have efficacy!" On the flip side, they also don't admit, "I don't feel efficacious in X, Y, or Z." Instead, if we feel efficacious, we simply move forward and do the work. If we don't have a strong sense of efficacy, we might delay, complain, or find reasons why we shouldn't do something. In other words, there are symptoms of a lack of efficacy to which you as a teacher team leader can pay attention to diagnose what's happening and identify potential remedies. Consider figure 1.3 with potential symptoms of a lack of efficacy and potential next steps to build capacity.

> The team has the power, and you are the servant of the team.

Potential Symptoms	Potential Next Steps to Build Capacity
Arriving late	• Establish team norms. • Create ways to hold each other accountable to norms. • Start and end meetings later (keep the same amount of time). • Begin with inclusion (chapter 3, page 65).
Regularly scheduling appointments during meeting time	• Reschedule meetings for a different time to ensure all can attend regularly. • Notice if this happens when specific agenda items are the focus (such as examining data).
Not bringing data to meetings	• Clarify expectations. • Set up a spreadsheet to organize data in advance. • Identify one staff member to remind others of this task. • Bring raw data to meeting and compile together (instead of separately) to model a process.
Making excuses for not doing assignments between meetings	• Do the assignment together the first time. • Clarify expectations. • Inquire as to what roadblocks can be reduced or eliminated.

Figure 1.3: Potential symptoms of a lack of efficacy and potential next steps.

*Visit **go.SolutionTree.com/PLCbooks** for a free reproducible version of this figure.*

You're likely familiar with John Hattie's (2023) work, *Visible Learning*. While he regularly updates his list of practices in schools that lead to increased student learning, the notion of collective efficacy consistently ranks at the very top. When the staff at a school, *collectively*, has a sense of effectiveness (or efficacy), student learning increases exponentially, and the behaviors of staff lead to the conclusion of effectiveness or the lack thereof. In order to be effective, to have individual or collective efficacy, we need to have the knowledge and skills to be able to do the work. We have to have our capacity built. This is your number two responsibility as a teacher team leader.

> In order to be effective, to have individual or collective efficacy, we need to have the knowledge and skills to be able to do the work.

As noted previously, these first two responsibilities are rarely mentioned, yet they are the most important of your responsibilities, since you can't get to that third responsibility without these first two.

Responsibility 3: Do the Work

Finally, the responsibility of doing the work is real. And there is plenty of work to do. In a PLC, the primary work of teams revolves around answering the four critical questions (DuFour et al., 2024).

1. What do we want students to know and be able to do?

2. How will we know when they have learned it?

3. What will we do when they don't learn it?

4. What will we do when they do learn it?

Each of these four critical questions has specific actions that the team takes in order to effectively answer that question. In a systematic and logical fashion, the team will need to do this work. Table 1.1 outlines some of the specific work that teams do, connected to each critical question.

There are excellent resources to assist you with doing the work, including (but not limited to) the following.

- *Learning by Doing: A Handbook for Professional Learning Communities at Work, 4th Edition* (DuFour et al., 2024)

- *Make It Happen: Coaching With the Four Critical Questions of PLCs at Work* (Bailey & Jakicic, 2018)

- *Help Your Team*: Overcoming Common Collaborative Challenges in a PLC (Bayewitz et al., 2020)

- *Amplify Your Impact: Coaching Collaborative Teams in PLCs* (Many, Maffoni, Sparks, & Thomas, 2018)

- *The Big Book of Tools for Collaborative Teams in a PLC at Work* (Ferriter, 2020)

Table 1.1: The Work of a Team

Critical Question	Work that the Team Does
1. What do we want students to know and be able to do?	• Distinguishes between essential and non-essential content or skills • Unpacks the essential content into specific and discrete learning targets • Sequences and prioritizes learning targets • Schedules when essentials and learning targets will be taught
2. How will we know when they have learned it?	• Creates or revises an End of Unit (EOU) assessment • Creates or revises Common Formative Assessments (CFAs) based on 1–3 learning targets
3. What will we do when they don't learn it?	• Analyzes CFA and EOU results by learning target • Plans and implements interventions and extensions, student by student, skill by skill
4. What will we do when they do learn it?	

Any or all of these books will be of tremendous value for you as you work toward pursuing that third responsibility of a teacher team leader.

Conclusion

A teacher team leader has three responsibilities, and this chapter laid those out: (1) make it safe, (2) build capacity, and (3) do the work. This entire book is about your first two responsibilities, first and foremost, so that you can get to that third responsibility. Making it safe involves two things: (1) increasing social sensitivity through both being and doing and (2) ensuring equity of voice through effective protocols and processes. Building capacity involves understanding *why* the team is doing *what* it is doing, which is to increase instructional effectiveness and results for students by enabling your team members to develop the skills to do the work. In the next chapter, be prepared to raise assumptions about your approach and clarify mindsets to effectively lead the work you do with others.

People will forget what you said, people will forget what you did, but people will never forget how you made them feel.

—Maya Angelou

CHAPTER 2

Understanding Your Approach

In deciding the subtitle for this book, I toyed around with many terms to describe the simple strategies, tools, actions, tips, and more that are described herein. The final subtitle most fully describes what it takes to transform collaboration: habits. This is because transforming collaboration goes beyond the moves, techniques, and strategies in the following chapters and begins with how you approach leading the team. As part of this approach, this chapter will raise what I believe to be fundamental assumptions to productive team leadership. We will frame your intentions and parallel mindsets to maximize effectiveness. And we will ultimately ensure clarity on how the foundations of chapters 1 and 2 lead to the effective utilization of the moves, techniques, and strategies shared in subsequent chapters. With this in mind, let's take a closer look at how to approach your responsibilities.

Assumptions

In all situations, we make assumptions. Assumptions are things that we hold to be true (Sparks, 2007). While sometimes assumptions are considered judgmental and therefore bad, they really are neither good nor bad—they simply are. Most of the time, our assumptions remain buried and unexamined, and most of the time, our assumptions don't get in the way of positive interactions. However, when conflict emerges, there are typically unexamined assumptions that are in direct opposition to each other. Becoming aware of those assumptions will often assist with navigating that conflict; going forward, you can make deliberate assumptions that lead to conscious decisions and ultimately better teamwork that results in improved student performance.

> **Make deliberate assumptions that lead to conscious decisions.**

To inform your approach as a teacher team leader, let's surface some assumptions about groups and the role that the team leader plays in ensuring effectiveness.

Raising these assumptions will also help you identify any additional assumptions that you naturally hold. These are assumptions that I hold to be true, and offer them for your consideration. While there is research to support each of these separately, I have not seen anyone compile them in a list like this to guide your work as a teacher team leader. My experience in my own leadership work is that these assumptions will be helpful to you as you lead your team. Here are five positive assumptions that improve a teacher team leader's approach to leadership.

1. People do the best that they can.

2. You can only control you.

3. Behavior communicates.

4. People want to get stuff done.

5. Conflict is good.

While I hold these to be true, that doesn't necessarily mean that they are fact. In reality, some of these assumptions may be flat out wrong depending on the people with whom I'm working. However, I have found that if I hold these assumptions, it helps *me* behave more productively. In other words, even if my assumptions are wrong, holding them will help increase effectiveness and move the team toward the goal of improved student learning.

Assumption 1: People Do the Best That They Can

Paulo Freire is one of my favorite educational philosophers and greatly influences who I am and what I do. In his seminal work, *Pedagogy of the Oppressed*, Freire (1970) states that "faith in people" is a necessary prerequisite to dialogue. He goes on to assert that this calls for believing in others "even before he meets them face to face." This first assumption, then, that people do the best that they can, is my own framing of a primary assumption necessary to transform collaboration—a belief in others, their intentions, and the actions that they take.

We all have many things going on in our lives. Some of this is public, while most aspects are private and therefore hidden. No one knows what anyone else is going through—physically, mentally, or spiritually. If I hold that even the most obstinate person on my team is doing the best that they can, I will treat them differently than if I assume they are "out to get me," or working to sabotage the team, or just limping toward retirement. In some circles, this assumption is known as having positive presuppositions (Garmston & Wellman, 2016), and the assumption or belief that they are doing the best that they can helps me to treat them with dignity in all interactions, thereby assisting with goodwill that leads toward greater productivity. Regardless of whether or not the other person *actually* has positive intentions in the situation, my adoption of positive presuppositions and assuming that they are doing the best that they can will help to advance the work of the team.

Assumption 2: You Can Only Control You

While our job as the teacher team leader is to ensure team effectiveness, it's really the group that decides how it will best function (Garmston & McKanders, 2022). While you have a great deal of influence over the group—and if you use the simple, go-to actions in this book, you will see your influence expand—it is really the group that is in charge. You will learn how to leverage your abilities, and, at the end of the day, if the group doesn't come along, you must be ready to support the group's decision. Don't attach yourself to specific methods. As dichotomous as it might seem, you have to be detached and know that the group is its own group. You cannot control others' thoughts and actions, so to avoid disappointment and heartache, don't try to control the group you have been asked to lead. You can only control yourself.

Assumption 3: Behavior Communicates

You may be familiar with the phrase, "All behavior is a form of communication" (Michigan Alliance for Families, n.d.). While not entirely accurate in all circumstances (Godat & Czerny, 2021), the overarching premise of the phrase and assumption generally holds, which is why I have slightly modified that phrase to be an assumption that behavior communicates. We can *try* to cover over our true feelings with our words. Still, our nonverbal patterns will almost always override those words. You no doubt have had interactions with someone who was unhappy with you or a situation, and you could tell this by their nonverbals. Their tone was tense, or their words abrupt, or their gestures sharp. So, with this in mind, you asked them what was wrong, and their words might have been, "Nothing. I'm fine," but you clearly knew that this was not the case. That's because a person's nonverbal cues don't lie. If someone is saying one thing with their words, but is indicating something different with their actions, believe their actions. Behavior communicates.

Assumption 4: People Want to Get Stuff Done

I've yet to meet someone who leaves a completely unproductive meeting and says, genuinely, "Wow, I just love meetings that are a complete and total waste of time! I just live for gatherings where nothing is accomplished." As a matter of fact, as you were reading that just now, you probably added sarcasm to the tone because you, too, know that the only time you might hear those words is if someone is being facetious.

Freire (1970) notes that dialogue cannot happen in an atmosphere where nothing comes of our efforts, and that our interactions will become sterile, bureaucratic, and tedious if we do not see results. With this in mind, it's helpful to assume that others want to get stuff done, too. The team wants to feel a sense of accomplishment and they want to see progress. Assume that they want what you want: to get all students to grade-level essential outcomes effectively and efficiently, and with a bit of joy thrown in for good measure.

Assumption 5: Conflict Is Good

Here's a likely shift in perspective: If there are three people in a room and everyone agrees, two of those people are unnecessary. Conflict is an essential element to being more productive. It enables us to push each other's thinking, challenge each other's assumptions and practices, and come to better decisions and actions. In brief, conflict helps to avoid so-called "group think," or the psychological phenomenon of making dysfunctional decisions as a group due to a desire to maintain a sense of harmony (Paul, 2023).

When most of us think of conflict we think of *affective*, or emotional, conflict (Black & Bright, 2019a). This is the kind of conflict where our blood pressure rises, our volume and intensity increases, and our emotions become entangled in the conversation. Sometimes we become flustered, other times we become angry, and in very few situations does this lead to productive growth. Affective conflict causes harm to relationships and damages the work of the team.

Many of the moves, techniques, and strategies in this book are about helping you lead the team in such a way as to avoid conflict that is harmful, and to instead have productive, cognitive conflict. This text will help you and your team be hard on ideas and soft on people—to make sure that you're challenging each others' thinking and practices while maintaining relationships, because cognitive conflict is good.

I offer these five assumptions as a way to prompt your own thinking about what you hold to be true about other people and your team. In addition to the assumptions I have shared, what others might you add? Take a moment to consider assumptions that you hold about yourself and others that might be helpful to surface in your journey toward becoming a more effective teacher team leader. Write them down, and be sure to come back to them periodically for revision based on your experience and learning.

Intentions

Having raised potential assumptions for you to consider as a teacher team leader, and prior to identifying productive mindsets to guide your leadership, let's take a moment and think through your intentions as a teacher team leader. The first two definitions of intention (Intention, n.d.) involve what "one intends to do or bring about" or "a determination to act in a certain way." As such, this section asks you to both (1) consider what you want to bring about and, therefore, (2) determine how you will act in order to make that happen.

I'm reminded of the Haim Ginnot (1972) quote that states the approach of the classroom teacher creates the climate and their mood makes the weather. So it is, too, with you as a teacher team leader. You possess tremendous potential to inspire, to humor, to heal, and to bring joy. And these outcomes come back very directly to your intentions. As you apply the contents of this book, I encourage you to think about this: What do you want to accomplish? Consider these answer options.

- A highly collaborative team, even though this will inevitably involve muddiness?

- Colleagues who better understand themselves and each other, even though this might involve conflict?

- Professionals who are engaged in meaningful improvement of their craft, even though this implies learning, growth, and acknowledgment (and celebration!) of mistakes?

As you consider your intentions, know that others do not know what you are thinking. They see your behavior and then draw conclusions based on those actions (see assumption 3 on page 31). And, unfortunately, lackluster execution of good intentions can lead to an interpretation by others that your intentions are not good. It is important for you to be explicit about your intentions, in both word and deed. Which means that you may need to reflect on your actions by asking questions such as the following.

> **Be explicit about your intentions, in both word and deed.**

- How might you ensure that others perceive you as being open and collaborative instead of directive and telling them what to do?

- In what ways will you help the team make meaningful choices in doing the work and not potentially get caught up in just "doing the work?"

- What steps might you take to ensure that others see you as a servant of the team and not their supervisor?

Of course, these questions are phrased as one extreme or the other. Nevertheless, thinking of these extremes might help you to clarify, for yourself, what you desire of the team. With this clarity in mind, then, choose methods that will get you there. The moves, techniques, and strategies described in chapters 3 through 6 will assist you, but only if you are clear about your intended result. In other words, know your intended results and then choose congruent behaviors to get you and your team there (Garmston & Wellman, 2016). For the sake of our students, we need teams who are getting more done, in less time, and with loads and loads of joy. Be clear on who you are, where the team can go, and your role in making it happen. Then choose the moves, techniques, and strategies to get there.

Use figure 2.1 to assist you in reflecting on your intentions and actions.

What Are My Personal Intentions?	Where Can the Team Go?	What Actions Might I Take in Making Those Happen?
To serve the team in drawing out the best from others	A highly collaborative team that accesses the expertise and voice of everyone in coming to consensus and being a team	Before every meeting, remind myself of my three responsibilities. Every month, reflect with a colleague on how I'm doing with actualizing my assumptions and mindsets.
To intentionally create safe opportunities for cognitive conflict	Colleagues who push themselves and each other to be and do better	Intentionally plan for using group rapport, laughter and humor, the pause, and third point.
To build momentum for improving our effectiveness as a team	Recognition and celebration of successes and mistakes	Use the agenda to build in reflection. Use anonymous reflections to ensure deeper reflection and get everyone's voices in the reflection. Ask the team how to regularly and systematically celebrate our accomplishments and learning.

Figure 2.1: Example reflections on intentions.

*Visit **go.SolutionTree.com/PLCbooks** for a free reproducible version of this figure.*

Mindsets

Assumptions and intentions are important to raise so that we are able to ensure our own personal clarity about how we go about working with a team, and mindsets are equally important. Very simply put, mindsets are attitudes that lead to actions (Mindset Works, n.d.). While mindsets are shaped by our beliefs, assumptions, and values, they focus our work by giving a few distinct lenses through which we take action. I propose that three mindsets are key to the effective functioning of a teacher team leader. Just like with the assumptions shared earlier, there is research to support each of these mindsets separately, though I have not seen anyone compile them in a list like this to guide your work as a teacher team leader. My experience is that these attitudes leading to discrete actions will be helpful to you as you lead your team. Notice that they each begin with action, "to see," "to be," and "to spread."

1. To see what others don't (yet) see in themselves

2. To be humble with a posture of learning

3. To spread the contagion of joy

Mindset 1: To See What Others Don't (Yet) See in Themselves

In order for a team to transform, they need to become more than what they currently are. This goes for the individual people on the team, as human beings and professional educators, as well as the team as a whole. By seeing and drawing out the best in others, including yourself, you will draw on the inherent excellence of each person as they strive for greater levels of excellence. The hope that others will feel coming from you because you believe in them will be contagious. As a teacher team leader, the more potential that you see in others, and in some cases what they don't (yet) see in themselves, the more the team will transform. As Ken Williams (2023) puts it, "You cannot be your best if you think that you are working with damaged goods."

Sometimes people don't behave in alignment with their innate excellence. A key mindset of the teacher team leader is to look beyond the behavior and to see that person for who they can become. An effective tool in your toolbox is the following idea shared with me many years ago: praise and reframe.

Praising is just as it sounds: finding areas of strengths and recognizing and celebrating those strengths. Reframing means that we look for strengths, search out opportunities, and identify ways that we can leverage those strengths and opportunities to best meet the challenges before us. Consider this as seeing opportunities in difficulties. It can be taking a bad event or situation and turning it into something positive. As an example, a teacher team leader I was working with shared how one particular team member was constantly against everything the team wanted to do. Other team leaders were able to help praise and reframe the situation by helping the team leader see that that member has decades of experience, including through pendulum swings with administrators (four in the last six years alone!). Through this reframing, the teacher team leader was able to then access the resistant teacher's expertise and leverage it in moving the work forward. Instead of seeing that teacher as an obstacle, the teacher team leader shifted their mindset to see what that teacher maybe didn't even see in themself.

Mindset 2: To Be Humble With a Posture of Learning

To be in the learning profession means that we, as educators, must also engage in learning (Learning Forward, 2023). And learning requires the humility to say, "I don't know" or "Let's explore a specific topic." In all things, a humble posture of learning is a critical aspect of not just being a teacher team leader, but a teacher in general.

A corollary to being in a humble posture of learning is our relationship with failure. In a learning team, the fear of failure has no place. This is because we know that failure is necessary for learning. If failure is a prerequisite to learning, then we should not fear it. And if we are in a humble posture of learning, then we know that failure will come, and we will welcome it—because failures are not set in stone, and because we are learning!

Now take that previous sentence and replace the *we*s with *I*s: If *I* am in a humble posture of learning, then *I* know that failure will come, and *I* will welcome it—because failures are not set in stone, and because *I* am learning! Assume a humble posture of learning for yourself, too. Failures provide feedback to make small or larger changes right now and over time.

Related to this notion of adopting a humble posture of learning where the fear of failure finds no place is the development of trust on your team. Many times, folks will say that *if* there were trust on their team, *then* they could open up and be vulnerable. The research on this actually finds the opposite (Coyle, 2018). In order to build trust, we have to be vulnerable. Demonstrate your vulnerability by expressing your learning, areas of growth, mishaps, and more. As you do this, trust will build.

A funny visual for this idea is a "giraffe conversation." As you know, giraffes have long necks. So when you have a giraffe conversation, you are sticking your neck out. You are being vulnerable by saying that you don't know something or that you messed something up. And it's often helpful to label your vulnerability by saying, "I'm gonna be a giraffe here" or "I am just being vulnerable in sharing that I'm uncomfortable with . . ." Making your vulnerability explicit builds trust as others see that you are trusting them with your willingness to express your weaknesses.

Of course, there is a limit to expressing vulnerability. There can come a point of oversharing—a point when folks start to lose confidence in you because you are sharing too much and dwelling too frequently on mistakes and areas of growth. Balance this need to build trust by being vulnerable with the spirit of confidence that someone who is competent also projects (see Approachable and Credible Voice, chapter 4, page 96, for more considerations on this topic). Be sure that when you demonstrate vulnerability to build trust, it is in a professional manner that actually does lead to increased trust. Humility is different from humiliation.

> **The fear of failure has no place.**

Mindset 3: To Spread the Contagion of Joy

You may be familiar with the term *mirror neurons*. Mirror neurons are a fascinating, specialized neuron. When we observe someone doing something, our mirror neurons "fire" as if we are doing the very same thing. And it goes for feelings as well. When someone expresses an emotion, happiness or sadness for example, our mirror neurons "fire" with the same emotions (Ferrari & Rizzolatti, 2014).

Helen Riess (2018), an associate professor of psychiatry at Harvard Medical School and director of empathy and relational science at Massachusetts General Hospital, states, "Consciously or not, we are in constant, neural resonance with one another's feelings. When we are engaged in shared mind awareness, the possibilities for mutual aid and collaborative problem solving abound" (p. 30). Maybe this is why emotions are contagious. When another person is feeling an emotion—particularly if it's a strong emotion—others in the room pick up on it and feel the same thing. When you're at a movie, a character might weep over the loss of a loved one, and in the audience, we, too, begin to cry. According to Pier Francesco Ferrari and Giacomo Rizzollati (2014), we are literally hardwired to "understand the intentions of others" based on our "capacity to *infer* others' internal mental states and to ascribe to them a causal role in generating the observed behavior" (p. 1). That's science speak for, "We feel what other people feel."

All of this happens subconsciously, but that doesn't mean you can't be aware of your own emotions and intentionally spread the contagion of joy. When we are happy, everything is just easier. Time goes by faster, and difficult tasks are more pleasurable when we are joyful. And, at the risk of stating the obvious, joy does not have to look like clowning around, though it might occasionally. This isn't to say that there won't be times of tension and conflict. No doubt the team will struggle through challenges. But, overall, the team will experience joy as a thread through it all because you will have the mindset of spreading the contagion of joy. You will be mindful of others' states and infuse joy, as appropriate. You will smile. You will laugh. You will find ways to infuse happiness into everyday interactions (see chapter 3, page 52, on laughter and humor for more considerations on this topic).

Role and Approach

You have three jobs, as outlined in the previous chapter: (1) make it safe, (2) build capacity, and (3) do the work. In order to fulfill these responsibilities, certain context is foundational. Teams matter. What they do when they are together makes a difference in whether or not student learning will improve because of the team's existence, and the development of meaningful community is central to that improvement.

Who you are matters. Team leaders are critical in ensuring the success of a team. What you believe, say, and do make a difference. To be effective, you must be grounded in certain assumptions, intentions, and mindsets that will lead to your own and your team's effectiveness. As a reminder, the responsibilities, assumptions, and mindsets reviewed in these chapters are as follows.

- Responsibilities:
  1. Make it safe.
  2. Build capacity.
  3. Do the work.
- Assumptions:
  1. People do the best that they can.
  2. You can only control you.
  3. Behavior communicates.
  4. People want to get stuff done.
  5. Conflict is good.
- Mindsets:
  1. To see what others don't (yet) see in themselves
  2. To be humble with a posture of learning
  3. To spread the contagion of joy

> **What you believe, say, and do make a difference.**

With that summary in mind, let us now transition to actions. As noted in the second assumption, you can only control you. As much as each of us might want to control others, we simply cannot. However, we can most certainly *influence* others. This, of course, starts with who you are as a person and leader (your being). Now we will explore the three sets of actions (your doing) that this book describes for you to increase your influence with your colleagues: moves, techniques, and strategies. Let's clarify the differences between each.

What You Do: Moves and Techniques

Communication courses emphasize that the vast majority of the meaning attributed to our communication comes from nonverbals (Grinder, 2018; Stillman, 2024). Much of the research is attributed to Albert Mehrabian (1972), and it lays out the impact of nonverbal patterns of breathing, eye contact, and more on our attributions of likability (Stillman, 2024). In other words, nonverbal communication has a significant, and disproportionate, impact on how we perceive others and how we, ourselves, are perceived. This leads to the conclusion that you can have significant influence on the team through the intentional use of certain nonverbal communication patterns. What you do, and *how* you do it, is more important than what you say.

Moves and techniques are exactly that—nonverbal behaviors that will help the team get more done, in less time, and with greater joy. Some of these you might already use and are strategic in using them. Others you likely use but aren't necessarily consciously aware of them. And still others may be entirely new to you. Some of them may even feel like some kind of magic that surely won't work to improve effectiveness. But they will.

More specifically, *moves* are primary ways that you influence your team. As already noted, these are actions that you take, and many times your colleagues don't even realize that you're doing them. In a classroom, moves that you might take include individually welcoming students on their arrival to your room with a positive greeting or using proximity to address potential (or realized) classroom management issues. In a team meeting, there are a whole host of moves that you can make to focus the group and ensure improvement of functioning. Moves are part of the You Do It Yourself actions in each chapter.

Techniques are specific types of moves that involve one of the approximately fifty nonverbal communication patterns that are fairly universal (Zoller, 2024). While often extraordinarily subtle, you will find that the implementation of these techniques will dramatically improve your and your team's effectiveness.

What We Do Together: Strategies

Creating a collaborative PLC demands persistence and skillfulness of all members (Garmston & Wellman, 2016). It is not easy, just as nothing worthwhile is ever easy. It requires looking in the mirror at your own beliefs and practices in your quest for community and guaranteeing student learning. It insists on each of us—from the paraprofessional to the principal and everyone in between—learning new skills and applying them in private and public settings. And it demands that we acquire new tools and refine their usage as we clarify who we are and how we do it. It is hard work and requires dedication and persistence as we practice and rehearse these skills.

Strategies, like what happens in a classroom, are approaches that we all do together. In a classroom, strategies might be using a graphic organizer, engaging in structured note-taking processes, or facilitating cooperative learning. These are ways that we all work together to improve. And so it is with our teams—there are strategies that we use together to improve our functioning.

Most chapters will share a handful of simple strategies to improve your and your team's functioning. These are approaches that are about *us*, as a team, and are the actions listed as We Do It Together.

Category Labels

One of the things you'll notice about upcoming actions is that there isn't a clear distinction between some of the moves within a category. As a case in point, third point (chapter 3, page 57) is shared as a move that you take, for example, during a heated conversation. You might go up to a whiteboard and start jotting down key points. However, third point can also be used as a strategy where the team decides to project the agenda or data. The team created a third point, and they did it as a strategy to improve team functioning—even though I have categorized it as generally being a move. Categories are only present to help organize the actions available to you. Table 2.1 categorizes the actions detailed in this book by the general type of action that it is.

Table 2.1: Types of Actions You and the Team Can Take

	Moves	Techniques	Strategies
Description	Actions that you take as a leader to move the work forward	Very specific, often subtle, actions that you take to increase your influence and the effectiveness of the team	Actions that the team takes together, many times initiated by you
Actions Detailed in This Book	• Group rapport • Laughter and humor • Pause • Third point • Paraphrase • Questions • Approachable and credible voice • And (not but) • Specificity • Decontaminate space • Individual rapport • Anonymize it	• Breathing • Gestures and words of inclusion • Break eye contact • Attribution • Fourth point • Mode of communication • Frozen gesture • Beat gesture • Hand position • Whisper • I interrupt myself	• Physical arrangement • Norms • Roles • Inclusion • Landing page • Outcomes • Running agenda template • Write it down • Plan the work, then work the plan • Celebrations • Others as experts • Sentence stems • Who will do what by when • Data usage • Self-assessment • Fist to five • Forced choice

Conclusion

Both who you are as a person and what you do as a leader matters. This chapter explored key elements of your approach to the task of being a teacher team leader. Five assumptions were raised and offered for your consideration: (1) People do the best that they can, (2) you can only control you, (3) behavior communicates, (4) people want to get stuff done, and (5) conflict is good. We also explored the importance of your intentions and how you can ensure alignment between your intent and the actions that you take. We then raised three mindsets, or attitudes leading to action, to assist you in transforming collaboration: (1) to see what others don't (yet) see in themselves, (2) to be humble with a posture of learning, and (3) to spread the contagion of joy. Finally, this chapter differentiated between moves and techniques, those actions that you take as an individual, and strategies, or those actions that the team takes together. In the next four chapters, we will deeply explore some simple, go-to moves, techniques, and strategies to transform collaboration.

PART II

Teacher Team Leader Actions

Having founded the transformation of your collaboration with clarity on your role and approach, we now turn our attention to simple moves, techniques, and strategies. We will begin with those actions that are foundational to a team getting started in effective collaboration practices and then explore steps to gain momentum, followed by habits to overcome obstacles. Finally, some actions that you can employ to refine your own skills will be shared before moving into real-world challenges that pull together the learning from the entire book.

Get started. Then get better.

—Tim Brown

CHAPTER 3

Getting Started

In the summer just before the sixth grade, my parents hired a man named Lloyd as a contractor to oversee a project to add a big two-story addition to our home. I remember the process of figuring out the blueprints, marking out the yard, digging the trenches for the foundation, pouring the concrete footings, waiting a week for those to cure, and then starting to put the concrete foundation blocks on those footings. To my surprise, as a young lad of eleven or twelve, it felt like we wasted four or five weeks of summer! There were no 2×4s, no framing, no sheetrock. No apparent progress whatsoever.

Because my parents were educators, we only had ten weeks to make this addition happen, and yet almost half of that time didn't seem to see any real progress. Now, of course there was progress. Had my dad said to Lloyd, "Lloyd, we don't have time for this. Skip straight to the framing so we can get this done by the beginning of August," Lloyd would have laughed in his face and left the site, never to return again.

Yet, in our work in schools, we do just this. We often decide to skip building the foundation because it's not glamorous. It doesn't show immediate, quick-win results. It doesn't feel like we're making any progress. Don't make this mistake. Build the foundation. Ensure that the foundation is solid so that effective collaboration can result. If your foundation is a little iffy, come back to it. This chapter will help you solidify that foundation, regardless of where you are in the process.

As we have established and you know well, teams are the engine that drive the PLC process. In order to drive that process, they have to function effectively. There are a handful of simple, go-to ways to get the team moving in the right direction. That's exactly what this chapter is about—the foundation of ensuring effective teamwork.

Some of the following actions are such that you or your team may have these already more-or-less established. If that's the case, great! You will still no doubt pick up a few tidbits by exploring what is shared in this chapter. If you or your team does not have the following moves, techniques, and strategies down pat, this chapter is the place to start. Everything else in this book revolves around the foundation that is laid in this chapter.

You Do It Yourself

The moves and techniques shared here start with group rapport, which is different from individual rapport, and is vital in transforming collaboration (Zoller, 2024). Breathing is underlying and cannot be overemphasized in developing that group rapport, so we'll look at ways to get folks breathing together, including through laughter and humor (Grinder, 2018). The pause enables your brain to think, colleagues' brains to think, and better paraphrasing (chapter 4, page 88) to ensue (Grinder, 2018). We will close out this section with third point, something that helps to make sure that affective conflict becomes minimized and synchronicity (which is what happens when the group has rapport) can be developed (Grinder, n.d.a).

After exploring these moves and techniques, consider your own situation and reflect on what you will begin to use immediately, what you will need to practice before using, what sort of systematic schedule you might create for implementing, and which ones you will reserve for later on in your leadership journey. Please use the blank reproducible tools at the end of this chapter, pages 84 and 85, to complete this activity after reading You Do It Yourself on page 46 and We Do It Together on page 58.

Theory in Action

One of the best ways that I refine my own practice of these skills is to video record myself leading a meeting or training. Then, when I watch it back, I can assess my skills and consider areas for refinement. One tip on watching yourself: do it at a speed of 1.5X or 1.75X. This does two things for you: (1) it creates a little bit of psychological distance between you and "that person" on the screen, allowing you to focus on the behaviors instead of how you look and sound, and (2) it saves you some time. Saving time, in particular, is an appealing reason for doing this.

We will cover the following actions in this section.

- Group rapport
- Breathing
- Laughter and humor
- Pause
- Third point

Each move or technique in the following sections has an accompanying activity or reflective exercise you can use by yourself or with your team. We will review each move or technique, detail tools that are helpful for implementation, offer a few reflection questions, and leave with tips for advanced implementation, including how you might leverage moves, techniques, or strategies from elsewhere in the book for maximum impact.

Group Rapport

We begin our exposition of the actions that you and the team take to transform collaboration with the most foundational of them all: creating group rapport. In group rapport, we aim to establish synchronicity, similar emotions, and common breathing patterns, which then lead to the physical manifestation of rapport. Just like in individual rapport (chapter 5, page 131), group rapport manifests itself when the group is in sync with itself. It is the result of a number of actions that you can take, including all of the moves and techniques included in this chapter.

Synchronicity is one of the most powerful tools available to you in working to establish group rapport. Synchronicity happens when everyone in the group is doing the same thing at the same time. For example, when we all laugh together (detailed later in this chapter, page 52), we create synchronicity and group rapport. Laughter is particularly powerful because, when we laugh, we breathe from deep in our diaphragm muscles. It "enhances your intake of oxygen-rich air, stimulates your heart, lungs and muscles, and increases the endorphins that are released by your brain" (Mayo Clinic Staff, 2021). So finding and sharing uplifting stories that generate laughter is one way to create synchronicity and, thus, group rapport.

Other examples of synchronicity happen with any of the inclusion activities discussed later in the chapter (page 65)—for example, when everyone is turning and talking to a neighbor, this is synchronicity. When everyone is taking a moment to jot down their thoughts on a particular topic, this creates synchronicity. So if the group is out of sync—one person is looking at their computer, another is looking at a screen, another is looking at you, and so on—do something to create synchronicity. Get folks to laugh, or to look at a third point (page 57) together, or to pause (page 54) and write down their thoughts on a topic, and so on. Get everyone doing the same thing at the same time using the moves, techniques, and strategies described herein, and group rapport will either come back or manifest itself. The think-do-say-feel tool and synchronicity tool are a couple of tools to help get you started.

> **The most foundational action you and your team can take to transform collaboration is to create group rapport.**

Think-Do-Say-Feel Tool

Use the following tool in figure 3.1 to organize your thoughts for the start of an upcoming meeting. You can find a blank reproducible version of this frame on this book's website. What do you want your colleagues to think, do, say, and feel within those first few minutes of the meeting? Then craft the initial activity based on your thinking (see inclusion on page 65 in this chapter for more details on this strategy). And please note, your preparation for this activity does not mean that you will tell colleagues what to think, do, say, or feel. Rather, it is an organizer for your own thoughts to prompt the interactions.

Tips for Group Synchronicity Tool

Use the following tool in figure 3.2, to think through when and how you can create synchronicity within the group. Proactive considerations are used to establish group rapport at the start of a meeting. Reactive tips are those that you might need to consider when the group falls out of rapport.

Think	Do
What norms will I focus on today?	*Review the norms*

Say	Feel
The norm I will focus on today is . . . because . . .	*Focused* *Grateful that all of us will follow the norms*

Based on the above, how will you start the meeting to create synchronicity and group rapport? Use the space provided to create your script for the opening of the meeting.
"Thank you, brilliant colleagues, for being ready to start our meeting on time. To remind ourselves of our agreements for how we will engage with each other today, please silently and individually read through the norms and identify which one you will personally focus on today and why."

Source: Adapted from Zoller, 2022. Used with permission.

Figure 3.1: Think-do-say-feel.

*Visit **go.SolutionTree.com/PLCbooks** for a free reproducible version of this figure.*

Proactive Considerations	Your Notes for When or How You Might Use
Inclusion	*Start every meeting with a short inclusion (no more than five minutes, but many times less than three minutes)* *Vary inclusion so it's not the same thing every time*
Third point	*Project the agenda for all to see* *Include the norms and outcomes on the agenda to reference for inclusion*
Humor	*Propose that the team start meetings with a funny story from personal experience about themselves (professionally) or learning*
Turn and talk	*Designate on the agenda when we will turn to each other to access the expertise of a partner*
Reactive Tips	**Your Notes for When or How You Might Use**
Silent write	*Be sure to have sticky notes at every meeting to spontaneously do this when needed*
Turn and talk	*Create my own "cheat-sheet" of reminders of turn and talk so that I can remember in the heat of the moment*
Physical movement (stand and talk, walk and talk, etc.)	*Create my own "cheat-sheet" of reminders of physical movement so that I can remember in the heat of the moment*
Humor	*Make a sticky note to put on my computer screen to remind me to find humor in little things in the meeting — including laughing at my own mistakes*

Figure 3.2: Tips for group synchronicity.

*Visit **go.SolutionTree.com/PLCbooks** for a free reproducible version of this figure.*

Reflection Questions

When you have finished using one or both tools, use a journal or notebook to reflect on the following questions.

- When do you notice that the group goes out of sync? How does this impact the ability of the team to get more done, in less time, and with greater joy?

- How effective have your efforts been to get the group into sync?

- What refinements might you make to your practice to increase the rapport of the team?

Next-Level Tips

The use of electronic devices has, by and large, increased the effectiveness of teams. However, the challenge of everyone having a device at a meeting is that we can lose interpersonal connection and rapport. We get fixated on our screens, and it's hard to tell if folks are focused on the topic at hand or surfing the net. Yet, the importance of group rapport cannot be overstated. We need to be in sync to be effective and meet the promise of ensuring every student attains grade-level essential outcomes.

In addition to the considerations shared above, think about also adding in the pause (page 54) and I interrupt myself (an advanced technique in chapter 6, page 167). The actions detailed in this section on group rapport are significant changes to whatever is going on, whereas pausing and I interrupt myself are much more subtle. Yet, with practice, they can be equally effective at gaining group rapport.

Breathing

Of the more than fifty nonverbal communication patterns in which we engage as human beings, breathing is by far *the most important and impactful* (Grinder, 2018), which is why it is second—right after establishing group rapport. It has an impact not only on communication and physiology, including respiration and the level of oxygen in the bloodstream (and, hence, oxygen that makes its way to the brain), but also on *other people's* heart rate, metabolism, and blood pressure. People who are doing good work and enjoying it are breathing together (Grinder, 2018). Not in unison, but from the same location—low in the diaphragm. When people are upset, they breathe shallowly and from their shoulders. They also tend to breathe more quickly.

> **People who are doing good work and enjoying it are breathing together.**

Having said all of this, as you can likely surmise, breathing is also one of the most subtle of the techniques. So while it is the most impactful, breathing is something that you likely don't even notice in others, and they almost surely won't notice *your* breathing. In other words, you can leverage the power of breathing, and it is highly likely that no one will ever know. If you're as fascinated about nonverbal communication as I am, consider visiting Michael Grinder's website at www.michaelgrinder.com, where he expands on this work. He's one of the world's premiere experts in this area, especially as it relates to education.

By now, you may be wondering how you get people to breathe together and to get a level of rapport that will be helpful for the team. This is where an audible inhale comes into play. This is not to say that an exhale is not helpful, but it can be easily perceived as a sigh of exasperation, and exasperated colleagues do not lead to higher levels of performance or happiness. So when you exhale, be sure to do it silently, or it may turn into a sighing sound.

Take a deep breath right now—low and slow. Breathe in through your nose, out through your mouth (or nose). Almost instantly, your heart rate decreases, blood pressure comes down, and a sense of calm tends to come over you. And, guess what? It has the same impact on others! A long, deep, audible inhale through the nose generally gets others to also take a deep breath. And this common breath leads to better thinking and engaging with each other.

Finally, please note that you are *not* overtly asking your colleagues to take a breath with you (for example, "Before moving on, let's all just take a deep breath together"). That might be weird, although on some teams, it might work just fine depending on the makeup of the team.

For this particular technique, you are the only one taking a deep breath, and you are doing it audibly through the nose to communicate thoughtfulness and create a space for that thinking. What will likely happen is that your colleagues will unconsciously take a breath with you, although it will probably not be as deep nor as audible. This breathing together will help to move the team forward.

Breathing Tool

Use the tool in figure 3.3 to remind yourself of potential times to take a deep audible breath to help create synchronicity on the team.

Reflection Questions

When you have considered the preceding tool, use a journal or notebook to reflect on the following questions.

- When will it be important to use this technique?

- What did you notice about the team's response when you engaged in an audible inhale?

- How might you combine this technique with others in order to maximize effectiveness?

When to Use Breathing
• Starting a meeting
• Beginning a new topic
• Posing a question that requires a thoughtful response
• When tensions are high
• When group rapport is absent

Figure 3.3: Breathing tool.

Next-Level Tips

It is difficult (maybe impossible?) to take a deep, audible breath through the nose while also talking. A pause will naturally occur. However, what might not be natural is keeping your mouth closed while you take that breath in. In order to increase the perception of your credibility, keep your mouth closed to the greatest extent possible (Grinder, 2018). In addition, consider breaking eye contact (chapter 4, page 102) with your colleagues. When you break eye contact and look up (or down), this signals thoughtfulness (Zoller, 2024). Of course, it's also helpful to actually be thoughtful as you use this technique.

Likely, this technique will be natural for you, but, if not, consider practicing breaking eye contact when you take this breath.

Finally, consider adding the frozen gesture (chapter 6, page 160) as well. This way, you are pulling many techniques together for this next-level tip: an audible in breath, a pause (with closed mouth), breaking of eye contact, and a frozen gesture. Try it out, practice it, and see how it impacts your team in developing synchronicity and rapport that leads to increased effectiveness.

Laughter and Humor

Laughter has been around a long time, and researchers have even found that animals engage in laughter (Wood, 2023)! According to those same researchers, laughter smooths social interactions and can communicate certain messages like pleasure, reassurance, and even threat. Part of the physiological reason for laughter helping with the team is that it develops synchronicity, as noted earlier in this chapter under group rapport and breathing (Grinder, 2018; Zoller, 2024). With this in mind, let's think about how you might engage with others to bring out their best with the use of humor.

People feel better when they are happy (Mayo Clinic Staff, 2021), and laughter, or humor, is one of those activities that helps with happiness. Laughter helps everyone breathe from the same place, in addition to the endorphins that are released when we laugh (Mayo Clinic Staff, 2021). If we want to get our work done efficiently and with greater joy, wouldn't it make sense to intentionally include that which makes people happy?

Let me be clear: I am not advocating for team meetings to become comedy central. While telling jokes can get the ball rolling, teams that laugh with each other *while* they engage in the work (not *instead of* engaging in the work) seem to be the most productive. Humor is a tricky thing, however. While authentic humor and laughter, including self-deprecating (but not self-belittling) humor can be helpful to a team, sarcasm and denigrating jokes directed at students or colleagues are categorically harmful.

Genuine laughter in which teams might engage to bring about joy often occur during simple interactions. Work to find joy in small places. For example, if you are an Apple computer-based school, you know well about the sheer number of dongles needed to hook your computer up to a projector or audio. This can be humorous. If you forget to bring something to a meeting that you intended, instead of getting upset, consider laughing it off and making a comment about your forgetfulness. If the projector isn't working well and it's dark, perhaps joke about needing to be bats. Teachers are good at humor in their classrooms, so find ways to insert that humor into your conversations and the work of the team.

Laughter and Humor Tool

Use the tool in figure 3.4 to consider when humor might be appropriate to provide levity, synchronicity, and a breath (literally!) of fresh air. Some possibilities are included in the sample tool to get you thinking.

Situation	How You Might Generate Laughter in the Situation	Reflection on How It Went
Start of the meeting	• A meme • A story • A quote	The meme worked really well to generate laughter, though it took us down a rabbit hole. I need to be thoughtful about what I do to start the meeting to make sure it connects with what we will be doing later on.

Figure 3.4: Humor in specific situations.

*Visit **go.SolutionTree.com/PLCbooks** for a free reproducible version of this figure.*

Here is a list of other situations you might reflect on when you are filling out this chart.

1. Transitioning between agenda items

2. Addressing the first critical question: What do we want students to know and be able to do?

3. Addressing the second critical question: How will we know when students know and can do it?

4. Addressing the third critical question: What will we do when students don't know and can't do it?

5. Addressing the fourth critical question: What will we do when students do know and can do it?

6. Reflecting on the successes and challenges of the team

7. Setting the next agenda

Use the tool in figure 3.5, page 54, to reflect on the types of humor currently found on your team. Over the course of one or more meetings, consider using it to keep track of how much and what kind of humor is most common by placing a tally mark in the appropriate box. Additional rows are provided for you in an online version of this figure.

Type of Humor	Tally Marks to Track How Often It Occurs
Genuine and natural	
Sarcastic and possibly forced	
Self-denigrating	
Insulting to others (students, parents, and colleagues)	

Figure 3.5: Types of humor.

*Visit **go.SolutionTree.com/PLCbooks** for a free reproducible version of this figure.*

Reflection Questions

When you have finished using one or both tools, use a journal or notebook to reflect on the following questions.

- To what extent is it easy or natural for you to generate laughter?

- What kind of humor is typical on your team—that which is genuine or that which is denigrating? In what ways does this impact the work of the team?

- How can you try to create an atmosphere where everyone is engaging in joyful behavior, including using humor?

- How can laughter become embedded in your tasks?

- How might you bring joy to the mundane?

Pause

Pausing in dialogue with someone is exactly what it sounds like: pausing. And when done well, it's like magic.

We tend to be bombarded all day long with this problem or that issue. Our gut instinct, many times, is to jump in and solve others' problems. Don't. Don't immediately jump in with your solution, and certainly don't interrupt them. Instead, give them space to think—five seconds may feel like a long time *to you*, but it's important to give that time and space. Oddly enough, five seconds won't feel that long *to them*, if you engage in this move with the right techniques. When you give people the gift of space and time to think, they will come up with far better solutions than you ever will. Give them the gift of space, of silence.

Our brains, while miraculous and very fast, require time to think meaningfully about issues. The prefrontal cortex, the front, "thinking" part of the brain, is slower than the rest of the brain. The prefrontal cortex's functioning is something Daniel Kahneman (2011) researched and labeled System 1 and System 2. System 1 is fast, intuitive, and emotional, and it tends to work on autopilot. System 2, on the other hand, is slower, more deliberate, and more logical—it's the brakes of autopilot, and it requires conscious tapping on those brakes in order to activate. Pausing allows System 2 to kick in and enable better conversations, decisions, and relationships. Recognize this and give both yourself and others time to think using System 2.

> **Give people the gift of space and time to think.**

In addition to giving System 2 a chance to process, when you pause before saying something, it increases the credibility and importance of what you are about to say (Grinder, 2018). For example, you might get people's attention, draw in a deep and audible breath through the nose—coupled with a frozen gesture (chapter 6, page 160) and broken eye contact (chapter 4, page 102), for good measure—and after your pause, begin speaking.

A pause after speaking, on the other hand, has the interesting impact of increasing long-term memory. To increase the likelihood of a productive pause after speaking, be sure to use that frozen gesture (chapter 6, page 160).

Types of Pausing Tool

When pausing, there are four broad categories of pausing in which you and your team can engage. These four types can be found along two continuums that intersect each other: (1) individually and collectively and (2) consciously and subconsciously.

As an individual, you, of course, at any time, can take a pause. You might do this consciously by saying something like, "Let me think about this for a minute," or "That's an interesting point, give me a chance to reflect for a moment." A subconscious pause happens when you take a deep, audible inhale that is typically accompanied by breaking eye contact and possibly including a frozen gesture.

A collective pause can also be helpful at times. This might mean saying something like, "So before we proceed, let's just take a moment and think silently and individually about the topic . . ." A collective pause can be particularly needed if the learning is intense or challenging, and you notice that the group has fallen out of rapport or synchronicity. And, of course, that subconscious collective pause can also happen by you facilitating that pause with your nonverbals, as noted above.

Use the tool in figure 3.6 to remind yourself of the types of pausing that might be helpful for you and the team. If this is a technique you are working to implement, consider printing it out and having it with you to remind yourself.

	Individually	Collectively
Consciously	• Say, "Give me a second to think about this." • Say, "By when do we need to make this decision or have this conversation? Given that, let me think about this and get back to you."	• Say, "Let's take a moment to think about this before moving forward." (Break eye contact and take a deep inhale through the nose.) • Say, "Given that we have some time to think about this, let's come back to it [later in the meeting, week, month, or year]."
Subconsciously	• Take a deep, auditory breath in through the nose. • Break eye contact. • Use a frozen gesture.	• Take a deep, auditory breath in through the nose. • Break eye contact. • Use a frozen gesture.

Figure 3.6: Types of pausing tool.

*Visit **go.SolutionTree.com/PLCbooks** for a free reproducible version of this figure.*

Reflection Questions

After considering and using the types of pausing tool, use a journal or notebook to reflect on the following questions.

- Did your pause cause others to also pause? Based on what you've learned for this technique, why might that be?

- What was the effect of your pause on yourself? On the group?

- What refinements might you consider for your use of this technique to increase your effectiveness?

Next-Level Tips

As briefly mentioned, a good, intentional, and purposeful pause is typically accompanied by a couple of other nonverbal moves: a deep inhale, breaking eye contact, and occasionally a frozen gesture. Move your eyes away from theirs (see Break Eye Contact; chapter 4, page 102), and use a frozen gesture (chapter 6, page 160) if you think it is helpful to communicate that you are pausing with that nonverbal cue.

Remember those mirror neurons discussed in chapter 2 (page 29)? Mirror neurons start "firing," and the same thing happens in the brains of different people. If you take a deep inhaling breath to accompany the pause, it's likely that they, too, will take a deep breath with you, and you end up pausing together. Further, pausing with a breath gets the blood oxygenated, and the brain needs oxygen. Specifically, the prefrontal cortex (System 2) needs oxygen to think well and clearly. So take a breath and pause. Finally, be sure your mouth is closed when you take the pause. In western cultures, pausing with your mouth open decreases your credibility (Grinder, 2018).

Third Point

Of the simple, go-to tools shared in this book, this one is probably not only the easiest to implement, but it is also one of the most impactful. It's easy to implement because you probably already do it in many situations without even being aware of it. By becoming conscious of this strategy, you can now use it purposefully to help transform collaboration.

The term third point comes from the notion that you, your own self, are the first "point" in any given interaction (Grinder, n.d.a). The other person or people are the second "point." The third "point," then, is another object. For example, when you use an agenda and have it projected on a screen, the screen is your third point. If you have data posted on chart paper, the data on the chart paper is your third point. When you are studying state standards and rating them individually and then compiling results on a marker board, the ratings on the marker board are your third point.

A third point does two things for a group: (1) it shifts energy and (2) helps with psychological safety. Regarding shifting energy, when we are focused on each other—especially in tense conversations—a third point enables that energy to be directed toward the third point instead of each other. This helps maintain relationships as we engage in a focused conversation where we can be hard on ideas and soft on people. This shift in energy facilitates psychological safety, then, because we have now shifted our energy to this "thing"—our third point—instead of at each other. This psychological safety makes it far easier to engage in productive conflict.

The tool for this strategy is simply having chart paper and markers in your meeting space. Of course, whiteboards can also work, but a piece of chart paper can be saved and brought back to your next meeting. A document projected on a screen can also work as a third point; just be aware that, depending on what you're doing, it might require you to take extra steps to remove any negative associations connected to what has been projected (see the decontaminate space tool, chapter 5, page 126) before or after using that same projected space. So make your life simpler and use chart paper if at all possible.

Reflection Questions

At some point after having engaged intentionally in using third point, use a journal or notebook to reflect on the following questions.

- When have you used third point before?
- As you prepare for your next meeting, at what points will you intentionally use a third point?
- What impact on the team did you notice when using a third point?

Next-Level Tips

Most cultures have an unwritten norm that when someone is looking at something, others will also look. That is to say that listeners' eyes follow the speaker's eyes (Grinder, 2018; Zoller, 2024). This also happens with direct eye contact and when informally interacting. If you are with a friend, and they look across the room at something for a period of time—even for just a few seconds—you will tend to follow their eyes and look at what they are looking at. It's instinctual.

As you use third point, use this instinct to draw attention to the third point. In other words, look at the third point with your own eyes as you are seeking to draw people's attention to it. You will likely feel awkward because you will probably want to look back at your colleagues while talking about the third point—whether data or essential standards or norms or the agenda. You'll feel the strong urge to make eye contact with your colleagues, not the third point. However, push through your own feelings of awkwardness and keep your eyes on the third point while you want them to be looking at that third point. Remember, eyes follow eyes.

We Do It Together

This portion of the chapter focuses on strategies that *the team takes together* to lay the foundation for effectiveness, efficiency, and joy in seeing your students excel. We start with the physical arrangement (MacDonald, 2023) to be sure that the physical space that we occupy is conducive to a learning meeting. Norms ensure that our work as human beings can be done while meeting each other's needs (DuFour et al., 2024), and clarity of roles ensures that everyone has a purpose during the meeting (DuFour et al., 2024; Ferriter, 2020). The use of inclusion (Garmston & Wellman, 2016) ensures that psychological safety is built into the meeting from the get-go, while also making sure that we aren't wasting valuable time on icebreakers that tend to tick many people off. A landing page increases efficiency as there is one place with all the team's important documents. Outcomes clarify the purpose for meeting, and the use of an agenda facilitates the attainment of those outcomes (Garmston & Wellman, 2016). This section will cover the following strategies.

- Physical arrangement
- Norms
- Roles
- Inclusion
- Landing page
- Outcomes
- Running agenda template

Each strategy in the following sections has an accompanying activity or reflective exercise you can use by yourself or with your team. Each strategy will describe the actions, detail tools that are helpful for implementation, offer a few reflection questions, and leave with tips for advanced implementation, including how you might leverage moves, techniques, or strategies from elsewhere in the book for maximum impact.

Physical Arrangement

Just as the physical arrangement of a classroom greatly influences the learning of students, the physical set up of the room in which adults meet directly impacts how the meeting will proceed (MacDonald, 2023).

Consider the effect of walking into a room with rows like a "traditional" classroom. Think about the effect that having the teacher team leader standing at the front talking to colleagues has. What happens if those rows are slightly shifted so that a circle or semicircle is formed where all members see each other? And what if members are spread throughout the room, on their devices, and are not close to one another? You can see how, depending on the arrangement of the room, team members may or may not be able to see each other's nonverbal communication patterns. The effect that this has on the team's ability to function is tremendous.

Use the continuum in figure 3.7 (page 60) to think about options that may be available to you for arranging the physical environment of the meeting space. On one end is an arrangement that may be most conducive to being directive, and on the other end is a depiction of a physical arrangement that is most collaborative. Consider which one might work best in which situation. For example, if the meeting is focused on simply conveying information, a directive meeting format might work well. If the focus is on learning, collaborative arrangements will work best.

Reflection Questions

When you have finished using the preceding tool to reflect on the physical arrangement of your meeting space, use a journal or notebook to reflect on the following questions.

- How is your team's meeting space typically arranged?
- What options are available to you to make it more collaborative?
- What steps might you take to engage your colleagues in a conversation about setting up the meeting space to maximize team effectiveness?

> **The effect that physical space arrangement has on the team's ability to function is tremendous.**

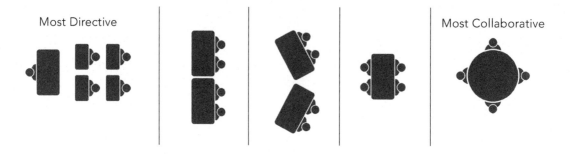

Figure 3.7: Directive versus collaborative scale.

> ### Theory in Action
>
> In thinking about the physical arrangement of a room, I am reminded of a school I was working with where the meetings for the leadership team happened in a classroom that was arranged with typical rows. At the first meeting I attended with them, staff sat in those rows, all facing forward. The underlying tenor of the meeting was one with a clear hierarchy and very little dialogue. Of course, as I worked with the school, we used protocols to proverbially level the playing field and get all voices in the room.
>
> Fast forward to my next visit a couple of months later, and staff automatically rearranged the desks to be in a circle. The tone was very much one of collaboration, even though they had not spoken about changing the physical arrangement of desks. And my next visit, a few months after that, was even more collaborative as members spontaneously stood around the same table to engage in the learning focused on a singular task.

Next-Level Tips

One of the most powerful actions you can take as a teacher team leader is to engage in third point (page 57). When you are setting up the physical arrangement, consider where and how you might be able to utilize this powerful tool in your teacher team leader toolbox.

Norms

Every group has "normal" interactions that are part of who the group is and how it functions. We want those norms to be productive. If norms are not written down, are not followed, and people aren't holding each other accountable to them, then the normal interactions of team members can become counterproductive. Quite frankly, the basic work of collaboration isn't that hard. Teams focus on improving their practice with each other and getting better results for students. It's a matter of reflective practice and action research, and the success of collaboration very directly relates back to creating a psychologically safe environment (Duhigg, 2016).

What's hard about the work of collaboration is that we are doing it with other people (W. M. Ferriter, personal communication, August 5, 2022). The interpersonal dynamics, personal proclivities, internal beliefs, and past experiences all contribute to how we engage with each other. And we want these to assist in the productive accomplishments of the team.

One way to think about norms is that they are an expression of each other's needs (Ferriter, 2020). If our needs are not met, we become grumpy. So think about how to ensure that norms are (1) an expression of the needs of folks, (2) followed, and (3) maintained through systems of mutual accountability.

The basic work of collaboration isn't that hard.

Norms Creation Tool

Identifying team norms on an annual basis is a key part of improving functioning. Use the tool and process in figure 3.8 to collectively establish written norms for team meetings, which is based on a process shared by Richard DuFour and Rebecca DuFour in 2005.

1. Each person has a 3×5 note card. On one side, they individually and silently write three to five pet peeves that they have about meetings. A sentence stem might be: "It really irks me when . . ." and a sample might be: "It really irks me when people are checking their email instead of engaging in the topic at hand." (1–2 minutes)

2. Each person flips the note card over. On this new side, then, they individually and silently write norms that, if followed, would solve their pet peeves. A sentence starter might include: "I would be super pumped if . . ." and a sample might be, "I would be super pumped if the agendas were meaningful and everyone engaged fully." (1–2 minutes)

3. With one other partner, share the norms (ignore the pet peeves and do not share! These are no more) and combine into one list. (3–5 minutes)

4. Repeat by having partners "square" with another partner to share and combine norms. (3–5 minutes)

5. If necessary, repeat the combining of groups and norms until one set for the team remains.

Figure 3.8: Norms creation tool.

Tips for Following Norms

Over the years of working with many teams, I have found that establishing norms can be a formality and is checked off a list of tasks to accomplish with minimal impact on team functioning. As such, I have picked up and identified a few tips to help you, the team leader, and the team itself bring the norms to life and avoid becoming a dusty artifact placed in a binder. These come from Richard DuFour, Rebecca DuFour, Robert Eaker, Thomas Many, Mike Mattos, and Anthony Muhammad (2024) and William M. Ferriter (2020), in addition to my own experience.

- Set new norms every year. (Do not just pull out the old ones and make it a formality to adopt. Create them from scratch—it doesn't take that long.)

- Review norms at the beginning of every meeting until they become internalized.

- Reflect on adherence to norms at the end of each meeting.

- Set up a process to hold each other accountable to the norms, possibly including:

  - A verbal or nonverbal signal of some sort

  - Someone who has the role of norm monitor

  - Holding each other accountable in fun and light-hearted ways

- Thank each other for following norms.

- Formally review and reflect on norms at least twice per year.

Reflection Questions

When you have finished using the norms creation tool in figure 3.8, use a journal or notebook to reflect on the following questions.

- What challenges does your team have in setting and following norms?

- How can you be sure that everyone is holding each other accountable to the norms, and not just you?

Next-Level Tips

Use the norms at the beginning of the meeting as an inclusion (page 65). When you do this, please, please, please do *not* just read the norms out loud. Your colleagues can read. Use that third point (page 57) and be sure to pause (page 54) so that people have an opportunity to reflect before speaking.

Roles

Just as it is important for you to be clear about your role as a teacher team leader, what your role means and what it does *not* mean, it is also helpful for members of the team to have identified and specific roles (Ferriter, 2020) in order to maximize working together. While your team may identify additional or different roles, a few starting points might include a norm monitor, a facilitator, a taskmaster or timekeeper, and a notetaker.

The norm monitor helps the team monitor norms, raising "points of order" to help the team stay on track. While all members are collectively responsible for the establishment and monitoring of adherence to norms, it's sometimes helpful to have one person more focused on the norms than others. Depending on the team, this norm monitor might simply verbally address norm violations, for example, if the team veers off task, the norm monitor might just say, "Just a quick note that we wanted to stay on task, and it seems we've gone down a rabbit hole." Or if a norm is to access everyone's voice and expertise, the norm monitor might call on specific people to share their perspectives if those individuals haven't shared their considerations.

A facilitator is a key role for ensuring that everyone's voice is heard. They also help keep the meeting moving forward while minimizing tangential conversations. While the facilitator is technically charged with keeping everyone on task, sometimes they (or you) are busy ensuring everyone's voice is heard and don't necessarily notice how much time is spent on different tasks. So a taskmaster or timekeeper may be helpful to monitor how much time is spent on each agenda item. In some cases, they might provide a warning to let the team know how much time is left on a topic—whether one, two, five, or ten minutes (depending on how much time the item is allotted). Or, they might announce when the allocated time for an agenda item has passed.

Finally, a note taker records decisions made by the team in the team's notes. They also may assist with the development of products associated with the team—for example, what essential standards the team has agreed on for an upcoming unit, the list of unpacked and prioritized learning targets from essentials, the common formative assessments (CFAs) that have been developed and when they will be administered, and so on.

Please know that when a person takes on a role, it is not a lifetime sentence. Roles can (and probably should) periodically rotate. While weekly is probably too often for this rotation to occur, consider a process where the roles change or rotate monthly, bi-monthly, or quarterly.

Finally, not all teams have four or more people on them to take on these four roles separately. As a team, decide which roles you need. In some cases people will take on more than one role at a time. In other cases, not everyone will have a distinct role identified (other than being an engaged colleague).

Possible Roles, Tasks, and Reflections Tool

Use the following tool in figure 3.9 (page 64) as a starting point for the team to clarify the roles of team members. A reflection column is also provided

> **All members are collectively responsible for the establishment and monitoring of adherence to norms.**

Role	Responsibilities and Tasks	Reflections

Norm monitor	• The norm monitor must:
	  ▪ Be clear on what each norm means in practice (or gain clarity as the need arises)
	  ▪ Lovingly point out when one or more norms are not being followed
	  ▪ Reflect with the team on how adherence to the norms is going
		This is a challenging role, and we need to provide each other with grace in doing it. Maybe we can intentionally praise our norm monitor for making sure we stay on task?

Facilitator	• The facilitator must:
	  ▪ Ensure everyone's voice is heard
	  ▪ Keep the meeting moving forward without distractions
	  ▪ Make sure that topics not on the agenda have a place or way for being addressed
		While we want this role to ultimately rotate, maybe we start with someone who is already good at this role. This way we can be sure to get habits in place before rotating to others.

Taskmaster or timekeeper	• The taskmaster must:
	  ▪ Be clear about how much time the team wants to spend on each agenda item
	  ▪ Keep track of how much time is spent on those agenda items
	  ▪ Share with the team how much time is spent on each agenda item
	  ▪ If needed, provide an advance warning to the team of how much time has been spent on each agenda item
		Sometimes it's helpful to have this role be fulfilled by someone who struggles with staying on task. Other times not so much. It may be important for the team to regularly reflect on the roles and who is fulfilling them to be sure that we are maximizing each other's skills while building new capacities.

Note taker	• The note taker must:
	  ▪ Be clear about the decisions of the team
	  ▪ Record those decisions accurately
	  ▪ Record additional commentary or discussion as decided on by the team
	  ▪ Ensure all members have access to team notes
	  ▪ Access prior notes to remind the team of previous decisions to not duplicate efforts and conversations
		We need to be sure that just because we have one notetaker, everyone else doesn't disengage.

Figure 3.9: Roles, tasks, and reflections chart.

*Visit **go.SolutionTree.com/PLCbooks** for a free reproducible version of this figure.*

for the team to reflect on the implementation of team roles. A blank version of the tool is available online.

Reflection Questions

When you have finished completing the possible roles, tasks, and reflections chart, use a journal or notebook to reflect on the following questions.

- What roles might be helpful for you and your team members to identify and assign?
- How will the team monitor the effectiveness of those roles?

Next-Level Tips

Sometimes it can feel like drudgery to identify team member roles. But it doesn't have to be this way. Have fun with it! Instead of a "taskmaster" or "facilitator," what about "flight control?" You and your colleagues can come up with some clever titles and bring about some laughter and authentic joy in the process.

Inclusion

When I was a first-year principal, one of the teachers came to me privately and said, quite bluntly, "Chad, people don't care about your meeting." After getting over the initial blow to my ego, I realized they were right. When people go into a meeting, they aren't thinking about the meeting. They are thinking about the interaction they just had with a student, an angry email that they just received from a parent, a celebratory phone call from a family member, or any number of topics not related to the meeting. They, quite literally, don't care about your meeting. So one of the tasks of a team leader is to get your colleagues to care about the meeting. And that's where inclusion comes into play.

First of all, inclusion (Garmston & Wellman, 2016) is very different from an icebreaker. Icebreakers tick off half the people in the room. Ticked off people don't help get more done. And, at the risk of stating the obvious, don't contribute to a joyful atmosphere. Don't do an icebreaker. Do an inclusion.

An inclusion activity does three things: (1) it focuses the mental energy of each person in the room, (2) it gets everyone's voice in the room, and (3) it starts to build community as we connect with each other and the content. Icebreakers, many times, will do two of those three things, but they typically don't focus our mental energy. And while it's possible that they build community for those who aren't angry, they don't often connect us to the content.

The second important thing to keep in mind about an inclusion activity is that they are quick, sometimes as little as thirty seconds, but probably between one and three minutes.

One more quick note about inclusion: it facilitates starting meetings on time. Even if everyone isn't there, start with an inclusion when the meeting is scheduled to start. This act sends the message that the team will start on time. People tend to enjoy this novel way to start meetings, so they will work harder to be on time. Plus, it allows for a start that doesn't require the repeating of content because someone missed critical discussions about the work of the team.

Inclusion Activity Ideas Tool

In order to (1) focus our mental energy, (2) get everyone's voice in the room, and (3) build community connected to the content, consider using one of the inclusion activities in figure 3.10 for an upcoming meeting. Then use the tool as a resource to generate ideas for future inclusion activities.

Reflection Questions

As you use the inclusion activity ideas tool, use a journal or notebook to reflect on the following questions.

- What about the inclusion activity helped to focus the mental energy, get everyone's voice in the room, and build purposeful community?

- What didn't work terribly well that you want to change for next time?

- In what ways might you change the type of inclusion that you use to ensure variety and engagement?

Next-Level Tips

Use a third point (page 57) to both create synchronicity and a greater likelihood that colleagues will look at the prompt, quote, norms, commitments, or agenda and outcomes. This synchronicity not only creates rapport, but it also enables people to think more deeply about what they are being asked. Consider coupling the use of a third point with an audible deep breath (page 50), being clear that this isn't perceived as a sigh and therefore a sign of frustration.

Landing Page

Once upon a time, teams had three ring binders of their team materials. When I started working as a central office administrator, we actually purchased binders with pre-printed tabs for every new staff member in the district (veterans

Type of Inclusion	Script
Review agenda and desired outcomes	• "As you review today's agenda and outcomes, what are you most looking forward to?" • "Looking at today's agenda and outcomes, what needs to be added, changed, or deleted to make today's meeting successful for you and us?"
Connections to norms	Start with allowing a silent review of the norms. Then use one of the following prompts. Alternatively, you could start with the prompt and then allow for silence to reflect, think, and then share. "What needs to be added, changed, or deleted to meet your needs today?" "Which of our norms do you think will be a . . ." (choose one) • "Struggle for you today?" • "Struggle for us today?" • "Focus for you today?" • "Focus for us today?"
Celebrations related to team commitments	As the team reflects so it can celebrate its collective commitments, it is sometimes helpful to only look at a handful, such as the first three or four, to focus the thinking and celebrations. After such a focus, then consider a prompt like: "As you look at the commitments that we have made to each other and our students, what celebrations would you like to share about your own work or others on the team or school?"
Quotes	Choose a quote related to your team, the school mission, the PLC process, and so on, then say something like: "As you think about this quote, what practical applications do you see for us today?" Some go-to quotes might include the following. • "Ralph Waldo Emerson is reported to have asked friends, 'What has become clear to you since last we met?' In that vein, what has become clear to you about our work as a team since last we met?" • "John Dewey has said that 'We don't learn from experience. We learn from reflecting on experience.' What does this make you think about today?" • "Michael Fullan says that groups can be powerful, which also means that groups can be powerfully wrong. How might this concept apply to our work as a team?" • "Ken Blanchard states, curlyPeople should learn less more and not more less.' What are your thoughts about this idea, and how might it relate to our practice as teachers and as a team?" • "There's an African proverb that says if you want to go fast, go alone. And if you want to go far, go together. In what ways might this apply to our work? And how can we try to go both far and fast?"
Prompts	Choose a prompt from the following for colleagues to reflect on for a few seconds. Then consider also including a follow-up question like, "Given . . ., how might we leverage these in our work as a team today and this year?" • "What might your family say are your greatest strengths?" • "What is the wisest thing you've ever heard?" • "Who has been the most influential teacher in your life?" • "Where is the most peaceful place for you and why?" • "What are some things we take for granted on this team?" • "What do you admire about people who show empathy and loving kindness to others?" • "If you had to choose one word to describe you, what would it be?"

Figure 3.10: Inclusion activity ideas tool.

already had one). There was a tab for norms, a tab for the list of essentials, one for SMART goals, and so on. Teachers were expected to bring this binder to every team meeting and use it to house all of the products of the team. While the impact on trees was negative, every team member had their documents and knew exactly where to find them.

While digital resources save trees, this added value sometimes leads to fumbling around from a lack of a paper trail. How many times do we get to meetings and spend precious and limited time searching for this or that document? And then, once someone finds what they think is the right document, we open it up and find out that it's a previous version, owned by someone else, or realize some other reason it is not able to do what we need it to do. So we continue searching, wasting valuable collaboration minutes. The solution? A landing page!

A landing page is one page (sometimes two or three) that houses links to all documents that the team needs. See figure 3.11 (pages 69–70) for an example. Some teams, once they have their links generally set up, will download the document as a PDF and put it on their desktop. The PDF format will preserve the links so that, if the document is simply on their desktop, they don't have to even search their folders for it every meeting. If you choose to do this, I might suggest that you also add an additional link at the top with a link to the landing page, itself. This way, if the other links change, the team can still access the landing page from the PDF document and then access the updated links from there.

Reflection Questions

When you have finished creating a landing page, use a journal or notebook to reflect on the following questions.

- What additional links would be helpful to include on your team's landing page?

- What changes might you make to the landing page so it is more beneficial to you and your team?

- How might you use the concept of a landing page for other aspects of your work to improve effectiveness and efficiency?

Next-Level Tips

As the team gets used to having a landing page, consider having one person whose team role (page 62) is keeping it up to date. In this way, you will start to build ownership in the work of the team by having multiple people taking responsibility for tracking and documenting the team's learning, instead of just you.

Outcomes

There are three most important things to always keep in mind for any meeting (Garmston & Wellman, 2016). The first most important thing about any given meeting is to *have clear outcomes*. People want to know *why* they are in the meeting. The second most important thing about any meeting is to *have clear outcomes*. People want to know *what* the meeting is about. No one likes to have their time wasted. They want to know what they are there to accomplish—outcomes do just this. And, finally, the third most important

---

INSERT YOUR SCHOOL LOGO

Team Action Record Form
(Copy and paste for each meeting on the same document with the most recent meeting at the top)
INSERT SCHOOL/DISTRICT WEBSITE LINK(S)

Our Data Dashboard

	Essential 1		Essential 2		Essential 3		Essential 4	
	Where we started	Where we are now	Where we started	Where we are now	Where we started	Where we are now	Where we started	Where we are now
Percent of Students Proficient								

Contacts	Name	Team Role	Phone Number
Resources	allthingsplc.info https://www.solutiontree.com/free-repros		

Periodically Reviewed Resources
(Create links to each document)

Norms
Commitments
SMART goal(s)
Critical issues for team consideration
Quarterly reflection tool

Figure 3.11: Landing page template.

continued ▶

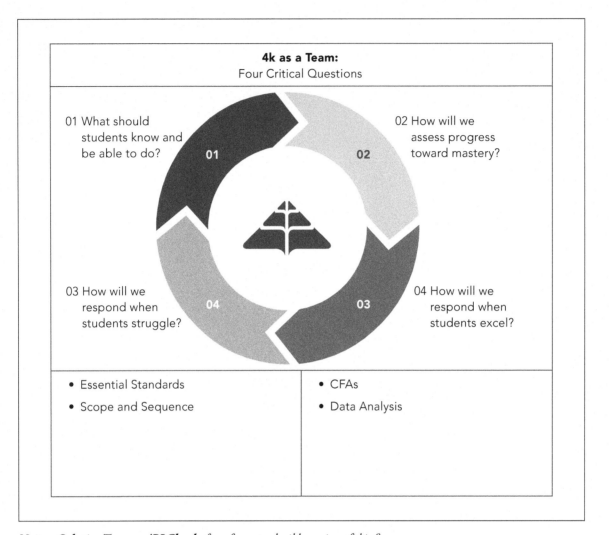

*Visit **go.SolutionTree.com/PLCbooks** for a free reproducible version of this figure.*

thing about any meeting is . . . you guessed it! To *have clear outcomes*. People want to know *how* their knowledge, skills, and talents will contribute to the greater good of the team and organization. They need to know the expectations for the meeting.

Setting outcomes doesn't take long and can very easily be done when setting the agenda (at the end of the previous meeting). And, as a point of emphasis, always remember that the purpose of the team is to guarantee that all students learn team-identified, grade-level essential outcomes. This is the entire reason for the existence of the team.

Before going any further, let's briefly explore different types of outcomes, as there are many (Van Soelen, 2021). For the purposes of teacher teams, I think it's helpful to think of outcomes as three different types: (1) to learn (or understand), (2) to decide, and (3) to inform. In a PLC, the first two are laudable outcomes for a team meeting. The third should be a rarity. While it may sound harsh, if folks need to be informed of something, put it in a memo or email (or, at the very most, reserve the last five minutes of the meeting for information and managerial type outcomes).

Because we are engaging in the work of a professional *learning* community, outcomes around *learning* will be a priority. Start with learning..Maybe we need to learn about grading practices, assessment types, kinds of learning targets, or specific instructional techniques. We might be seeking to understand each other, our system, a practice or policy, or the implications of a current or future practice or policy. Start with learning, and then move into the second type of outcome (decide) after coming to some common understandings.

This leads to the second type of outcome, and that is to make a decision. We are good at this. Research indicates that the average teacher makes more than 1,500 decisions per day, or roughly four decisions every minute (Continental Press, 2023)! We make a lot of decisions.

Unfortunately, many times we jump to decisions too quickly. We fail to engage in adequate learning, and we neglect seeking to understand each other's perspectives. Some of us, too, take longer than others to understand *our own* thoughts about a subject and need time to think about it before we can offer our opinion, why one thing doesn't seem right, or why another is better. This all leads to a failure to consider the impact of decisions on our individual and collective practices. As a result, we make decisions that end up not sticking. Sound familiar?

You may have heard of the *pendulum effect* in education. We get hit with this year's fad or another school district's program, and then, in short order, it disappears, and we swing in a different direction. Just like a pendulum. And if you've been in education long enough, you've been hit by the same pendulum a couple of times! Part of this, I believe, is because we make decisions without first learning and developing collective understanding. Teams need to have clear outcomes that make sure they are focused on the right work, that the agendas are aligned to those outcomes, and that the team starts with the right types of outcomes and then works their way through them: learning and understanding, followed by making decisions. As noted earlier, there is one more type of outcome for meetings. For the sake of emphasis, in a PLC, this type should rarely (if ever) be used: to inform. Table 3.1 (page 71) lists some possible outcomes associated with the critical issues of a team in a PLC at Work.

Critical Issues and Their Outcomes Tool

As noted earlier, in a PLC at Work, the work of teams revolves around the four critical questions. More specifically, eighteen actions of teams were identified by DuFour and colleagues (2024), and these are identified as "critical issues." The tool in table 3.1 connects the critical issues of the work of teams with the types of outcomes in which a team might engage in order to accomplish those critical issues. Please note that these are only samples and not an exhaustive list of possible outcomes for the critical issues.

Outcome Tracking Tool

Use the tool in figure 3.12 to track the dates of the types of outcomes your team is focusing on over the course of a semester or year. Do this by putting the date of the meeting where the team addressed that type of outcome in a box below that type of outcome. Then reflect on what the data says about the team and consider potential next steps. Remember that outcomes that inform should be rare and take minimal time if you want your team to be high performing. To assist you, a sample is included for one team in one semester.

After you've completed the outcome tracker tool, consider the following questions. This will precede your reflection question prompts.

- Which types of outcomes do your team spend the majority of time on?

- What next steps might be appropriate based on this?

Reflection Questions

When you have finished reflecting on the critical issues and their outcomes tool (table 3.1), as well as the outcome tracker tool (figure 3.12), use a journal or notebook to reflect on the following questions.

- How has clarity of outcomes assisted your team with becoming more effective and efficient?

- What next steps will be important for you and your team to ensure that everyone is clear about the outcomes of each meeting?

Learning or Understanding Outcomes						Deciding Outcomes						Informing Outcomes					
8/24	8/31	9/6	9/14	9/21	10/12	8/31	9/7	9/14	9/21	9/28	10/5	9/20	10/5	12/14			
10/19	11/2	11/30	12/14			10/19	11/2	11/9	11/16	11/30	12/7						
						12/14											

Figure 3.12: Outcome tracker tool.

*Visit **go.SolutionTree.com/PLCbooks** for a free reproducible version of this figure.*

Table 3.1: Critical Issues and Their Outcomes

Critical Issues	Possible Learning or Understanding Outcomes	Deciding Possible Outcomes
1. We have identified team norms and protocols to guide us in working together.	• To explore a protocol for identifying norms • To learn about possible protocols to make our work more effective • To better understand each other's needs	• To establish norms for our meetings • To choose a data analysis protocol
2. We have analyzed student achievement data and established SMART goals to improve on the level of achievement we are working interdependently to attain. (SMART goals are strategic and specific, measurable, attainable, results oriented, and time bound)	• To learn what is involved in setting SMART goals • To understand our current levels of performance • To understand our current strengths and areas for growth	• To establish our long- and/or short-term SMART goals
3. Each member of our team is clear on the knowledge, skills, and dispositions (that is, the essential learning) that students will acquire as a result of (1) our course or grade level and (2) each unit within the course or grade level.	• To study the standards • To see the connections between grade-level standards • To recognize connections between content areas	• To identify priority essential learning that we will guarantee for all students
4. We have aligned the essential learning with state and district standards and the high-stakes assessments required of our students.	• To identify explicit connections between external assessments and our standards • To understand what we need to emphasize as part of instruction and assessment	• To decide on what will be priorities for learning
5. We have identified course content and topics that can be eliminated so we can devote more time to the essential curriculum.	• To learn about the importance of identifying content to de-emphasize or even eliminate • To better understand what content might be de-emphasized or even eliminated • To understand where in our curriculum materials non-essential content is found	• To decide what we will de-emphasize or even eliminate from our curriculum materials

continued ▲

74 THE TEACHER TEAM LEADER HANDBOOK

Critical Issues	Possible Learning or Understanding Outcomes	Deciding Possible Outcomes
6. We have agreed on how to best sequence the content of the course and have established pacing guides to help students achieve the intended essential learning.	• To understand our current scope and sequence • To understand how early concepts contribute toward learning later in the course	• To decide on the sequence of our essential learning standards • To decide on what type of pacing guide works best for our team (Quarterly? Monthly? By unit?)
7. We have identified the prerequisite knowledge and skills students need in order to master the essential learning of each unit of instruction.	• To come to a common understanding of the prerequisite skills we will preassess to ensure student success	• To decide what prerequisite knowledge and skills we will make sure students have before starting the unit
8. We have identified strategies and created instruments to assess whether students have the prerequisite knowledge and skills.	• To learn about ways we could find out what students already know about our upcoming unit	• To select or create the tool(s) to assess prerequisite knowledge and/or skills • To decide on when we will administer our tools
9. We have developed strategies and systems to assist students in acquiring prerequisite knowledge and skills when they are lacking in those areas.	• To learn from each other how we have or might help students acquire prerequisites • To learn from others how to best help students acquire specific prerequisites • To study scheduling options for helping students acquire prerequisites	• To decide how we will individually help students acquire prerequisites • To decide how we will collectively help students acquire prerequisites
10. We have developed frequent CFAs that help us to determine each student's mastery of essential learning.	• To come to a common understanding of what constitutes a CFA • To learn about Depth of Knowledge (DOK) or Bloom's levels and how to best measure these	• To decide what assessment tool will best measure student learning based on the DOK or Bloom's level • To schedule when we will administer our CFAs
11. We have established the proficiency standard we want each student to achieve on each skill and concept examined with our common assessments.	• To study exemplars (national, state, or district) to learn what proficiency might look like • To clarify what evidence would be best to determine proficiency on each learning target (a cut score, criteria, checklists, rubric, exemplars) • To share what we think proficiency looks like for each learning target on each CFA	• To decide what we will accept in common to determine proficiency on each learning target

12. We use the results of our common assessments to assist each other in building on strengths and addressing weaknesses as part of an ongoing process of continuous improvement designed to help students achieve at higher levels.	• To understand how each of our classes of students performed on our CFA • To identify areas of strengths and growth for us as individuals • To identify areas of strengths and growth for us as a team	• To select learning for us as individuals to get better results • To select learning for us as a team to get better results
13. We use the results of our common assessments to identify students who need additional time and support to master essential learning, and we work within the systems and processes of the school to ensure they receive that support.	• To understand student needs based on specific learning targets • To consider misconceptions that students have about specific learning targets	• To identify students who need additional time and support • To decide how we will provide that time and support
14. We have agreed on the criteria we will use in judging the quality of student work related to the essential learning of our course, and we continually practice applying those criteria to ensure we are consistent.	• To learn from each other about how we judge the quality of student work	• To make a decision on the criteria we will accept for different levels of student performance
15. We have taught students the criteria we will use in judging the quality of their work and provided them with examples.	• To understand the criteria we will use to judge student work • To share possible examples of student work that we might share with students	• To decide which exemplars we will commonly share with students
16. We have developed or utilized common summative assessments that help us assess the strengths and weaknesses of our program.	• To understand how each of our classes of students performed on our common summative assessment • To identify areas of strengths and growth for us as a program	• To identify changes that we want to make for next year • To identify changes that we might make yet this year
17. We have established the proficiency standard we want each student to achieve on each skill and concept examined with our summative assessments.	• To study exemplars (national, state, or district) to learn what proficiency might look like • To clarify what evidence would be best to determine proficiency on each learning target (e.g., a cut score, criteria, checklists, rubric, exemplars) • To share what we think proficiency looks like for each learning target on each	• To decide what we will accept in common to determine proficiency on each learning target for the summative assessment
18. We formally evaluate our adherence to team norms and the effectiveness of our team at least twice each year.	• To understand each other's perspectives on how we're doing as a team	• To make changes (if needed) and recommit to our mutually agreed-on norms

Source: DuFour et al., 2024.

Next-Level Tips

As your team gets used to being clear about the outcomes for each meeting, take a few seconds at the end of the meeting to revisit the identified outcomes. Reflect together on how the team did and what it could have done differently to better meet them.

Running Agenda Template

You might be surprised at the number of meetings I get to visit where an agenda is absent. Unfortunately, if you and the team are not clear about what you're doing, you won't be able to do it. Have an agenda in advance of each meeting.

Without an agenda, we show up unfocused, unprepared, and unable to maximize our own and each other's productivity. Further, without an agenda, the likelihood of us meeting the identified outcomes drops dramatically. An agenda helps increase the likelihood that we will meet our outcomes.

However, any old agenda won't do. The agenda has to be focused on topics and activities that will help the team accomplish its outcomes. In other words, tie the agenda to the outcomes. Just like it is good instructional practice to engage in backward design, so, too, is it good practice to engage in backward design for meeting planning. First, identify your outcomes. Then, identify the agenda items and activities that will get you there.

Remember the notion of the landing page (page 66)? Link your agenda document on that landing page for easy access.

In addition to linking your agenda, have *one* agenda document for the entire year (or maybe even two or three years) as your running agenda (and notes). Then, at the top of the document, create a table of contents that will update automatically (if in Google Docs) when new dates are added. Finally, and this is counterintuitive but will pay dividends down the road, go backward. Start with the most recent meeting date at the top of the document (right after the table of contents). This way, when people open the document, the first thing they see after the table of contents is the agenda and notes for the current meeting.

Here's why: Your team will learn and make decisions over the course of the year (or multiple years). When it comes time to remember what was learned or decided, who will remember the exact date of that topic? Almost no one. You'll spend time searching through multiple documents trying to figure out if you talked about that topic on September 16 or 23, or was it October 5 or 15? Or maybe we did that in August? Meanwhile . . . time is ticking. Precious collaboration time. If you have *one* document that keeps both your agenda and notes, a simple Command + F on a Mac (the "F" is for "Find") or Control + F on a PC will enable a quick keyword search of the entire document. Within seconds, you'll be able to recall that prior learning or decision (as an added tip, this search function works on websites, Excel spreadsheets, and PDFs, as well). Many agenda templates abound, and two are provided for you here to consider.

Agenda Templates

Use the template in figure 3.13 (page 78) for setting the team meeting agenda (what needs to get done) and recording what was accomplished during the meeting.

This first template is fairly broad in nature, yet it contains all of the essential elements necessary for effective functioning. Some teams appreciate more detail in their agenda, for which the following template may be helpful.

Template Option 2 Sample

You'll notice a few aspects of this alternate agenda template in figure 3.14 (page 80). First, it is clear who will be leading or facilitating each portion of the meeting. Second, the team is clear about what they're doing and why they're doing it, and there is a written, step-by-step procedure for how the team will go about doing it. The use of written directions is very helpful for learners, as we then have something we can refer back to when we forget what the next step is that we are supposed to do. Finally, there is a portion for materials so that participants know what is being used in each part. It also helps the meeting planner think through what materials are required (sticky notes, note cards, chart paper). And, as a bonus, if it is created in a Google Doc, digital materials can link directly to those resources, whether they are Google Docs in a drive, website articles, videos, or other kinds of resources.

Reflection Questions

As you consider your current agenda template and the two offered here, use a journal or notebook to reflect on the following questions.

- Which of the agenda templates best aligns with your and your team's style?

- What changes to that agenda template might make it more useful to your team?

- How does having an agenda improve your and your team's effectiveness?

- In what ways does being clear about next steps help your team?

> **If you and the team are not clear about what you are doing, you won't be able to do it.**

THE TEACHER TEAM LEADER HANDBOOK

Agenda Template

Team name: _____

Start time: _____ End time: _____ Today's date: _____

Team members present:

_____

_____

_____

Team members absent (reason):

_____

_____

_____

Team SMART goal:

_____

_____

Today's outcomes:

To Learn or Understand	To Decide	To Inform

Agenda:

1. Norm review

2. Celebrations (here or at the end)

3. Review of the agenda (our outcomes)

4. DO THE WORK (One or more of the critical questions)

5. Set next agenda and outcomes

    a. Learn or understand

    b. Decide

    c. Inform

6. Celebrations (if not at the beginning)

7. Review norms

We agreed on the following actions (Who will do what by when):

Who	Will do *what*	*By when*

Our next team meeting is scheduled for: Date: _____ Time: _____

Figure 3.13: Sample agenda template 1.

*Visit **go.SolutionTree.com/PLCbooks** for a free reproducible version of this figure.*

Next-Level Tips

Having an agenda is an important first step for a team. Once you have it, use a third point (page 57) and display the agenda, so it is not just on your computers. Either have hard copies for each person or project it. Projecting is particularly helpful for having a visual reference of where you are in the agenda. Finally, stop the meeting three to five minutes before the designated time to close the meeting with clarity around next steps and reflection.

Putting It All Together

Use the tool in figures 3.14 (page 80) and 3.15 (page 81) to reflect on your work. To assist you in pulling together your learning from this chapter, following is a story of a teacher team leader and a description of the team and its members. Consider what content from this chapter might best assist her in leading the team.

> Tamisha is a high school teacher team leader who is new to this role, but not to teaching. Her team of three other ninth-grade teachers meet weekly for one hour as part of a regularly scheduled early release that the district has for all teachers to collaborate. While Tamisha is in her sixteenth year of teaching, two of the three others are new. One is fresh out of college, another has four years of experience but is new to this school, and the fourth is a veteran of twenty-eight years who speaks regularly of retirement being right around the corner.

> The team has traditionally met in the team leader's classroom for their meetings, and Tamisha's is organized in three rows with two desks side-by-side and parallel to each other in each row, facing a whiteboard at the front of the room. Tamisha's desk is at the back of the room.

> While the team is mostly collegial (they enjoy each other's company), the team struggles with following through on decisions. Significant chunks of time are spent trying to remember what has been decided previously. Frequent refrains you might hear from members of the team include, "What do we need to talk about today?" or "Do we even need to meet this week? I sure could use the time to grade papers," or "Do I need to bring my laptop today?"

> The teacher with four years of experience rarely speaks up, and the brand new teacher is a proverbial wild card for how they might interact with the team because no one has served with them previously.

Based on this scenario, use figure 3.16 (page 82) to circle the responsibilities, assumptions, and mindsets that you believe will be most critical for Tamisha to keep at the forefront of her mind. How might you suggest she does this? Having considered the responsibilities, assumptions, and mindsets, which of the moves, techniques, and strategies do you think would be most useful for Tamisha at the team's first (and subsequent) meetings? How would you suggest she go about using them?

80 THE TEACHER TEAM LEADER HANDBOOK

Who	What	Why	How		
			Materials		
Meeting Expectations, Norms, and Working Agreements: We will . . .					
Name	Inclusion, outcomes, agenda: Collective commitments	☐ To bring our best selves into this space and ground ourselves in relationship to the content and each other	• Individually: Review the collective commitments that we generated last time we were together. • Share with a partner an example of work done within the past few weeks that embodies one of the drafted commitments.		
			Collective commitments		
Name	The work	☐ To improve our own practice and results for students ☐ To decide on essential standards for our next unit and unpack those into discrete learning targets	• Follow the attached R. E. A. L. criteria protocol to select essential standards. • Use the attached unpacking tool to identify learning targets.		
			State standards District curriculum guide Textbook R. E. A. L. criteria Unpacking tool		
Name	Set next agenda	☐ To maximize our effectiveness by continuing our work from week to week with minimal wasted time	• Use our timeline and learning cycle expectations to determine our next agenda.		
			Agenda Timeline Learning cycle expectations		
Name	*Who* will do *what* by *when*	☐ To build in mutual accountability that ensures our work continues between meetings	**Who**	**What**	**By When**
Name	Celebrations	☐ To leverage our individual and collective strengths and leave our meeting celebrating each other	Who would you like to honor, based on one of our schoolwide or team commitments, this week? This could be students, staff, parents, or yourself!		

Figure 3.14: Sample agenda template 2.

*Visit **go.SolutionTree.com/PLCbooks** for a free reproducible version of this figure.*

Responsibilities, Assumptions, and Mindsets	Notes for How to Keep This in Mind
Responsibilities: 1. Make it safe. 2. Build capacity. 3. Do the work.	
Assumptions: 1. People do the best that they can. 2. You can only control you. 3. Behavior communicates. 4. People want to get stuff done. 5. Conflict is good.	
Mindsets: 1. To see what others don't (yet) see in themselve. 2. To be humble with a posture of learnin. 3. To spread the contagion of joy	

Figure 3.15: Pulling together your learning reflection chart.

*Visit **go.SolutionTree.com/PLCbooks** for a free reproducible version of this figure.*

Possible Next Steps

Please note: Even though this vignette highlights multiple moves, techniques, and strategies as part of the first meeting, this is not meant to imply that, after the first meeting, they can be ignored. On the contrary, these moves, techniques, and strategies will need to be employed throughout the course of the year.

Having considered the strategies mentioned in this chapter, Tamisha decides that the physical arrangement of her room, while suited for her fifteen-year-old students and her instructional style, is not best for adult team meetings. Prior to the first meeting of the year, she quickly moves a few of the desks at the front of her room, near the whiteboard, to create a circle for the meeting. She does this knowing that the set up of the room communicates to others that they are all equals, while also having access to the whiteboard as a third point when that time comes. She does not sit at her desk, but instead joins the circle she just created.

She decides to set this first agenda herself, with minimal input from colleagues, to ensure that a solid foundation is laid for future success. That agenda includes the following.

- Clear outcomes

- An inclusion that is focused on developing norms (using the tool and process provided in this chapter to ensure equity of voice)

- The identification and assignment of team member roles (using the tool provided in this chapter)

- Clarity around the work of the team (including the use of a landing page and running agenda template).

You Do It Yourself	
Moves and Techniques	**How and When Might Tamisha Use It?**
Group rapport	
Breathing	
Laughter and humor	
Pause	
Third point	
We Do It Together	
Strategies	**How and When Might Tamisha Use It?**
Physical arrangement	
Norms	
Roles	
Inclusion	
Landing page	
Outcomes	
Running agenda template	

Figure 3.16: Do it yourself and we do it together vignette chart.

*Visit **go.SolutionTree.com/PLCbooks** for a free reproducible version of this figure.*

First Meeting Outcomes

- To better understand each other and our needs so that we can function effectively

- To identify ways to hold each other accountable (and celebrate!) adherence to norms

- To identify and assign team roles

- To clarify processes we will use to maximize our work, including next steps and next agendas

Tamisha projects the agenda onto a screen so all can see, thereby creating a third point that they can reference together. Prior to the inclusion activity, she plans to show a humorous slide that reads as follows.

"Are you lonely? Do you work on your own or hate making decisions?"

"Hold a meeting! You can see people, draw flow charts, feel important, and impress your colleagues . . . all on your organization's time!"

"Meetings . . . the practical alternative to work!"

Tamisha figures that this slide will generate some laughter, which also leads to similar breathing patterns. She then plans to use the inclusion activity, consisting of developing the norms, to further develop group rapport as synchronicity takes place when everyone writes down their thoughts. To remind herself to pause and give people a chance to think, she writes "P-A-U-S-E" large on a sticky note and places it on her computer screen as a reminder. She has learned that one of the secrets to transforming collaboration is in laying a solid foundation for team productivity.

Summary Reflective Questions

When you have finished pulling together your learning, use a journal or notebook to reflect on the following questions.

- What lessons might you take from Tamisha's experience and plan?
- What will you apply to your setting?
- What next steps do you see yourself taking?
- What criteria will you use to determine whether or not you are being successful in that implementation and what course corrections you might need to make?

Conclusion

Getting started in any endeavor, overcoming inertia or the habits of past practice, is sometimes the hardest part of improvement. Kudos to you for starting, and for working to ensure that a foundation is solidly established. This groundwork includes you using the moves and techniques to establish group rapport, like paying attention to breathing and using laughter and humor to establish synchronicity. The pause and third point were also highlighted in this effort to illuminate moves and techniques to transform the work of the team. In terms of strategies that the team might use, setting up the physical arrangement of the room, together with collectively establishing norms, clarifying the roles of team members, and starting every meeting with a brief inclusion are key. A landing page, clear outcomes, and the use of a running agenda template will also facilitate meetings where more can be done in less time, leading to greater joy.

REPRODUCIBLE

84

Chapter 3: You Do It Yourself
Planning and Reflection Tool

Now that we have explored these moves and techniques for getting started, consider your own situation and reflect on what you will begin to use immediately. Which moves and techniques will you need to practice before using? What sort of systematic schedule might you create for implementation? And which ones will you reserve for later on in your leadership journey?

You Do It Yourself				
Move or Technique	To Start Immediately	Needs Some Practice	When and How Will I Practice?	Save for Later
Group rapport				
Breathing				
Laughter and humor				
Pause				
Third point				

The Teacher Team Leader Handbook © 2025 Chad M. V. Dumas • SolutionTree.com
Visit **go.SolutionTree.com/PLCbooks** to download this free reproducible.

Chapter 3: We Do It Together
Planning and Reflection Tool

Now that we have explored these strategies for getting started, consider your own situation and reflect on what you will begin to use immediately. Which strategies will you need to practice before using? What sort of systematic schedule might you create for implementing? And which ones will you reserve for later on in your leadership journey?

We Do It Together				
Strategy	**To Start Immediately**	**Needs Some Practice**	**When and How Will I Practice?**	**Save for Later**
Physical arrangement				
Norms				
Roles				
Inclusion				
Landing page				
Outcomes				
Running agenda template				

The Teacher Team Leader Handbook © 2025 Chad M. V. Dumas • SolutionTree.com
Visit **go.SolutionTree.com/PLCbooks** to download this free reproducible.

*Coming together is a beginning;
keeping together is progress;
working together is success.*

—Edward Everett Hale

CHAPTER 4

Gaining Momentum

At this point, you have been working to lay a solid foundation for your own leadership skills that will help the team to (1) create psychological safety, (2) build capacity, and (3) get work done. Now you will want to gain momentum in the work while continuing to refine the skills you have learned from chapter 3 (page 45).

You Do It Yourself

This section shares potential moves and techniques that will continue to increase your influence and the effectiveness of the team. With the foundation of pausing (from the prior chapter), paraphrasing and the use of questions will be exponentially helpful for you and the team (Garmston & Wellman, 2016). Being clear about your choice of voice will make sure that you are perceived in ways that you want when you are engaging with your colleagues, while gestures and words of inclusion implicitly and explicitly help people to feel included in the work (Grinder, 2018; K. Zoller, personal communication, April 6, 2023). "And (not but)" creates space for thinking and learning, and breaking eye contact is an important tool to develop in your arsenal (Fisher, Ury, & Patton, 2006; Grinder, 2018).

This section will cover the following.

- Paraphrase

- Questions

- Approachable and credible voice

- Gestures and words of inclusion

- And (not but)

- Break eye contact

After exploring these moves and techniques, consider your own situation and reflect on what you will begin to use immediately, what you will need to practice before using, what sort of systematic schedule you might create for implementing, and which ones you will reserve for later on in your leadership journey. Please use the blank reproducible tools at the end of this chapter (pages 120–121) to complete this activity after reading You Do It Yourself and We Do It Together.

Paraphrase

One of the most powerful moves of an effective teacher team leader (or any leader, for that matter) is the paraphrase (Garmston & Wellman, 2016). The process of paraphrasing for another person does two very simple things: (1) it ensures that they feel heard, and (2) it ensures that you understand. This communicates to them their value as a person, as well as their value as a professional. Finally, this greater understanding builds relationship and community.

Quality paraphrasing requires that you pay careful attention to the speaker so that you can accurately paraphrase. The paraphrase cannot be contrived or shallow, but, rather, it must be a sincere acknowledgment of the other person's concerns or needs and then a reflection back. In order to be effective, and to give our brains a chance to think, a pause (chapter 3, page 54) is typically useful before commencing a paraphrase. As you engage in this practice, you'll see that it's virtually impossible to engage in quality paraphrasing without a pause to think, get the blood flowing, and engage that prefrontal cortex—to tap the brakes and give the slower, conscious thinking (System 2) part of the brain a chance to do its thing. One of the benefits that comes from paraphrasing others is that it buys you time to think. When paraphrasing, Garmston and Wellman (2016) counsel us to avoid the term "I," as in "I think I hear you saying." Instead, use stems like, "So you're thinking that . . . ?" or "You feel as though . . . ?" or "You're seeing this . . . ?" Finally, the paraphrase should not be longer than their statements. It's not about you; right now, it's about them.

More specifically, there are three types of paraphrasing: (1) acknowledging, (2) organizing, and (3) abstracting (Garmston & Wellman, 2016). An acknowledging paraphrase recognizes the thoughts or feelings of the other person. "You're frustrated that . . . ?" or "You're really excited about . . . ?" or "You're livid that . . . ?" or "You think it's really important that we . . . ?" or "You are struggling with how to . . . ?" It simply acknowledges the thinking or feeling of the other person.

An organizing paraphrase organizes the thinking of the other person into chunks. Often, when folks are sharing concerns or issues with you, they are addressing a number of things at once, and it can be all jumbled up. An organizing paraphrase can be useful in helping both you and them see categories of ideas. For example, you might say, "So, it seems important to you that we address three big concerns. Those concerns are [first category]? [Second category]? And [third category]?" You might pause in between each one, gesturing

> **Paraphrasing to ensure you understand someone communicates to them their value as a person, as well as their value as a professional.**

with your hands to distinguish between each of the points. Or you might use the words "first," "second," and "third." The clearer you are in your own thinking about paraphrasing for them, the better off you and they will be.

Finally, an abstracting paraphrase is one that shifts perspective up or down a proverbial ladder from specific and concrete to that which is abstract: goals, values, or beliefs. I personally find this type of paraphrase to be the most difficult, although, when it is employed effectively, it has the greatest potential for increasing and shifting thinking toward greater effectiveness. Let's imagine someone expressing frustration at the number of students in their kindergarten classroom—that twenty-five is too many. They list off all of the needs of specific students, from behavioral to academic, social to cognitive, emotional to other specific challenges, all of which are valid barriers to meeting the needs of each and every one of those five-year-olds—even the "easy ones," who don't have as big of needs but shouldn't be ignored just because they aren't drawing significant amounts of energy. Regardless of how *you* specifically feel about the issue, or whether or not your hands are tied on being able to solve the problem, an abstracting paraphrase might be helpful: "So, you're struggling with managing all of the needs of students because you value the importance of meeting each and every student's personal needs, and you're struggling with differentiating for their needs?" Notice how this paraphrase addresses the *value* of meeting each student's needs.

On the other hand, maybe this same teacher comes to you with the frustration that the district expects teachers to differentiate, and that they don't have time and are really struggling with so many students in their classroom. An abstracting paraphrase going the "other way" on the proverbial abstracting ladder might go like this: "So, you're wanting to figure out the specific needs of each student and how you will go about addressing each of those needs?" In this case, we went from values down to specific needs.

As you can probably see, this type of paraphrasing is more difficult in the moment of the interaction. It requires you to truly understand what the other person is saying and translate that understanding either into values or take it into concrete day-to-day practice. Because of this challenge, it requires more practice. However, hopefully you can see the potential for greater understanding between colleagues and the possibility to shift perspectives to improve our practice and results for students.

Three more notes about paraphrasing. First, did you notice the question mark at the end of each of the sample paraphrases that I provided? This is because you're not telling them what they are thinking or feeling, but inquiring if you understand correctly. Second, because we are finding out if we understand correctly, the paraphrase (a question), is accompanied with an approachable voice (see page 96). Finally: don't be surprised if, after you have paraphrased, the speaker then expounds on their thinking. If you have been successful in paraphrasing, they will frequently keep speaking. That means that you simply keep listening and continue to pause and paraphrase.

Paraphrase Tool

Use the following tool in figure 4.1 to remind yourself to paraphrase and to identify what types might be helpful. Access a blank version of this template for your own use by following the link at the end of the figure.

Reflection Questions

After having used the types of paraphrase tool to improve your own effectiveness, use a journal or notebook to reflect on the following questions.

- What challenges do you find yourself facing as you work to better understand others and help them feel heard using paraphrasing?

- What do you notice about yourself when you engage in paraphrasing?

- Which type of paraphrasing do you find yourself most proficient in? What evidence do you have to support this assessment?

- Which type of paraphrasing would you like to improve your practice in? How might you go about doing that?

Next-Level Tips

As suggested previously, a paraphrase is best posed as a question. If your paraphrase is a summary statement, you can append a question like, "Do I have that right?" This can work wonders at communicating to the other person that you (1) are indeed paraphrasing and (2) want to be sure that you understand them (Knight, 2023).

While the tendency is sometimes to focus on one type of paraphrase at a time to improve your practice, it doesn't have to be this way. It is perfectly legitimate to combine types of paraphrases in the same paraphrase. For example, "Because it's important that we [insert value], we want to be sure that [insert multiple action steps identified by the colleague]. Do I have that right?" This combines an abstracting and an organizing paraphrase into one.

Additionally, the examples shared in the description above are focused on one-on-one paraphrasing, because this is the bedrock of effective paraphrasing. However, as you can see in the tool for implementation, these ideas also apply to paraphrasing the work of the group. For example, if the team has been prioritizing essential standards, your role in paraphrasing that work might be to say something like, "So, it seems like we have identified these three standards as our priority for the next unit, and that we will begin with this one

Types of Paraphrase

Key Characteristics	Acknowledge	Organize	Abstract
Key Characteristics	• Feelings • Thinking • Impact	• Most important points • First, next, last • Three things	• Values • Beliefs • Priorities • Specifics
	As a transition, consider adding the word, "So . . ." in front of the stem. **Or, if appropriate, "Wow . . ." or another transition word**		
Sentence Stems	• "You're frustrated that . . ." • "You're thinking that . . ." • "You're concerned about the ramifications of . . ." • "You're really excited for . . ."	• "A few important points for you are . . ." • "Some important next steps for you are . . ." • "There are three things that you're thinking about . . ."	• "Because you value [insert value, belief, or priority] you want to be sure [insert practice] aligns with that . . ." • "This [insert practice] concerns you because of your desire for [insert value, belief, or priority]."
Considerations for Paraphrasing a Group	• Change "you," "you're," and "your" in the above sentence stems to "we," "us," or "our" • Paraphrase throughout learning and decision making to ensure all are understanding the work of the team. • Paraphrase at times you might consider "ending points" where consensus has been (or needs to be) reached.		
Notes to Self	Be sure to listen for key words that they might use, like see, hear, or feel, and use those same words in my paraphrase. I want to really get good at this type, so I will try to use it in many individual interactions, both personally and professionally.	This comes fairly naturally to me, so a refinement to my practice might be to use my gestures to distinguish between the different "buckets" that I am helping to organize for the other person.	Because I'm not good at this one (yet), I want to practice it more. I will start by trying to do abstracting paraphrases when I am watching movies or television shows (silently and to myself). As I get better, I will then use this type when with my family, as appropriate, starting by just identifying (in my head) when this might be useful. I might also ask my spouse to help me with practicing this skill.

Figure 4.1: Types of paraphrase.

*Visit **go.SolutionTree.com/PLCbooks** for a free reproducible version of this figure.*

because it is our highest priority. Is that correct?" Another example might be to paraphrase a sharing of instructional strategies by saying, "So, we have talked about these three instructional practices today: [state the practices]. Do I have that right?" Such paraphrasing not only ensures that everyone is on the same page as each other, but also gives the record keeper a chance to make sure that the thinking, learning, and decisions of the team are accurately recorded in the notes.

Questions

The process of posing questions (Garmston & Wellman, 2016) allows other people to feel valued, heard, and dig deeper into their own thinking. Colleagues can talk through what they already know and come to their own conclusions. Used in combination with pausing (chapter 3, page 54) and paraphrasing (page 88), posing questions is really helpful in building relationships and meaningful community. As you know, collective understanding is critical in building community and transforming collaboration.

> **Instead of serial advocacy, consider ongoing inquiry.**

As you work to lead your team, prompt their thinking with questions. This can be a challenge as you will likely want to advocate for your own perspective. But instead of serial advocacy, consider ongoing inquiry. Probe their thinking to gain clarity and understanding. Ask questions that you genuinely do not have "the answer" to, ones where you authentically want to know what others think. And, as noted before but as a reminder for emphasis, engage in a paraphrase to be sure you understand and they feel heard. You will find that this also tends to give them a chance to clarify their thinking.

There are four key elements, as I see it, of quality questions to prompt thinking, build relationships, and strengthen community: (1) use open-ended questions, (2) consider tentative language, (3) inquire with plurals, and (4) avoid "Why?"

For open-ended questions, avoid phrasing questions in a way that a person can answer the question with a "yes" or "no." This means to avoid starting questions with the word "do" or "is" or "are" as this is automatically a yes-or-no question and by definition closed-ended: "Do you think students want you to meet their needs?" or "Are you frustrated by the lack of support for your individual students?" Neither of these examples are open-ended. Instead, consider starting with "when" or "what." For example, "When you think about meeting the needs of all your students, what are some of the biggest obstacles that you are facing?" Or consider, "What are some of the strategies you have tried previously?" and not, "Have you tried X, Y or Z?"

The second element helpful for posing questions is using tentative language. When we are asked to come up with one "right" answer, the amygdala's fight-or-flight response can kick in (Garmston & Wellman, 2016). When that happens, the thinking from the prefrontal cortex is shut down. You have now bypassed the logical part of the brain for that which is reactive, and getting back from that fight-or-flight response can be a challenge. Tentative language allows the brain to have so-called wiggle room and not have to come up with one right answer, and words like "might" or "could" or "possible" are key terms to use. In a question form, these might look like, "What strategies might we try?" or "What next steps could we consider?"

Theory in Action

As a concrete example, parents know, before even asking, what the answer will be when they ask their (especially middle school aged) students at the dinner table, "What was the best part of the day?" It is too much pressure on the brain and not even worth thinking about, so they say, "Dunno."

Instead, try, "What might be some of the highlights of your day that you could share?" or "If you were to choose a few things, what might be some of the more notable events from the day?" Notice the use of the words could, might, and some. These are tentative and indicate that there may be multiple options. Of course, your student is likely trained to say, "nothing," so they might initially look at you oddly for asking a longer question than normal, and then say, "Nothing." At which point, you can press, "If there were some things you might choose, what might they be?" It may take a few meals, but eventually they'll come around (and, while you haven't learned about it yet, use an approachable voice as discussed on page 96).

This leads us to the third element of effective questioning practices: the use of plurals (Garmston & Wellman, 2016). Tentative language and plurals go hand in hand. We're looking for multiple options, so having plural endings creates options that increase thinking. "When you think about meeting the needs of all your students, what are some of the biggest obstacles that you are facing?" or "What are some of the strategies you have tried previously?" use plurals in each of them (such as "biggest obstacles," "strategies," and more).

The final element of questions: Avoid the use of "why" to start your questions. This word can trigger defensiveness, and that's not what we want. Even worse is to start with "Why did you . . . ?" or similar phrases. We want open and viable relationships as part of our team. For example, for a question like "Why did you decide to . . . ?", start with "what" instead, such as, "What were (or might be) some of the things you were thinking about when . . . ?" Table 4.1 (page 94) gives examples of potential stems for open-ended questions and recommends tentative language to soften the delivery of your inquiry.

Table 4.1: Questioning Considerations and Potential Stems

Open-Ended Questions	Tentative Language	Plurals
Use: • When . . . • What . . . • Which . . . **Avoid:** • Did . . . • Have . . . • Why . . .	**Use:** • Might • Could • Some • Hunches • Seem **Avoid:** • Is • Was	**Use:** • Plural versions **Avoid:** • Singular versions

Similarly, figure 4.2 offers examples of potential questions to ask your team based on needs that you might identify. Use this figure to guide your own development of questions to advance the work of the team. Please know that this list is not exhaustive in either the work of the team or the potential questions that could be posed, nor should the list of questions be considered a checklist of queries to ask for the sake of asking.

While many educators use questions as part of their instructional practice, the four elements identified here will greatly enhance the effectiveness of those questions. Whether with students or colleagues, consider the inclusion of those four elements as part of your practice.

Reflection Questions

When you have finished considering the questions in figure 4.2, use a journal or notebook to reflect on the following questions.

- What do you notice about your use of questions in relation to these criteria? Which are more natural for you? Which ones do you want to work on?

- How might you ensure that you remember to keep these criteria in mind?

- What steps might you take to ensure that you ask questions with an approachable voice?

Next-Level Tips

At least one paraphrase is typically helpful in order to ensure that the other person feels heard, that you understand their thinking, and that there is psychological safety to proceed with a question. Once you have done this, one or more questions might be helpful.

The Work of the Team	Potential Questions
Results	• Which essential learning outcomes have students learned? • What evidence do we have that we've ensured mastery of essential outcomes? • What are the specific names of students who require additional time and support? Extension? What actions will we take to do this?
Norms	• Which of the norms do you think we might need to focus on for our meeting today? • What are some team norms that we have excelled at? • What might be some next steps for us to improve our team functioning?
SMART Goals	• As we look at our data, what might be a good stretch goal for us to pursuethis unit or year? • What are some actions we could take to help us meet our SMART goals? • In what ways might we demonstrate our commitment to these SMART goals?
Critical Question 1: What do we want students to learn?	• What are your hunches about some of the prerequisite knowledge or skills students need to be successful on this standard? • What documents might be helpful for us to study in order to increase our understanding of what students should know and be able to do? • What deadlines could we set for ourselves to ensure that we are continuing to move the work forward?
Critical Question 2: How will we know when they have learned it?	• How might we determine whether or not students know a specific learning target? • Which of these learning targets does it make sense to combine? • Which of these learning targets might we need to eliminate from our CFA plan? • What deadlines could we set for ourselves to ensure that we will keep moving forward? • What patterns do we see in the data? • What criteria might we look for to determine that students are learning what we want and progressing toward mastery of the standard?
Critical Questions 3 and 4: How will we respond when students learn (or do not learn) it?	• What are some approaches that have seen success in student learning? • What strategies might we individually or collectively use to improve student learning? • Which of our colleagues are seeing success on which learning targets? • What steps might we take to ensure that students are learning these essential learning targets? • What might be some of the reasons students are not achieving as we had hoped? • What might be some strategies that we can use to extend learning for students? • What approaches seemed to work for us in getting more kids to this level of learning that we can use in the future?
Reflection	• When we come back to this unit next year, what are some of the things we want to be sure to remember to come back to? • Thinking about our team functioning this quarter, semester, or year, what were some of the things that worked really well? • Thinking about our team functioning this quarter, semester, or year, what might be some steps we could take to improve?

Figure 4.2: Sample questions based on the work of the team.

When using your approachable voice to pose a question, consider also having gestures (page 98) that are open and inviting for thinking and responding. Be sure to pause after asking your questions, as well, to give the person time to respond. For me, I keep a water bottle by my side in meetings so that I can take a sip of water, forcing me to pause and provide time for people to think, especially after asking a question.

The use of eye contact (or lack thereof) is also something to keep in mind as part of next-level implementation. As noted on page 102, eye contact can be perceived as intimidating or even threatening. So breaking eye contact to pose your questions can open up relationships and, ultimately, improve the functioning of the team.

Approachable and Credible Voice

One of the more important considerations in nonverbal communication patterns is that of the credibility-approachability continuum (Grinder, 2018; Zoller, 2024), which has to do with the intonation of the voice. On one end is approachability, and when we use this voice tone, the intonation goes up and down quite a bit and typically ends on an upswing (sometimes resulting in statements that sound like questions). A by-product of the approachable voice is that the head typically moves up and down quite a bit—a movement that shortens and stretches the vocal cords, creating the up and down modulation of sounds.

On the other end of this continuum is the credible voice. It has very little modulation and typically ends with a downward pitch. It also generally has limited head movement, and many times, it is accompanied by a slight downward motion of the chin at the end of statements. Think of James Earl Jones saying, "This is CNN." News broadcasters are very good at the credible voice, as are athletic coaches and angry stakeholders.

Try this—say the following phrase two different ways. Once, use an approachable voice (and imagine twenty-five prekindergarten students in the room): "OK, kids, it's time to put the toys away." Now, try it again. This time imagine you're addressing your own children; it's late at night, you're tired, and you've asked them many times to put their toys away: "OK, kids, it's time to put the toys away." Notice the difference? You likely said the first one with a very approachable voice, and no one (or very few people) would listen and respond. The second one grabbed some attention. You meant business.

Notice approachable versus credible voice in others and in yourself. When you want to be sure that you are understanding the work of the team, the perspective of an individual, or opening up a conversation for learning and thinking, use an approachable voice. When you're sharing something that isn't up for debate, such as the agenda at the beginning of the meeting (which was set by the team at the last meeting, so you are simply the "enforcer," if you will, on behalf of the team), then it will be helpful to use a credible voice.

> **Theory in Action**
>
> Two extreme examples of the approachable-credible continuum can be seen when most people engage with pets or with babies. When an adult wants to be perceived as approachable with a baby or a pet, we crouch down, turn our heads to the side, and many times change our pitch to go into falsetto (that higher pitched voice) with lots of modulation. This is extreme approachability.
>
> On the other hand, if the pet (or child) is misbehaving, our intonation changes. We stand up more straight (or if we crouch we do so with stiffer angles in our body as opposed to curves), lower the pitch of our voice, speak in more succinct statements accompanied by swift gestures, and end our phrases with the pitch going down. Credible to the extreme.

Voice Continuum Tool

Using the following continuum in figure 4.3 circle where you see yourself defaulting most of the time. Consider asking colleagues to also assess where, from their perspective, you fall on the continuum most of the time.

Figure 4.3: Voice continuum self-assessment.

*Visit **go.SolutionTree.com/PLCbooks** for a free reproducible version of this figure.*

Approachable and Credible Voice Tool

There are certain typical characteristics associated with the extremes of an approachable voice and credible voice. The following shows those differences, as well as potential purposes for each type of voice. Use table 4.2, page 98, to help discern the differences and consider your own choices depending on the context.

Table 4.2: Approachable and Credible Voice

	Approachable Voice	**Credible Voice**
Purpose	• Understanding others • Opening up a conversation for learning and thinking	• Stating a fact • Enforcing a previous decision
Characteristics	• Lots of modulation • Phrases end with pitch going up • Considerable head movement • Accompanied by open hand gestures and arm movement	• Minimal modulation • Phrases end with pitch going down • Minimal head movement • Many times accompanied by beat gesture

Reflection Questions

When you have reflected on the voice continuum tool and considered implications for the approachable and credible voice tool, use a journal or notebook to reflect on the following questions.

- Knowing your default on the approachable-credible continuum, what steps do you need to take to ensure that you vary your voice to match your intended outcomes?

- What reminders do you need to have for yourself in order to be able to utilize a voice tone that will lead to the intended results?

Gestures and Words of Inclusion

All of us want to feel that we are respected and have an important role to play in the work of the team. A subtle way to create this sense of team is through using words of inclusion accompanied by gestures that also indicate a sense of belonging (Grinder, 2018; K. Zoller, personal communication, April 6, 2023; Zoller, 2024). For example, when you say something that begins with one of the following stems, it communicates a sense of "we" that wouldn't exist without it.

- "All of us . . ."

- "We already know that . . ."

- "Because we value . . ."

By the way, did you notice how I started the description for this move? It was with, "All of us. . . ." Words of inclusion in action—you likely didn't even notice it, yet agreed with the sentiment.

To move further, combine the use of a sentence stem from above with a sweeping gesture that includes an open, palm-up hand with fingers slightly curved. Or, alternatively, gesture toward your heart or head while gently tapping on your chest or temples and speaking the sentence stem. Depending on your point, you have now indicated to your colleagues, through a gesture and words of inclusion, that we are in this together. And, of course, as a team, you are.

Words of Inclusion Tool

Use figure 4.4 (page 100) to consider the following scenarios and considerations for gestures in planning implementation for yourself. A blank version is provided online for you to identify your own scenarios, statements, and gestures.

Reflection Questions

Using the words of inclusion tool will take some practice, and you will want to apply this learning and create your own scenarios, script, and considerations for gestures. Having practiced extensively and applied this learning to real scenarios, use a journal or notebook to reflect on the following questions.

- What gestures and words of inclusion are particularly natural for you to use in team meetings?

- When might you need to be particularly prepared to use this move?

- How will you remind yourself to use this move to its full effect?

Next-Level Tips

As part of the planning tool for this move you will have already noticed some next-level tips—for example, using the pause (chapter 3, page 54), beat gesture (chapter 6, page 162), and fourth point (chapter 5, page 137). Consider also using the "I interrupt myself" technique (chapter 6, page 167) for added emphasis and to ensure that folks are really listening and considering the point. For example, "While a part of us [pause; break eye contact; take an audible breath; or re-start with a lower pitch, volume, and intensity]. While a part of us is frustrated . . ."

Be sure to practice this move—especially as you start to combine moves and techniques, as suggested in this next-level tip. Video record yourself and watch it to see where you need to refine the moves and techniques so as to make it as natural as possible. Further, have someone else watch the video with you, providing critical feedback as to how you can refine your skills to be more effective in using words and gestures of inclusion to maximize your impact and increase the team's effectiveness.

Scenario	Statement	Considerations for Gestures
A mandate has been issued that the team likely doesn't want to comply with.	"While a part of us is frustrated by another mandate, we all know that everyone is doing their absolute best to improve student learning. With that in mind, what might be some best next steps for us as a team?"	• Touch the heart when saying "part of us" • Point outside the room with "frustrated" • Broad, open gesture to the team with "everyone" • Beat gesture with "best next steps" • Frozen gesture after statement
The team is struggling to determine how to respond to a challenging situation (such as a difficult standard, the motivation of a handful of students, a chunk of the population that is already proficient, challenges with time, and so on).	"Considering that we have all faced extremely challenging situations before and have been successful in overcoming them, what lessons can we apply from those challenges that might help us with this one?"	• Broad, open gesture to the team with "we have all" • Gesture in a direction away from the group with an open hand, palm up, fingers slightly curved, when referring to "extremely challenging" • Gesture back into the group on "successful in overcoming them" • Point back outside on "those challenges," then come back to pointing downward in front of you, when saying "with this one"
A small yet persistent group of students remains below proficiency on certain essential standards.	"Given that all of us are committed to ensuring that every student learns at high levels, what next steps might we take to meet this promise that we have made to each other and to these students?"	• Broad, circular gesture with your hand, palm up, fingers gently curved, signaling "all of us" and again on "might we take" • Pause after "us" and "committed" • Tap your heart with "committed" and "we have made" • Beat gesture on "every," "student," and "learns" • Gesture to outside the room on "these students students"

Figure 4.4: Words of inclusion.

*Visit **go.SolutionTree.com/PLCbooks** for a free reproducible version of this figure.*

And (Not But)

Use words and gestures of inclusion to maximize your impact and increase the team's effectiveness

I was once introduced to a "game" where, in a large group, everyone was divided into pairs. One person in each pair was given the task of sharing ideas for a party. The other person's job was to simply give reasons why every idea for the party was a bad idea. After a couple of minutes of pure agony in this entirely contrived situation, the facilitator then changed the directions. This time, one person would share ideas while the other person would say, "Yes, and . . ." followed by additional ideas. The point was clear. The energy, excitement, enthusiasm, and idea generation were clearly far better when folks were *adding to* each other, rather than diminishing and coming up with (or even simply identifying) obstacles.

Every time you use the word "but," you are negating everything that was said before that (Fisher, Ury, & Patton, 2006). For example, "That's an important task that we need to do, but . . ." or "We want to do this work, but . . ." or "Students are well-behaved, but . . ." or "It was a nice meal, but. . . ." Every single "but" negates what comes before it, so why even say what comes before it if your intent is to be critical? While there is a time and place to push our own and each other's thinking, be transparent about this without trying to sugarcoat your comments with a "but."

Instead, use the word "and." Here are some examples.

- "That's an important task that we need to do, and first, we need to be clear about what it is we need to accomplish."

- "We want to do this work, and there are some obstacles we need to overcome."

- "Students are well-behaved, and they are struggling with lunch recess."

Words matter. Use *and*, not *but*.

Having said all of this, there are times when you will disagree with your colleagues. Please don't try to gloss over this disagreement with an "and" when you really hold a different opinion. Instead, use one of the sentence stems (this is a strategy on page 113 later in this chapter) to push the thinking of the team further along. For example, "That's interesting . . . I see it another way." Or, "In addition to your comment, I'm wondering about . . ." As a team, it's not necessary to agree on everything all the time. Indeed, this can be a red flag for folks not providing their true opinion or not engaging in critical thinking on the topic at hand. You want the clash of differing opinions to be a regular part of learning, and that clash needs to be productive. The use of "and" and sentence starters can assist with this.

"And" Tool

Use the following reminders in figure 4.5 (page 102) to help you use "and" instead of "but."

Reflection Questions

When you have finished examining your use of "and" with the tool provided, use a journal or notebook to reflect on the following questions.

- When do you notice yourself feeling the urge to say "but?"

- What impact does other people saying "but" have on you, your thinking, and your feelings?

- What changes do you notice in other people when you say "and" instead of "but?"

Break Eye Contact

Eye contact, or lack thereof, is a subtle nonverbal behavior that can communicate a number of things (Grinder, 2018). In most western cultures, eye contact signifies respect, but in some cultures, looking down is the most respectful way to speak with others. Your awareness of the cultural background of those with whom you engage will most definitely impact this particular action.

With that understanding, know that eye contact can also signify a threat. So being aware of your own level of eye contact with your colleagues is a good first place to start when considering how to help transform collaboration.

Another consideration is how and when you break off eye contact with the group. Almost universally, when someone needs to think, they will break eye contact and look away (in certain cases and people, they may not break eye contact, but their pupils will dilate and they will look "through" you). This breaking of eye contact, then, intuitively signals thoughtfulness. Given this, to create a pause in the conversation, break eye contact to help facilitate a pause and create space for thinking. Further, if you ask a question, by breaking eye contact with everyone, you signal that you are not expecting a certain person to answer. If, when asking a question, you maintain eye contact with one person, that person will assume that you intend for them to answer (and others will also assume that you intend for that person to answer).

Pausing and breaking eye contact go hand in hand. You'll likely find yourself doing both simultaneously, naturally. Now, you will also notice when you do them, and you can become intentional about using this technique to help the pause become more effective.

When to Use "And"
• Instead of "but"
• In lieu of "however"
• In place of "what about"
• To replace "On the other hand"
• Whenever you feel a contrary opinion coming on
• To transition to a sentence stem, like ". . . and I'd like to offer a different perspective"

Figure 4.5: When to use "and."

Breaking Eye Contact Tool

Use the following topics in figure 4.6 to think through when it might be helpful to break eye contact with your team. Sample scripts are provided for a few, and the blank version online will offer you space to create your own.

Have you been able to come up with your own examples? If not, consult this handy list for some helpful times to break eye contact in a team meeting.

- At the beginning of a meeting after greeting everyone

- After posing a question

- Between agenda items

- Whenever people (or you) need a chance to think

Topic	Potential Script
Inclusion	[After introducing the inclusion (see chapter 3, page 65) break eye contact with a pause]
Outcome and agenda clarity	"As you look at today's outcomes and agenda, please individually and silently identify which one(s) you want to be sure we emphasize." [Break eye contact and use the outcomes and agenda as a third point for added emphasis.] "After a few seconds for us to think, we will share."
Identifying essential standards	
Creating CFAs	
Analyzing data	
Determining intervention and extension activities	
Identifying the next meeting's agenda items	
Add your own	
Add your own	

Figure 4.6: Planning to break eye contact tool.

*Visit **go.SolutionTree.com/PLCbooks** for a free reproducible version of this figure.*

Take some time to think of other scenarios where breaking eye contact can be beneficial for communicating a specific emotion or message or for creating space for people to think. Because this is usually a subconscious or instinctual act, it might take you some time to become fully aware of when you typically break eye contact.

Reflection Questions

When you have finished completing the breaking eye contact tool, use a journal or notebook to reflect on the following questions.

- When do you notice yourself needing space and time to think in a meeting?

- Do you break eye contact when you need a chance to think, or do you look "through" the other person?

- Do people let you think, or do they interrupt you? If they interrupt you, what actions might you take to signal that you need that time and space to think?

Next-Level Tips

One combination of techniques you might consider is taking a deep audible breath (chapter 3, page 50) when you break eye contact. Remember that the inhale needs to be audible and not the exhale, which potentially might give the impression that you are exasperated. The combination of these actions (pause, audible breath in, and breaking of eye contact almost simultaneously) will almost certainly cause others to pause also. As an additional step, you might consider bringing your hand to your face or chin, combined with freezing that gesture (chapter 6, page 160) as you inhale.

We Do It Together

Now that you and your team have laid the foundation for team effectiveness, and you have been working on implementing some skills from the preceding You Do It Yourself section, you might find that you're really gaining momentum and need some additional strategies for the team to do together. That's exactly what this section of the chapter explores as you find five strategies to help your team gain momentum in (1) creating psychological safety, (2) building capacity, and (3) doing the work. Of course, there is no need to fully master the actions described in the previous chapter or section before starting to engage in the strategies shared here. Keep moving forward with adding tools to your toolbox and increasing your effectiveness, thereby transforming collaboration.

Part of being able to gain momentum is seeing progress in the work. When the team plans the work, they can then work the plan, see progress made, and celebrate accordingly. Writing it down ensures that everything that the team does is recorded in such a way that time is saved in ensuring that learning is recorded and decisions are implemented. Others as experts makes sure that you're building shared knowledge and not simply pooling opinions (DuFour et al., 2024; Garmston & Wellman, 2016). Sentence stems will help you and the team to focus the conversation and figuratively get out of your amygdala, if that's where members' brains have gone. Finally, who will do what by when will ensure that everyone is clear about next steps when leaving the meeting (Garmston & Wellman, 2016).

This section will cover the following strategies.

- Plan the work, then work the plan
- Celebrations
- Write it down
- Others as experts
- Sentence stems
- Who will do what by when

After exploring these strategies, consider your own situation and reflect on what you will begin to use immediately, what you will need to practice before using, what sort of systematic schedule you might create for implementing, and which ones you will reserve for later on in your leadership journey. Please use the blank reproducible tools at the end of this chapter (pages 120–121) to complete this activity after reading You Do It Yourself (page 87) and We Do It Together (page 104).

Plan the Work, Then Work the Plan

Teams gain momentum when they see the results of their work, and this happens when they create a plan for what the team needs to accomplish, then work that plan to make it happen. Of course, the team itself needs to establish its own timelines based on the units of study they have, the essential standards being considered, the amount of time allocated for collaborative meetings, and more.

So what might be a reasonable timeline for doing the work? First of all, let's assume that your team meets for roughly forty-five minutes once per week (which is what we advocate for, as a minimum, in the PLC at Work process). At least initially, many teams spend one to two meetings on critical question one—clarifying essential standards, unpacking them, and sequencing the resultant learning targets—all for an upcoming unit. Then the team will spend one to two meetings on critical question two—creating or revising an end-of-unit assessment and one or more common formative assessments (CFAs) for that same upcoming unit. Finally, the team is now ready to implement their unit plan with CFAs in hand, and the next two to six meetings, depending on the length of the unit, will involve looking at data and making decisions about interventions and extensions after each timely CFA.

> **Teams gain momentum when they see the results of their work.**

At the conclusion of the unit, the team will spend a portion of a meeting reflecting on the process—including how the team did on meeting its SMART goals—and then restart this recurring cycle again. Of course, when reinitiating the cycle, the team will be looking ahead two to four weeks to the next unit so that their time spent on critical questions one and two are in preparation for the unit, and not while the team is engaged in actually teaching that unit.

Notice that this timeline implies that not every standard, nor even every unit, necessarily, will be the subject of the PLC process every year. As a team, you will identify standards that are essential and focus your efforts on guaranteeing students learn those. The key is to shift your mindset from teaching to learning while establishing those non-negotiables for what students will *learn*. Then draw the line in the sand and move heaven and earth to get students there.

> **Shift your mindset from teaching to learning.**

Potential Work Timeline Tool

By having a plan in place, the team can have forward movement in doing the work. Plan the work, then work the plan. Figure 4.7 presents a sample potential work timeline you can use as a basis for creating your own.

Reflection Questions

After having reflected on the potential work timeline tool to create the team's timeline, use a journal or notebook to reflect on the following questions.

- What obstacles can you foresee in helping the team create a timeline for doing the work? How might you overcome them?
- What actions will be helpful to keep the team on track for implementing their plan?

Next-Level Tips

The third point move (page 57) is a great one to use when facilitating the creation of a timeline. Stand up, use some chart paper (it's easier to initially cross out and make changes to the plan than in an electronic document), and guide the team through creating their timeline. It may be helpful to use others as experts (page 111) so that, instead of you imposing this timeline, the team is learning and developing a common understanding before deciding on a plan.

As the team writes down their plan, some folks might feel undue pressure with a perceived lack of flexibility in the work of the team. Pause. Paraphrase. No doubt the team will come to a common understanding that having a plan is better than not. They will no doubt come to the conclusion that if the plan isn't fully achieved, they will at least have made more progress than without a plan. And, of course, they will learn as part of the process. Perfection is not the end result—learning is.

Date	Outcomes (chapter 3, page 69)
Before school starts (or at end of previous year)	• Create norms and establish draft timeline. • Identify essential standards for the upcoming unit. • Unpack essential standards.
First week of collaboration	• Finish unpacking essential standards. • Sequence learning targets and determine schedule for assessment administration. • Start creating and revising CFAs for identified learning targets.
Second week of collaboration	• Finish creating and revising CFAs. • Set SMART goals for unit and year.
Third week of collaboration	• Examine data from CFAs. • Share effective practices based on results. • Identify intervention and extension practices.
Fourth week of collaboration	• Examine data from CFAs. • Share effective practices based on results. • Identify intervention and extension practices.
Fifth week of collaboration	• Examine data from CFAs. • Share effective practices based on results. • Identify intervention and extension practices.
Sixth week of collaboration	• Reflect on processes from this unit, including SMART goal attainment. • Make note of changes to unit for next year. • Identify essential standards for the upcoming unit.
Seventh week of collaboration	• Finish identifying essential standards for the upcoming unit. • Unpack essential standards for the identified upcoming unit.
Eighth week of collaboration	• Continue the process . . .

Source: Adapted from DuFour & DuFour, 2008.

Figure 4.7: Work timeline sample.

> **Celebrate both the efforts made and the results of those efforts.**

Celebrations

As educators, it seems that many times we just keep doing our work and rarely pause to collectively recognize both the efforts we are putting forth and the improved results of that labor. Recognizing small efforts and changes, however, is critical to not only our own social-emotional wellbeing, but also to building momentum for future growth and development (Johnson, 2022). So the team needs to find ways to celebrate both the efforts made and the results of those efforts.

Just like in life, there are occasions for formal celebrations as well as informal appreciations. The school year has built-in opportunities to celebrate, such as the end of a unit, term, or year. In addition to these, there are lots of informal chances to recognize and appreciate each other, like when the team has identified essential standards, unpacked them, created CFAs, administered those same assessments and has data to look at, after actions were taken and more students learned, when a team planned for intervention and it either went off without a hitch or lessons were learned, or . . . You get the picture. Find ways to celebrate the work of the team, and embed those celebrations into the structure and routines of the team. Celebrating small wins stimulates the brain to release dopamine, a feel-good chemical that reinforces the learning experience and strengthens our sense of connection to those we work with (Johnson, 2022).

Please note that we're talking about celebrations and recognition as part of *both* efforts expended *and* results attained. It seems that, too often, we only celebrate results, when in reality effort is needed to get those results. Celebrating effort is what builds momentum toward results. Please note, also, that I'm not talking about a participation trophy for every little step the team takes. Genuine effort to do the work of the team will lead to improved results, and a little recognition can go a long way in furthering that work and the results.

Finally, celebrations can be simple appreciations. A little "well done" or "congratulations, we did it" can have an oversized impact on the team. The vast majority of the time team celebrations will not be elaborate parties with cake and ice cream. They will instead be a small recognition acknowledging the work of the team and individuals on the team. That said, in my book, there's no prohibition against special treats.

Opportunities for Recognition or Celebration Tool

Use the following tool in figure 4.8 to identify when and how the team might celebrate based on the work it is doing and results that are being achieved. Some examples are provided, and additional space is provided for the team to note other considerations for these celebrations, as well as to identify more ways to celebrate.

Reflection Questions

After reflecting on and implementing some considerations from the opportunities for recognition or celebration tool, use a journal or notebook to reflect on the following questions.

- What are some characteristics of effective recognition and celebration that you want to embed in this practice?

- How might you engage your colleagues in celebrating each other (and not having this fall solely on your soldiers)?

Opportunity for Recognition or Celebration	When and How to Do It	Other Considerations
After coming to consensus on norms	• Implement immediately after establishing norms. • As a team, decide how to celebrate the work of the team. • Celebrate based on the decision of the team.	• What materials might be needed? • Who else should be included? • Who else needs to know about this achievement?
After coming to a successful decision after an intense deliberation	• Implement either right away, first thing at the next meeting, or in a follow-up email from the meeting. • "Friends, I just want to thank each of you for sharing your frank opinions on matter X. It was intense, and I think it shows a healthy culture when we can disagree without being disagreeable. Thank you."	• What kind of follow-up might be needed? • Is there a place or need to acknowledge that if the decision proves to be wrong, the team will absolutely revisit it? What criteria will show that? And after what time period?
After a tense deliberation but where all points of view were shared and heard		
After identifying essential standards for an upcoming unit		
After unpacking one or more essential standards		
After creating one or more common formative assessments		
After administering one or more common formative assessments		
After compiling and examining data from a common formative assessment		
After making instructional decisions based on data from a common formative assessment		
After seeing student results improve from the work of the team		

Figure 4.8: Opportunities for recognition or celebration tool.

*Visit **go.SolutionTree.com/PLCbooks** for a free reproducible version of this figure.*

Theory in Action

One school that I get to work with starts every day, in every classroom, with "good things." Students (and teachers) share things that are good in their life or day, and it's as simple as that. Meetings at this school, too, start with good things from staff. It's a nice, simple way to acknowledge each other and recognize improvements.

For a small refinement to focus the efforts of the team, it might be that those good things be related to the work of the team (collective commitments). This step, employed in your own team, could help that recognition move from purely personal to professional celebration.

When I am personally with teams, I typically do a little "woot woot" to recognize and celebrate effort and results. It is accompanied by a gesture of my hands upward, as if lifting an object above my head. The gesture goes up twice, just as there are two syllables to "woot woot," and the vocal inflection is in falsetto. This little act typically engenders smiles, laughter, and, as desired, a genuine appreciation for the work being done. As you can imagine, this naturally leads to having more joy in the work of the team, and it's fun when I return to teams and they look to me for my little "woot woot" celebration. It's small, yet significant.

Next-Level Tips

Recognition and celebration may start with you, but this is listed as a strategy that the team does together. In this vein, it will be key for you to help the team take collective ownership of celebrations. As such, consider the role that self-assessment (chapter 5, page 143) plays, together with data usage (chapter 5, page 141), in giving the team itself ways to monitor and celebrate both effort and achievement. Further, the use of gestures and words of inclusion (page 98) can be quite impactful in nonverbally attributing (chapter 5, page 129) the excellence of the team to others on the team.

Write It Down

You're busy. Your colleagues are busy. You need your brainpower to focus on the most important task of raising up our next generation of teachers, secretaries, plumbers, electricians, nurses, artists, social workers, and more. So free up your brain to focus on this most important work by writing down the work of the team. Then, you don't have to try to remember what was talked about when, what decisions were made and the factors that went into them, and so on.

You have a written agenda (chapter 3, page 76). Now use that same template to also take notes. Write down your team decisions. Write down key points from the conversation. Write down your identified essentials standards, your unpacked standards, your CFAs, when you will administer them, when data will be brought to the team, what protocol you use for the data analysis, what next steps you decided, and your reflections on what worked. Write down everything. This way, in a week (or month or next year), you won't be using your memory to try to remember, and instead, you can focus on refinements and next steps for those decisions and practices.

At some point in my career, I heard a colleague say, "If it's not written down, it doesn't exist." Too true. Here's the standard for which I think we should strive: If everyone on the team was hit by an ice cream truck tonight, would the substitutes and new teachers coming in be able to pick up where you left off? If so, great! If not, start writing it down.

Use one of the running agenda templates (chapter 3, page 76) as the place to record the work of the team. Of course, if the team wants separate documents for different decisions, simply link them on the agenda (and landing page—chapter 3, page 66).

Reflection Questions

Use a journal or notebook to reflect on what the team writes down and where it is written (whether on an agenda or linked to a landing page) using the following questions.

- What work does your team need to be sure to write down so that it isn't lost?

- How might you engage your colleagues in taking ownership of writing down the work so that it doesn't fall only to you?

Next-Level Tips

If you use Google Docs, the products that your team creates can easily be linked within the document. Be sure that they are shared so that others on your team can access them without having to request it. Finally, linking on your landing page (chapter 3, page 66) will ensure that nothing gets lost within the deep dark recesses of files and folders on your electronic management system.

Others as Experts

Maybe you've heard the saying that no one is a prophet in their own land. People tend to take for granted those that they are with day in and day out. For many teacher team leaders, this phenomenon plays out as colleagues tend not to see you as an expert. This means that you have to access others as experts and bring those voices into the room.

Others as experts can be as simple as a journal article that you found online, a short video clip, quoted excerpts from the field, or a resource from this or other books. And you will no doubt identify these (and other) resources through your networks, professional associations, colleagues, and more. As a specific example, for a strategy to plan the work and work the plan, you might bring the blog and response referenced in that section to the team to read and discuss. As part of that dialogue, you might use the upcoming say something strategy to access everyone's expertise around the topic. In other words, instead of you just imposing a timeline, the team accesses someone else as an expert through the written text and learns before making a decision.

As part of an outcome around learning, others as experts becomes really important. We don't want to simply pool opinions and go with whoever has the loudest voice. Rather, we learn. We build shared knowledge around the work of the team and then take action. Others as experts is what helps ground our new learning in evidence and research.

Say Something Tool

Building shared knowledge is more than just handing people a handout and having them read it. Building shared knowledge involves engaging with expert thinking in a meaningful way. The following process is a simple strategy (adapted from www.thinkingcollaborative.com/as-resources) that works very effectively whenever you want to engage in learning around a piece of text.

1. Start by pairing up with another person in the room.

2. Decide on who is A and who is B.

3. Partner A reads a previously agreed amount of text (article, quotations, or blog), typically out loud, and then says something.* Partner B listens silently.

4. Partner B reads the next agreed amount, typically out loud, and then says something*. Partner A listens silently.

5. Repeat the pattern.

6. When finished, what overall comments, questions, insights, applications, and so on do you have?

   Participants do not literally say the word "something." Rather, they share a comment, question, insight, application, and so on.

Reflection Questions

When you have finished using the say something tool, use a journal or notebook to reflect on the following questions.

- What were some of the strengths and challenges you found from using this protocol?

- What revisions or clarifications might be helpful for making this protocol more effective the next time?
- What other processes might you use to ensure that the team is building shared understanding from accessing others as expert?

Next-Level Tips

Combine others as experts with a third point (chapter 3, page 57). This adds credibility to the point you are trying to make, reinforcing that it is not your thinking, but that of the expert.

Sentence Stems

When engaging in conversations that might push our thinking, our brains can get caught in fight-or-flight mode. When this happens, the amygdala takes over and starts reacting instead of thoughtfully considering next steps (Black & Bright, 2019b). Sentence stems provide a frame to start our thinking and help bypass that reactivity, giving our prefrontal cortex a chance to catch up to the emotions of the moment. They give us the language of learning and of productive conflict. And they force us to consider our words carefully as we move forward in challenging our current practices and beliefs.

Sentence Stems Tool

Notice the tentative nature of these sentence stems, which allows for openness of thinking as opposed to closed statements of "facts" that tend to shut down learning and teamwork. Use the following tool in figure 4.9 to review some sentence stems; access the blank version of this tool online to create your own.

> **Sentence stems give us the language of learning and of productive conflict.**

Sentence Stems

- Say more about that . . .
- I'm not sure I understand . . .
- Another consideration might be . . .
- That's interesting. Tell me more . . .
- I'm thinking about this a little bit differently . . .
- I wonder if we might look at this from a different perspective?

Figure 4.9: Sentence stems.

*Visit **go.SolutionTree.com/PLCbooks** for a free reproducible version of this figure.*

Use the preceding link to access an online version of this tool that you can print out on cardstock and have available for yourself and colleagues as part of deliberations. It may be that, knowing that a difficult topic is coming up, you share these with colleagues as a tool to assist the learning and decision making. Modeling the use of the sentence stems will be an important part of using them, as is practice. I've heard of teams, in advance of their difficult conversation, playing around with the sentence stems and challenging each other to use a certain number in a meeting. In other words, have fun with it as learners.

Reflection Questions

When you have used the sentence stems tool, either for just yourself or with the team, use a journal or notebook to reflect on the following questions.

- When do you see yourself or your team using sentence stems to facilitate conversation?
- Which of the sentence stems seem most useful to you? What other ones might you add?
- When you used one or more sentence stems, how did it work?

Next Level Tips

Have you ever noticed how the same word or phrase can mean many different things depending on *how* it is said? Having taught middle school, I was keenly aware of not just the words that a student might use, but the intonation of their voice. It's the intonation that makes all the difference. Try this: say "Thank you" three or four different ways, out loud. First, say it genuinely. Then sarcastically. Then with annoyance. Do you hear the difference?

So it is with these sentence stems. Page 96 has details on using an approachable and credible voice. This tip is to be sure to use an approachable voice with sentence stems that are seeking input or desiring an open conversation. In other words, *how* you deliver the sentence stem with the inflection of your voice will make a significant difference in how people respond and engage in the conversation. In addition to using an approachable voice with this strategy, consider how you might use these stems for yourself, personally, before introducing them to the team. This will give you an opportunity to refine your own skills and set the stage, so to speak, for introducing this strategy to your colleagues.

Who Will Do What by When

The purpose of a meeting isn't just to meet, but ultimately to take action so that all students learn team-identified essential outcomes.

Some of the action will take place inside the meeting, and some will happen in between meetings. In many meetings that I have been in, people leave without a clear understanding of next steps. Ask someone what their meeting was about, and a likely response might be, "Good question! Wish I knew!"

At the conclusion of the meeting, everyone needs to be clear about next steps. A simple way to do this is to use "WHO will do WHAT by WHEN" (Garmston & Wellman, 2016). Being clear about this, and writing it down, will ensure that we set up mutual accountability to carry through on our decisions. For example, the team might decide that they need to have state standards, state test blueprint documents, their curriculum guide, and the textbook or curriculum materials at their next meeting in order to best decide on essential standards for the upcoming unit. Instead of relying on "someone" to bring these, they might decide that one person will bring the state standards and state test blueprint documents, another person might print out copies of the curriculum guide, and another person will bring the textbook or curriculum materials. This will all be done by the next meeting. Just like the use of one of the preceding templates (see the running agenda template, page 76) can help set up and facilitate meetings, so, too, can having this simple statement at the bottom of each agenda. See the running agenda template for two potential tools.

Reflection Questions

When you have finished using this practice, either with one of the tools in chapter 3 or by simply including the phrase on your current agenda, use a journal or notebook to reflect on the following questions.

- What obstacles do you anticipate to having this clarity around next steps?

- How has having clarity about next steps, and who is doing what by a timeline, helped with team functioning?

- What revisions to this practice might be helpful in implementation?

Next-Level Tips

While the agenda template has this strategy at the end of each agenda, it doesn't have to literally happen at the end of the meeting. Many times, as you're doing the work, it will become clear what next steps need to happen. Feel free to make note of those at the time without waiting until the end of the meeting. Closing the meeting with this brief reminder, however, will raise any additional next steps that might need to be taken that the team hadn't previously considered.

Putting It All Together

To assist you in pulling together your learning from this chapter, following is a story of a teacher team leader and a description of the team and its members. Consider what content from this chapter might best assist him in leading the team.

Joaquin is an elementary teacher team leader who has been in this role since the school started having teams meet twice per week to focus on the four critical questions of a team in a PLC. For the last fifteen years, the team has met during their common planning time, which means that, after transitions to get students to specials and a quick restroom break, they have about forty solid minutes of collaboration. The two other grade-level teachers on Joaquin's team have slightly less experience than him, clocking in with six and nine years of being in the classroom.

All three team members have strong personalities and opinions, and the team has therefore struggled to gain traction in finding meeting times productive. Team members generally dread their time together and find it difficult to arrive on time, let alone use the remaining time productively.

While being generally polite in the hallways and team meetings (a few significant outbursts have occurred previously), members leave meetings and do their own thing. Joaquin believes in engaging students in meaningful hands-on learning that could be perceived as poor classroom management. The second teacher is tightly organized with their classroom management and employs direct instruction practices almost exclusively. And the third teacher is in the middle and mostly keeps their head down and out of any possible disagreements.

Based on this scenario, use figure 4.10 to circle the responsibilities, assumptions, and mindsets that you believe will be most critical for Joaquin to keep at the forefront of his mind. How might you suggest he does this?

Responsibilities, Assumptions, and Mindsets	Notes for How to Keep This in Mind
Responsibilities: 1. Make it safe. 2. Build capacity. 3. Do the work.	
Assumptions: 1. People do the best that they can. 2. You can only control you. 3. Behavior communicates. 4. People want to get stuff done. 5. Conflict is good.	

Responsibilities, Assumptions, and Mindsets	Notes for How to Keep This in Mind
Mindsets: 1. To see what others don't (yet) see in themselves 2. To be humble with a posture of learning 3. To spread the contagion of joy	

Figure 4.10: Pulling together your learning reflection chart.

Having considered the responsibilities, assumptions, and mindsets, which of the moves, techniques, and strategies would you suggest to be most useful for Joaquin at the team's first (and subsequent) meetings? How would you suggest he go about using them? Use figure 4.11 to complete this activity.

You Do It Yourself	
Moves and Techniques	**How and When Might Joaquin Use It?**
Paraphrase	
Questions	
Approachable and credible voice	
Gestures and words of inclusion	
And (not but)	
Break eye contact	
We Do It Together	
Strategies	**How and When Might Joaquin Use It?**
Plan the work, then work the plan	
Celebrations	
Write it down	
Others as experts	
Sentence stems	
Who will do what by when	

Figure 4.11: You do it yourself and we do it together vignette chart.

*Visit **go.SolutionTree.com/PLCbooks** for a free reproducible version of this figure.*

Possible Next Steps

Joaquin knows well that, as a teacher team leader, who he is and what he does has an impact on others. Because of this, he spends some time considering the responsibilities, assumptions, and mindsets to make sure that he approaches interactions with his colleagues in a productive way. He decides that, given that one colleague just keeps their head down, he needs to be sure to make it safe. And since he can only control himself, assumptions numbers one and five, that people do the best they can and that change is good, will be critical. Further, all three mindsets will be important to move the team forward, so he prints these out and puts them on his computer as regular reminders to himself.

When Joaquin learns about approachable and credible voice, he decides to practice the skills everywhere he goes to ensure that he is choosing the voice that matches his intention. He practices at the grocery store, ordering food, with his students and colleagues, with his family and his neighbors—everywhere he goes!

He also gives himself a reminder to "paraphrase your butt off" so he can focus on this for his personal skill development. He decides to make this his focus for the month and then to shift to another move or technique to home in on every month of the school year. Of course, he wants to be sure that he applies specific skills to the best situations, so, at the beginning of each month, he looks through the list of moves and techniques and identifies which ones he will focus on for specific meetings based on the topics at hand. As part of this process, he scans the tools, reflection questions, and next-level tips to remind himself of, and pick up on, refinements to his own practice as a team leader. Given the undercurrent of previous conflicts, he decides that and (not but) will be pretty important to use sooner rather than later.

For the first meeting, Joaquin decides that norms, roles, and inclusion from chapter 3 (pages 60, 62, and 65, respectively) will be particularly important to implement, but he also sees real value in others as experts and sentence stems to help overcome the inertia the team experiences. Starting with the development of norms, he uses the sentence stems described in the norms section to facilitate that conversation. He also pulls a brief article on the importance of roles for the team to read so that they can decide on what roles they need to become more effective. Finally, he uses the roles tool as another expert perspective to facilitate the thinking of the team.

When the team is creating the norms, he is sure to voice the perspective that it is important to regularly celebrate so this can become a regular part of the work and part of instilling joy into team meetings. Further, the roles conversation will lend itself to the process of writing it down. And he decides that, on the agenda, it will be important to have a who will do what by when section. He adds this to the agenda without any further conversation with the team.

Joaquin realizes that these first steps will not be a cure all, and that how he proactively plans and responds will set the tone for future growth on the team. He has a plan to focus on responsibility number one, together with the identified two assumptions and all three mindsets, through the application of the moves, techniques, and strategies shared in this chapter and the previous chapter. He is excited to help the team get more done, do it in less time, and move beyond the tension that has been part of meetings, instead having them filled with joy. Most of all, he is excited to truly transform collaboration.

Summary Reflective Questions

When you have finished completing the pulling together your learning reflection chart, use a journal or notebook to reflect on the following questions.

- What lessons might you take from Joaquin's experience and plan?
- What will you apply to your setting?
- What next steps do you see yourself taking?
- What criteria will you use to determine whether or not you are being successful in that implementation, and what course corrections you might need to make?

Conclusion

With a solid foundation in place, the team is working to gain momentum in getting more done, in less time, and with greater joy. The actions you can take to continue the momentum involve paraphrasing and using questions after having engaged in meaningful pauses that were shared in the previous chapter. Simultaneously, consider your voice and the tone you employ on the scale of approachable to credible together with the use of gestures and words of inclusion. Finally, remember the power of and (not but) and how to strategically break eye contact to maximize effectiveness and efficiency. As a team, five strategies will help to build momentum, beginning with finding ways to recognize and celebrate both efforts made and achievements attained. Writing down the work of the team will ensure that there is a record of what has been accomplished, and accessing the expertise of others ensures that the team avoids simply pooling opinions. Using sentence stems will assist with maintaining cognitive (as opposed to affective) conflict, and, finally, the team will work to ensure clarity on who will do what by when. With the momentum that the team is gaining, you are no doubt keenly aware that obstacles will present themselves, which is the focus of the next chapter.

Chapter 4: You Do It Yourself Planning and Reflection Tool

Now that we have explored these moves and techniques for gaining momentum, consider your own situation and reflect on what you will begin to use immediately. Which moves and techniques will you need to practice before using? What sort of systematic schedule might you create for implementing? And which ones will you reserve for later on in your leadership journey?

You Do It Yourself				
Move or Technique	To Start Immediately	Needs Some Practice	When and How Will I Practice?	Save for Later
Paraphrase				
Questions				
Approachable and credible voice				
Gestures and words of inclusion				
And (not but)				
Break eye contact				

The Teacher Team Leader Handbook © 2025 Chad M. V. Dumas • SolutionTree.com
Visit **go.SolutionTree.com/PLCbooks** to download this free reproducible.

Chapter 4: We Do It Together Planning and Reflection Tool

Now that we have explored these strategies for gaining momentum, consider your own situation and reflect on what you will begin to use immediately. Which strategies will you need to practice before using? What sort of systematic schedule might you create for implementing? And which ones will you reserve for later on in your leadership journey?

We Do it Together				
Strategy	**To Start Immediately**	**Needs Some Practice**	**When and How Will I Practice?**	**Save for Later**
Plan the work, then work the plan				
Celebrations				
Write it down				
Others as experts				
Sentence stems				
Who will do what by when				

The Teacher Team Leader Handbook © 2025 Chad M. V. Dumas • SolutionTree.com
Visit **go.SolutionTree.com/PLCbooks** to download this free reproducible.

Obstacles don't have to stop you. If you run into a wall, don't turn around and give up. Figure out how to climb it, go through it, or work around it.

—Michael Jordan

CHAPTER 5

Overcoming Obstacles

Now that you have a solid foundation and are gaining momentum, in this chapter, we will explore what it takes to overcome obstacles that will inevitably reveal themselves. As before, this chapter will lay out moves and techniques that you will do as the team leader, followed by strategies that the team can take together. And as a brief reminder, these moves, techniques, and strategies are all in the service of (1) creating psychological safety, (2) building capacity, and (3) getting work done.

You Do It Yourself

Even when you have the best foundation and momentum is gathering, challenges will occur. I guarantee it. So how can your team work to overcome those challenges? The roadblocks that teams face typically require some skillful facilitation with specific moves and techniques that you alone will employ. While the skills you have learned up to this point will lay a solid foundation, and in many cases you can rely on those to help accomplish your objectives, this section of this chapter will lay out some more moves and techniques that you can consider in overcoming the challenges that will inevitably come your way.

Generalizations are the enemy of improvement, so making sure that you and the team are providing specificity as part of your meeting is a good first step to overcoming barriers. Decontaminating space (Grinder, 2018; Zoller, 2024) is a concept that is subtle but very effective in clearing away negative emotions associated with a location or term. Attribution is the opposite, making sure that we draw out each other's best by identifying and labeling that best, both explicitly and implicitly (Zoller, 2024). Individual rapport (Zoller, 2024) makes sure, particularly during conflict, that we are in relationships with each other and are able to move forward by engaging in cognitive instead of affective conflict. Anonymizing our work makes sure that we get everyone's voices in the room without certain opinions having more weight because certain people said it. Fourth point helps to keep negativity out of the room (Grinder, 2018). Finally, the mode that you use to communicate with others matters, so before you hit that send button on an email, think about what the best mode for that communication might be.

This section will cover the following moves and techniques.

- Specificity
- Anonymize it
- Decontaminate space
- Fourth point
- Attribution
- Mode of communication
- Individual rapport

As before, after exploring these moves and techniques, consider your own situation and reflect on what you will begin to use immediately, what you will need to practice before using, what sort of systematic schedule you might create for implementing, and which ones you will reserve for later in your leadership journey. Please use the blank reproducible tools at the end of this chapter (pages 155–156) to complete this activity after reading You Do It Yourself (page 123) and We Do It Together (page 141).

Generalizations are the enemy of improvement.

Specificity

Generalizations are the enemy of improvement. It's only when we get specific that we can identify what needs to be accomplished, how it will be done, and by when we will take action. And, yet, generalizations are where teams can get stuck. So use your paraphrasing and questioning skills (see chapter 4, pages 88 and 92, respectively), together with prompting, to get to specifics and avoid the vague comfort of general comments.

Generalization to Specificity Tool

Use the examples of generalizations in figure 5.1 to plan for how you might guide the team in getting specific. The first column provides examples of generalizations that I have heard in team meetings, followed by the second column detailing specifically why that statement is a generalization. Finally, the third column provides possible prompts that you can use with your colleagues to help get to specifics. As with other actions shared in this book, after this tool there are reflection questions to help you with implementation, and there is also a reproducible version online with blank spaces for you to reflect on your own examples of generalizations.

Generalization	Why It's a Generalization	Possible Prompts to Get Specific
Students just aren't getting this concept.	Which students aren't getting the concept? Which specific parts of the concept are they missing?	• "So you're frustrated that, after your best efforts, kids still aren't getting it?" [Pause] "Let's take a look at the data to see which kids and which specific knowledge and skills students are missing."
The standard that they need to learn is . . .	Standards are generally too broad to be instructionally useful. So, the team needs to break the standard down into specific, discrete, and measurable learning targets that make up the standard.	• "So, this standard is pretty broad. Let's break it down into specific learning targets so we can scaffold the learning for students."
The assessment showed that they don't have it.	Which parts of the assessment showed this? Which students didn't get it?	• "Let's first look at the learning targets to see how each student did on the assessment, by learning target. Then we can look at the specific items, too, to see first if they align with the targets, and then what misconceptions we can identify based on student responses."
I taught it, but I'm not sure why they aren't getting it.	What are students being taught, specifically? How was it taught?	• "This is challenging—giving it all we've got, and students still aren't getting it?" [Pause] "Let's talk about the specific instructional strategies we each used and see what we can learn from each other. Maybe seeing them in action might help, too."
I just don't know how to help the high kid.	There is no such thing as a "high kid." All students are capable of high levels of learning, depending on the content area, specific skills, time of the year, teacher, and more.	• "Based on the learning targets we're focused on at this time, who are the students we're thinking about? Let's look at both the learning targets and list of students and figure out, together, how we can extend or deepen learning for these students based on the specific learning targets."

Figure 5.1: Generalizations to specificity tool.

*Visit **go.SolutionTree.com/PLCbooks** for a free reproducible version of this figure.*

Reflection Questions

When you have finished reflecting on the generalization to specificity tool and implemented this practice in your team, use a journal or notebook to reflect on the following questions.

- When you prompted colleagues to get specific, how did it work? What was the response?

- Based on your colleagues' response, what changes would you make the next time?

- How did preparing in advance for potential generalizations help you in being able to move the team forward?

Next-Level Tips

How you say something is even more important than *what* you say (see approachable and credible voice; chapter 4, page 96). Prompting your colleagues can be genuine, or it can be perceived as snarky. Combine the prompt you are considering with the use of an approachable voice, and your prompt will be perceived as authentic and less intimidating.

> *How you say something is even more important than what you say.*

Practice using these (and other) prompts, by yourself, in a mirror, or video record yourself to see how you might be perceived. It will, likely, be very uncomfortable at first. Practice it anyway. As you practice, it will become more comfortable for you, and then when it's time to get specific, you can combine this with the appropriate approachable and credible voice for maximum impact.

Decontaminate Space

When we have an extremely emotional experience someplace, whether good or bad, the emotion stays with us. Maya Angelou is reported as having said something along the lines of, "I've learned that people will forget what you said, people will forget what you did, but people will never forget how you made them feel." Emotions are a powerful thing, and they stick with us. In a collaborative team setting, a common cause of negative associations is when the work of your team has not been productive. If this is the case, folks likely abhor (or strongly dislike, at least) going to the meetings. Therefore, it sometimes becomes necessary to decontaminate a physical space (Grinder, 2018; Zoller, 2024).

Decontaminating the space could involve changing the arrangement of the chairs, moving the focal point for the work (screen or whiteboard or chart paper), or changing the room in which the team is meeting. Judge the level of contamination, and then choose which version of decontaminating space you need to pursue based on the intensity of the negative feelings; the stronger the negative emotions, the more intensive your decontamination intervention will need to be.

Overcoming Obstacles 127

> ### Theory in Action
>
> There was a team that I was working with one time that, from the moment they entered the room, it was clear that they didn't want to be there. Unfortunately, the meeting did not go well. Knowing that the physical space of that area of the room was now contaminated with those negative feelings, for the next meeting, I intentionally changed where we were meeting. I rearranged and moved the tables about ten feet in a different direction from the first meeting. We used chart paper in a different location to note our work, and I purposely sat in a different location than before, but this wasn't enough. The emotions were strong, and we needed extra decontamination. So we started by doing an activity where everyone got up from their seats, moved into a circle to share their thinking, and then proceeded from there. The team was now at a point where we could move forward, and the rest of the meeting was pretty magical! We simply had to decontaminate the space.

Decontaminate Space Tool

Use figure 5.2 (page 128) to consider times when you may need to decontaminate space. Access a blank version of this template for your own use by following the link at the end of the figure.

Reflection Questions

When you have finished reflecting on and using the decontaminating space tool, use a journal or notebook to reflect on the following questions.

- When might you be sure to use this move?
- When you used this move, what did you notice about the impact on the team?
- What adjustments might you make to your usage of this move?

Next-Level Tips

In addition to decontaminating space after the fact, you can be proactive when you know that certain situations will stir up negative emotions. In this case, frame the interactions that you know will lead to negative reactions in a way that ensures you can shift back to the work of the team while leaving those emotions behind in that physical space. For example, if you know that the principal will be coming to deliver bad news, have that delivery happen in the hallway or in a room where you don't typically meet. While it's possible to just have everyone turn in a different direction than they typically look, you risk the emotions still contaminating the space of the team, and, therefore, the work of the team.

Situation	Considerations	Notes to Self
Budget cut news is being shared	<ul><li>Should this be in a team meeting?</li><li>Who should deliver the news?</li><li>How can we create a third or fourth point?</li><li>What is the room setup, including where team members sit and where the messenger delivers the news?</li><li>What will the physical movement of members be after the news is shared?</li></ul>	
Data that isn't good is being examined	<ul><li>How can we create a third or fourth point?</li><li>Should we use paper and pencil examination or a screen (a screen will contaminate the screen for the rest of the meeting and potentially beyond)?</li><li>What is the room setup, including where team members sit?</li><li>Should we use chart paper to capture thoughts on a third point and engage in some physical movement?</li><li>How can we identify next steps?</li></ul>	
Updates on the state testing requirements are being studied	<ul><li>How can we connect this to the work of the team?</li><li>How can we create a third or fourth point?</li><li>What is the room setup, including where team members sit and where the messenger delivers the news?</li><li>How can we identify next steps?</li></ul>	

Figure 5.2: Decontaminating space.

*Visit **go.SolutionTree.com/PLCbooks** for a free reproducible version of this figure.*

Attribution

A colleague of mine frequently begins her emails with something along the lines of, "Hello brilliant colleagues." I can't tell you the impact that the addition of the little word, "brilliant," has on the reader. Personally, I read her emails, and it just makes me happy. It feels good to be recognized for your experience, expertise, or skillset. Attribution is a technique you can make that does just this: It recognizes and assigns the attributes that others bring to the table—sometimes in subtle and subconscious ways, and other times explicitly (Zoller, 2024).

To explicitly engage in attribution, you simply verbally (or in writing, like the previous example) attribute a virtue to another person. For example, "Given your experience in this area . . ." or "With the collective wisdom of our group . . ." or "Given our dedication to student learning . . ." or "OK, brilliant colleagues . . ." In these statements you are attributing the virtues of experience, wisdom, dedication, and brilliance to your colleagues. You can also gesture toward them when uttering a particular word to give added attribution to them. This is explicitly assigning attributes to your colleagues.

One final note about attribution: It must be sincere. If you are trying to manipulate your colleagues, they will see right through you. Your authenticity as a human being and colleague will come through if you are truly trying to either (1) explicitly call out attributes worthy of highlighting or (2) drawing out from them what they might not (yet) see in themselves (mindset 1, chapter 2, page 35).

> **It feels good to be recognized for your experience, expertise, or skillset.**

Theory in Action

You may have noticed that, throughout this text, I have used attributions. Statements like, "You know well," or "As you are well aware," or "As you well know," or "Given your experience," are all attributions. There is an assumption that you know your stuff, and I am attributing that quality to you, the reader.

You can also subconsciously assign attributes to your colleagues, though this is far more subtle. In this case, you might refer to someone else's wisdom, kindness, dedication, and so on—but as you speak about that other person, when you want to attribute the virtue to the group, you gesture to your colleagues. For example, you might say, "Two of the greatest educational thinkers of our time, Rick DuFour and Bob Marzano, stated that...." When you say the words "greatest educational thinkers," gesture, with palms up and fingers slightly curved, toward the group. The combination of your gesture with those words subliminally assigns those attributes to the group.

Attributes Tool

Use the following list of attributes (listed in alphabetical order) in figure 5.3 to consider how and when you might assign these to your colleagues, depending on the topic. A few boxes are left blank for you to identify additional attributes. A blank version of this template is available on this book's website.

Attribute	When and How You Might "Assign" It
Adaptability	Consider using before or after a change of plans from the team. For example, "Because we are educators, our ability to adapt to curveballs is exceptional . . ." Before making a change, or after coming to a decision or implementing a change of plans, you could say, "Our adaptability is an excellent trait."
Brilliance	Use to start meetings and emails in the salutation. Also, consider using this at the end of meetings and emails, thanking people for bringing their best, brilliant selves into the space.
Collaboration	At the beginning of the year or a meeting, say, "Given our identities as collaborators, how might we go about preparing for _____?"
Creativity	When a challenge is confronted (for example, students not achieving what the team is wanting), say, "Since we're all creative beings here, what comes to mind about how we might approach this challenge?"
Dedication	At a difficult time of year (such as end of semester, the February doldrums, and so on), remind folks of their mission as educators with something like, "It is an honor to work alongside such dedicated professionals as you all."
Energy	When the end of the semester draws near, and energy levels seem to get lower, remind people of their innate energy sources with something along the lines of, "Given our ability to draw from deep within ourselves and desire to finish strong . . ."
Focus	If meetings are at a time when focus can be a challenge (for example, at the end of the day or before a break), consider saying, "Since we all want to be as focused as possible, how might we move forward?"
Leadership	
Passion	
Patience	
Problem Solving	
Wisdom	

Figure 5.3: Attribution assignment.

*Visit **go.SolutionTree.com/PLCbooks** for a free reproducible version of this figure.*

Reflection Questions

When you have finished using the attribution assignment tool to plan for and implement this technique, use a journal or notebook to reflect on the following questions.

- In what ways have you noticed your colleagues taking on the assigned attributes?
- How might you make the use of attribution a regular part of your routines with both adults and students?
- How does attribution contribute to adding joy to your team meetings?

Next-Level Tips

Remember mindset 1 (chapter 2, page 35), to draw out from others what they don't (yet) see in themselves? This technique is very powerful in this regard. Combine the thinking of praise and reframe from that mindset and work to draw out from your colleagues what they may not (yet) be exhibiting. For example, if the team seems inflexible, it may be worthwhile to strive to attribute adaptability to the team to increase flexibility. Or, if the team seems to struggle with being truly collaborative, consider assigning the attribute of collaboration to the group.

In addition to assigning attributes to the group, you can consider the individual members of the team. Assigning attributes to individuals in the group can also be powerful, and it can be a tool for recognizing the experience, expertise, or skillset of those members.

Individual Rapport

A funny thing happens when you are with someone and are comfortable with them—your body language starts to mirror each other's body language. It happens naturally and without you even thinking about it—the other person leans in, and you will also lean in. If they sit back, you will also sit back. This doesn't happen instantly, but rather a few seconds after each other. The mirroring of one's body movements is what it's like to have rapport.

Having rapport means there is a level of relationship between two people—a basic level of trust and ease in communication (Zoller, 2024). A lack of rapport signals the opposite—that communication is not happening, and that trust may also be lacking. Thus, it's critical for members of the team to have rapport with each other, to physically mirror one another. The challenge with this move is that you cannot tell people to simply have rapport. Rather, *you* must create it by being the one to create rapport with *them*. As uncomfortable as it may feel at first, you must mirror their physical movements. Now, notice that I said mirror, not mimic. The mirroring isn't an exact match, it's not at the exact same time, and it's not in the exact same way. Rather, the mirroring of body language is subtle and done over the course of a conversation.

There are many ways to pay attention to rapport (MindTools, n.d.; Tickle-Degnen & Rosenthal, 1990), and I have distilled these into three most obvious manifestations: (1) body language, (2) voice tone, and (3) volume and intensity. Up to this point, I've talked about body language and how observable this aspect of rapport is. Body language can be broken into two main components—(1) movement of the head and (2) size of the gestures. Regarding head movement, you will start to notice how some people have very little head movement when they speak. Others are highly mobile. When building rapport with someone, pay attention to how they move their head and mirror those movements. Additionally, notice if they hold their head at a slight angle to the side, or if it is straight up and down. Mirroring this positioning of the head can be helpful in developing rapport, as well.

In terms of gesture size, you will also notice how some people "talk with their hands," and others will have minimal or no movements with their arms and hands at all. Where do you fall? Notice how others talk and then mirror that to create rapport.

Voice tone is somewhat related to head movement, because when you move your head, your vocal chords also move, affecting the pitch as it goes up and down with the changes in the vocal chords. Because of this, in general, those who move their head a lot will also have voice intonation that goes up and down a lot more. On the other hand, those with minimal head movement will typically have little shift in intonation simply because the vocal cords are not moving as much (Zoller, 2022). To develop rapport, notice your colleague's intonation and mirror it (and for more on the approachable to credible continuum, see the move in chapter 4, page 96).

Finally, volume and intensity need to be matched to develop rapport. Let's take a person who is loud, intense, and possibly even angry. It just doesn't work to simply ask someone to "calm down." Instead, work to create rapport. Then, over the course of the conversation, you can mirror them and, through your actions, bring their intensity and volume down to a level that tends to be more productive.

You might find it fun to notice rapport when watching television shows or movies. You'll see these ideas present—mirroring of body language as a nonverbal (and unconscious) way of being in relationship. Notice when rapport happens in everyday life, then work to improve your own ability to get in rapport with others. This will assist you when it comes time for meetings where you absolutely need to leverage rapport to increase effectiveness.

Theory in Action

When I first learned about the idea of mirroring to build rapport, I had become a secondary principal. There was one parent in particular who I got to know really well and who was quite angry and intense toward me and the school on a nearly weekly basis.

My technique of asking them to calm down just wasn't working; they remained angry, and we had a very difficult time seeing eye-to-eye on just about anything. Conflict was high. So, I decided to learn more about the technique of rapport by focusing on volume and intensity. To learn, I had to practice and be ready and willing to try something new and uncomfortable—as in I, an adult in the school, had to learn to try getting into physical rapport by mirroring and focusing on volume and intensity.

The next time they came in, angry and worked up, I practiced mirroring. Since I'm naturally a calm person, I worked up all the intensity and volume I could, accompanied my volume with some large and forceful gestures, and said, "Wow, you're really angry. Why don't you come into my office, and we can talk about it."

At first, they were surprised by my new way of responding. And yet it worked. They quickly brought their level of anger down, intuitively perceiving that I recognized how important this situation was to them. We had a productive conversation, and, quite frankly, after that, our relationship was much better. I'm not sure they ever came back into the office like that again. Rapport. Mirroring. Volume and intensity.

One important note about volume and intensity is that you cannot actually have the emotion that you are placing in the room. You are simply placing that intensity into the room through your nonverbals. If you yourself become angry in the process, or your blood pressure starts to rise, or you start to feel intense, then you will have succeeded in simply intensifying the emotions, and you will not be able to work the situation back down into a productive one.

There is one final note about rapport, and that is that it can be misused. If you are using rapport to manipulate someone to get what you want, you're misusing this skill. Further, it will shortly stop working as people begin to suspect that they are being manipulated. Rapport is to build relationships so that the other person feels and is truly heard, valued, and respected. Any use of rapport for anything other than building community is a misuse of this wonderful tool that happens naturally for most people in most situations and can be leveraged to increase the effectiveness of your team.

> **Rapport is to build relationships so that the other person feels and is truly heard, valued, and respected.**

Rapport Building Tool

Use the following tool in figure 5.4 to observe others, bring awareness to your own natural tendencies, and remind yourself of actions you might take to build rapport with colleagues.

Body Language	Voice Tone	Volume and Intensity
• Head movement • Head tilt • Gesture size • Talking with the hands or not	• Lots of modulation? • More monotone? • Phrase ends with pitch going up? Or down?	• Place emotion in the room • Don't have the emotion
Observations of others and myself: *I noticed that I am generally approachable with my voice and head position, but when I start to become emotional, I present less credible attributes. This doesn't seem to help the situation.*		
Reminders for myself in the future: *When I go into meetings where I know I may become emotional, I need to continue to use approachable voice and gestures. Additionally, I want to reflect regularly on how I created rapport with colleagues.*		

Figure 5.4: Gaining rapport.

*Visit **go.SolutionTree.com/PLCbooks** for a free reproducible version of this figure.*

Reflection Questions

When you have finished using the gaining rapport tool in advance and after a particular conversation, use a journal or notebook to reflect on the following questions.

- What do you notice about rapport when the level of conflict is low? High?

- When can you intentionally practice getting into rapport in low-conflict situations so that you can practice those skills before higher-conflict situations arise?

- When working to build rapport during higher-conflict situations, what do you notice about yourself? About others? About the situation?

Anonymize It

In a perfect world, everyone could say what they think and not be influenced by their colleagues. We don't live in a perfect world. All of us are influenced by our peers—sometimes positively and sometimes negatively.

You've probably seen it happen where one person's ideas are always perceived by their colleagues as being the best (let's call them Person A), and another person whose ideas are consistently shunned (let's call them Person B). The reasons could be many, from experience (or lack thereof) to personality to family relationships to who knows what else. If Person B says something that everyone disregards, and then a few minutes or meetings later, Person A says *the same thing*, everyone nods in agreement. One of the results of this is a feeling of being devalued, and this can lead to either colleagues shutting down and not contributing or becoming more aggressive in their comments to force their ideas on the group. Who says what in a meeting matters, as does equity of turn taking in talking.

In addition to this fact, remember that your number one responsibility is to make the meetings psychologically safe. In an ideal world, psychological safety exists, and there is no need for anonymizing the work. We don't live in an ideal world. In my experience, when people share their thinking anonymously, they are more likely to share their own thinking more honestly without the influence of others. This isn't to say that anonymity guarantees full and frank sharing, but it greatly increases the likelihood of it.

Anonymity happens when folks write down their thinking and then have the results of that writing (sticky notes, 3×5 note cards, sheets of paper, and so on) anonymously mixed up and shared. In the Theory in Action from decontaminating space (page 126), in addition to holding the meeting in a different spot in the room with a different seating arrangement, individuals wrote down on a sticky note practices in which the team had engaged that year that they wanted to celebrate. On a differently colored sticky note, then, they wrote practices that they felt needed to be improved. Those sticky notes were all tossed into two little baskets (one for celebrations and one for adjustments) before we moved into a circle (which was a standing circle). In the circle, each person pulled out a sticky note and read the celebration to the group. While the celebration didn't *need* to be anonymous, it helped set the tone for the sharing of modifications, which was done after the celebrations (and those modifications definitely needed to be anonymous). Because the sharing was anonymous—no one knew who wrote what—the dialogue was much more productive than if each person had shared their own.

Anonymization Tool

Table 5.1 (page 136) identifies potential situations in which anonymizing the work might be helpful. It also includes potential steps for you to consider to maximize team effectiveness through the implementation of this move.

Table 5.1: When to Anonymize the Work

Situation	Steps to Consider
Setting norms	<ul><li>On 3×5 note cards, individually and silently write pet peeves for meetings that you attend.</li><li>On the flip side of the card, individually and silently write down norms that, if followed, would solve the pet peeves.</li><li>In pairs, share your norms (ignore the pet peeves now!) and combine into one set.</li><li>Pairs now get together with another pair to share and combine.</li><li>Share sets of norms to get one final list (if needed).</li></ul>
Reflecting on norms	<ul><li>On a sticky note, identify which one the team needs to work on this next month. Be sure to also write why you think this needs work.</li></ul>OR<ul><li>On a sticky note, identify which one we should celebrate because we've done a good job with it. Be sure to also write why you think we should celebrate it.</li><li>Place all stickies in a basket and pull out one at a time to see where the team falls. Consider using a third point to put up on a whiteboard or chart paper to see where the team is landing.</li></ul>
Identifying essential standards	<ul><li>Each person individually and silently prioritizes the content area standards. Use a process that works for your team.</li><li>Individuals place their priorities on a sticky note in a basket.</li><li>Compile results on chart paper with tally marks for the prioritized standards.</li></ul>
Making a decision (fist to five or otherwise)	<ul><li>Clarify what decision is being made, including the options before the team.</li><li>Individuals silently write their preferred decision on a sticky note and place it in a basket.</li><li>Results are shared out and tallied.</li><li>Further dialogue can happen, if needed.</li></ul>
Reflecting on team functioning	<ul><li>Individuals silently write their reflections on a sticky note or 3×5 note card. Be sure that people know that they will not be sharing their own, so their description on the sticky note needs to be precise enough that someone else reading it will know what they are saying.</li><li>Place reflections in a basket.</li><li>Each person draws out a reflection and reads it to the group. The team may engage in dialogue about each reflection if they want.</li></ul>

Reflection Questions

When you have finished reflecting on and using the anonymization tool, use a journal or notebook to reflect on the following questions.

- When will it be important for your team to anonymize their work?
- How did anonymizing the work improve the team's functioning, both in productivity and joy?

Next-Level Tips

Know that, when anonymizing parts of the work, some people will pipe up and claim what they wrote, saying something like, "I wrote that . . . and here's what I meant." While not ideal, there's nothing you can do about that. It happens. Just go with it. My experience is that this claiming happens on teams where, oddly enough, psychological safety isn't as great, and the person or people who tend to hold more sway over others are the ones who tend to claim their thinking. Again, it's OK. Observe the interactions and keep moving forward. The very act of writing down and having others share each other's thinking will start to increase psychological safety on the team.

> **In this room, we all believe that all students can learn at high levels.**

Fourth Point

Recall from chapter 3 (page 57) that a third point is an inanimate object that draws us out of ourselves and to that object. An agenda posted on the wall, data displayed on a screen, or a set of reading material in front of the team that we are all looking at together can be a third point.

A fourth point is something that is outside the room that you gesture toward while speaking about (Grinder, 2018; Zoller, 2024). Generally, it's in relation to something with a negative connotation. For example, you might say, "There are some people who don't believe that all kids can learn at high levels." When saying "some people," you would gesture outside the room to place "that group of people" out there. What this subconsciously signals to the group is that people who don't believe that all students can learn are not in this room. In this room, by contrast, we all believe that all students can learn at high levels. And you have signaled that without explicitly identifying colleagues.

Basically, any time you want to refer to a negative sentiment, feeling, or experience, gesture outside the room. We don't want that negativity in the room with us, so we quite literally place it outside the room with a fourth point and gesture outside the room. Once, I even saw a presenter walk to the door of the training room and speak about the negative concept outside of the room before returning. They were using nonverbal gestures to communicate that that sentiment doesn't belong in our space. By using a fourth point for anything negative, you'll find that the positive vibes in the room will increase, and so will the team's effectiveness and joy.

Fourth point is really very simple, yet effective. You may already do it, and this explanation of what fourth point is just helps you to be mindful of it and use it to keep negative energy out of the team learning and meeting space. You will note that using fourth point is related to the idea of decontaminating space (page 126), except that fourth point is really a proactive measure to keep negativity at bay to the greatest extent possible.

Fourth Point Tool

Use figure 5.5 to guide your planning for use of fourth point based on your own scenarios (or the ones provided). The first box is completed as an example of how you might use this tool. You will find a blank version of this tool on this book's webpage.

Reflection Questions

When you have finished using the fourth point tool to prepare for and implement it, use a journal or notebook to reflect on the following questions.

- When do you see yourself using this move?

- When you used it, how did it work? How do you know?

- What changes might you make when using it in future situations to make sure that you have the desired effect?

Mode of Communication

As you know well, face-to-face communication is very different from email communication. All of the moves and techniques that are being discussed in this book are what bring meaning to the words that we use, functioning as nonverbal communication skills that convey upward of 90 percent of meaning. In written communication, we can't convey or receive underlying nonverbals, so others infer them. And, because of the way our brains are wired, we naturally tend to go to worst-case scenarios (Chadwick, n.d.; Cherry, 2023). This goes back to the days of our distant ancestors, living in less safe conditions than we do today, when a movement or sound in the dark had to be assumed to be a threat. If we assumed that that sound or movement was not a threat, we may very well have ended up a predator's meal. Therefore, those who survived were those who assumed the worst.

Maybe this has happened to you: You got an email from your boss saying to please see them after the school day. Or maybe they saw you in the hallway and said to please stop by in the next day or so. While I'm not a betting man, I would wager that you didn't think to yourself, "Gosh, I'm gonna get

> All of the moves and techniques that are being discussed in this book are what bring meaning to the words that we use.

Scenario	Considerations	Your Notes
Schedule changes for next year mean that your high-performing team will be separated with new team members coming in.	• How to acknowledge this • Who is mandating the change • Where to gesture • How to bring the team back after acknowledging (without getting stuck in negativity) • Some might be happy about this—how to validate?	"As you know" (attribution, with a gesture toward the group, and a brief pause with credible voice) "There are many considerations" (gesture outside the room with approachable voice) "when making a master schedule." (approachable voice with pause after phrase) "Unfortunately" (pat my chest, pause), "this has practical implications for us" (pat my chest) "and our work" (credible voice, gesture back to the space and pause). "As we" (open-handed, palm up, circular gesture) "move forward with these constraints" (gesture outside the room, pause) "what possible solutions might we consider to continue to maximize our effectiveness?" (beat gesture on maximize, approachable voice)
One person regularly complains about the work of the team.		
Struggles with student behaviors are bogging down the work of the team as folks are spending time complaining about this.		

Figure 5.5: When to use fourth point.

*Visit **go.SolutionTree.com/PLCbooks** for a free reproducible version of this figure.*

a bonus!" or anything positive. Instead, you went to the worst-case scenarios, thinking, "Oh no, what did I do wrong?" This is because you are literally hardwired to assume the worst (Cherry, 2023).

So when, as a teacher team leader, you send an email, be aware that if it could be interpreted the wrong way, it likely will be. Consider the mode of communication. Limit email communications to announcements and those subjects that have minimal interpretive options. Reserve everything else for face-to-face interactions.

Mode of Communication Tool

Table 5.2 lays out some of the more frequent types of communication that might be more helpful in email versus face-to-face modes. Add to this list based on your experience.

Table 5.2: Email Versus Face to Face

Email	Face to Face
• Reminder* of upcoming meeting with team-developed agenda from last time	• Setting agendas
• Reminder* to bring curriculum materials to examine to identify essential standards	• Prioritizing standards
	• Unpacking standards
• Reminder* to bring possible assessment items for the to-be-developed CFA	• Developing CFAs
• Reminder* to bring analyzed CFA data to the meeting	• Analyzing data
	• Determining interventions
• Notice of change of time or location of meeting	• Determining extensions
	• Reflecting on practice
• Providing a reflection tool to use in a meeting that might be helpful to preview before the meeting	

Be aware that sometimes people can get in the habit of being reminded. When this happens (if you remind people all the time about every little thing), if you forget to remind them, they might blame you. This does not build capacity in team members, so carefully consider when you send reminders so as not to create dependence on you to remind folks of the work of the team.

Reflection Questions

When you have finished using the email versus face-to-face tool to reflect on your own practice and identify additional content for each mode of communication, use a journal or notebook to reflect on the following questions.

- When are times that you have sent emails that were misinterpreted?

- How can you be sure to use email communication to increase effectiveness and efficiency?

Next-Level Tips

Here's a very simple trick to help get more people to read your emails: a meaningful salutation. Don't just jump into the content of your email. Instead, say good morning or hello. Follow this up with a well wish, like, "I hope you're having a great day," or "I hope you had a fantastic weekend." It doesn't matter what you say, exactly, other than for it to be genuine and "you." By starting your email with a salutation that signals that you care, you will not only communicate that you care, but you also have a greater likelihood of having your email read (Goel, 2023).

We Do It Together

There are four strategies laid out in this section of the chapter that the team can do together to overcome challenges; we begin with the use of data, because data can be a powerful force for change (Garmston & Wellman, 2016). At the same time, data must be handled with care as you maintain a psychologically safe space focused on building capacity and doing the work. Honest self-assessments help the team to reflect individually and collectively on and refine their own practice because a team can't improve without identifying areas to improve. Fist to five is a process that will facilitate decision making when the going gets tough (or otherwise), as will forced choice.

This section will cover the following strategies.

- Data usage
- Fist to five
- Self-assessment
- Forced choice

As before, after exploring these strategies, consider your own situation and reflect on what you will begin to use immediately, what you will need to practice before using, what sort of systematic schedule you might create for implementing, and which ones you will reserve for later in your leadership journey. Please use the blank reproducible tools at the end of this chapter (pages 155–156) to complete this activity after reading You Do It Yourself (page 123) and We Do It Together (page 141).

Data Usage

Effective teams ground their work in evidence and reality, and this is where data come in (Garmston & Wellman, 2016). The use of some kind of data should be a part of the majority (yes, more than half) of your team meetings.

The term *data* is a four-letter word and, like certain other four-letter words, is unfortunately viewed with contempt by many. For this reason, I prefer to use the term *evidence*, as it opens the possibilities of what data can be. In this vein, let's be clear about what data are and what data are not. In possibly the broadest sense, data are qualitative or quantitative. When most of us think of data, we think of quantitative data, specifically student achievement metrics—"hard" numbers like percent of students proficient, numbers of students in certain classes, scale scores (like ACT, SAT, RIT, and so on), grade-level equivalents, and percentile ranks. However, quantitative data can also include results from student, staff, and parent surveys. It includes metrics monitored by the guiding coalition, such as the number of teams who have created norms, identified essential outcomes, developed CFAs, or who reflect on their team practices at least once a year. It also could be the results of self-assessments like the critical issues survey (the first column of table 3.1, page 7373), or even tallies when one person is charged with tracking interactions in a team meeting, like the number of times each person speaks and for how long, the norms that are specifically referenced, or the number of times colleagues praise or criticize each other. And, at the risk of stating the obvious, the most important quantitative data used by the team is the percentage of students who have met the team-identified, grade-level essential outcomes. These data have tremendous value in a team and school and need to be a regular part of our thinking and planning. And yet, if we limit ourselves to quantitative data alone, we severely constrain ourselves.

Qualitative data, on the other hand, is more narrative. In terms of student performance, it could be exit tickets that students complete after a lesson or series of lessons. It also could be the results of an open-ended questionnaire that a team gives to students at certain points in a unit to find out, from the students' perspectives, what's working and what's not. And it could be compiled narrative self-assessment results of the team (see the self-assessment strategy on page 143).

Both forms of data, or evidence, need to be used in team meetings if the team is to improve its practice and results for students, to overcome challenges that the team will have, and to bring more joy to the work. Aside from being a fairly objective tracking mechanism, it provides a focus for the work of the team and a tool to facilitate celebrations.

> **Effective teams ground their work in evidence and reality.**

Evidence Tracking Tool

Use figure 5.6 to track what types of evidence your team is using, as well as how often those types are being used. A couple of examples are provided for you here, and a blank printable version of this tool is available as a reproducible on this book's webpage.

Quantitative Evidence		Qualitative Evidence	
Date Used	**Description of How It Was Used**	**Date Used**	**Description of How It Was Used**
MM/ DD	*Results from the first CFA of unit X were used to examine our effective practices and learn from each other. They were then used to determine which students need which additional skills and how to do do that.*	MM/ DD	*The team asked students, on a 3x5 card exit ticket, which of the learning targets in the current unit they felt most comfortable with and why. The team then looked at these results to plan next steps for instruction.*

Figure 5.6: Evidence tracking tool.

*Visit **go.SolutionTree.com/PLCbooks** for a free reproducible version of this figure.*

Reflection Questions

When you have finished completing the quantitative versus qualitative tool, use a journal or notebook to reflect on the following questions.

- Review the data in figure 5.6. What patterns do you notice? How effective has your team's use of data been? What changes might you consider to improve that effectiveness?

- What do you notice about your team's comfort, or lack thereof, in accessing, displaying, analyzing, and using data?

- What steps might you take to increase that level of comfort?

- How will you know that the steps you are taking are having a positive impact? And how and when will you celebrate this positive impact?

Next-Level Tips

Double this strategy up with third point—especially if the data can be perceived as highly personal (like student performance data from a CFA). In addition, refer to the data as "the data" instead of "our data" or "our results." And, even more important, don't refer to a specific teacher's results. Instead, point to the data and say, "These results." While very subtle, the level of psychological safety this simple act creates is noticeable. It separates us, as human beings, from the data. And data can be very personal. Open up space for vulnerability, building trust, and identifying next steps by using these small, subtle, and powerful tips.

In addition to the third point tip, use the quantitative versus qualitative evidence tool (page 142) to monitor your team's usage of data in team meetings over time. Reflect on and celebrate any increases in using evidence. Remember, what gets measured is what gets results. And data (or evidence) is how we know that we're getting better at guaranteeing learning for all students.

Self-Assessment

Teams that fail to self-assess fail to grow (Garmston & Wellman, 2016). In other words, if you want to transform collaboration, the team has to self-assess where it is on its journey. This includes brief self-assessments at the end of most meetings regarding adherence to norms or the work of the team, as well as more in-depth reflections throughout the course of the year and at its conclusion.

Self-Assessment Tool

Figure 5.7 offers a sample potential timeline for regular self-assessment. Consider sharing it with the team to identify when and what intervals the team will self-assess to improve functioning.

Frequency of Self-Assessment	What to Self-Assess
Every Meeting	• Adherence to norms • Accomplishments of the meeting (related to outcomes)
Quarterly	• Ferriter's quarterly reflection tool (Ferriter, 2020, p. 44)
Mid- and End-of-Year	• Norm review • More done in less time with greater joy tool (figure 5.8) • Evidence tracking tool (see data usage strategy on page 142)
End-of-Year	• Critical issues for team consideration (see first column of table 3.1 on page 73)

Figure 5.7: Self-assessment timeline.

Visit go.SolutionTree.com/PLCbooks for a free reproducible version of this figure.

More Done in Less Time with Greater Joy Tool

Use the following process and figure 5.8 to assist the team with reflecting on what they have done, what they might continue to do, and what they might consider changing in order to get more done, in less time, with maximized joy. Possible responses are provided, and a blank version of the tool is provided online for you and the team to access.

1. Each person on the team silently and individually completes the second column for each of the following prompts (five to seven minutes).

2. In round-robin fashion, each person shares their thoughts to the first prompt while all others remain silent.

3. At the conclusion of the sharing for that first prompt, engage in open dialogue about what this sharing means for the team's next steps.

4. Repeat steps 2 and 3 for the remaining prompts.

Prompt	Individual Response	Team Next Steps
What are some of the strategies that we have used that have *proven successful this year* in terms of getting more done in less time? What evidence do you have to support this conclusion?	Having an agenda and sticking to it (with clear roles for people on the team, including the norm watcher) has really helped keep us focused and not going astray. While I sometimes don't like to reflect, the act of writing down these thoughts makes me grateful for our leadership and team, and "forces" us to identify ways to get better.	Keep using the agenda. Sometimes we forget to set the agenda at the end of the meeting (for next time), so that would help make sure that we are prepared for our next meeting.
What are some of the strategies that we have used that *need to be changed in order to help us get more done in less time?* What would those changes be?	Sometimes our inclusion goes long and cuts into our valuable time together. Making sure that we keep those short would be helpful.	Set a timer for inclusion. Start on time, and end the activity before the timer goes off (or shortly after). Consider projecting a timer so all can see.
What are some of the strategies that we have used *that have brought greater joy to our work?* What evidence do we have to support this claim?	Our celebrations are really great! I love that we have a mini-cheer that is silly to just acknowledge each other. And we have changed it a couple of times, which helps to keep our celebrations fresh.	Keep changing our celebration routines. I like how someone is in charge of what we will do as our mini-cheer each week. Keep doing that.
What strategies might we consider *adding or tweaking in order to create a more joyful atmosphere?*	We do a good job of celebrating each other, and I think it would also be good to celebrate those not on our team—like students, parents, other teachers, and administrators. It would also be good to be more intentional at celebrating the accomplishments of the team (as in, we plan our work, but we rarely celebrate the accomplishments of that work).	Be sure to celebrate the implementation of our plans for improvement.

Figure 5.8: More done in less time with greater joy tool.

Visit go.SolutionTree.com/PLCbooks for a free reproducible version of this figure.

Reflection Questions

When you have finished using either or both the self-assessment and more done in less time with greater joy tools, use a journal or notebook to reflect on the following questions.

- What is the "just right" frequency of self-assessment that is most helpful for your team?

- What additional or different sorts of self-assessment might be helpful?

- In what ways might you engage your colleagues in taking the lead on self-assessment?

Next-Level Tips

The result of self-assessment is data that can be used, over time, to improve team functioning and results for students. Even if you don't know if it will be helpful down the road, record the results of self-assessments in a way that they can be accessed again later on. The growth shown from self-assessments over time (whether that "over time" is over a few months or a few years) can be a wonderful source for celebrations. As a bonus, because the team is the one doing the self-assessing, the validity of the growth shown over time is not questioned by team members and therefore adds strength to the celebrations and momentum for growth that this creates.

> **Building consensus is a critical aspect of a team's work.**

Fist to Five

Building consensus is a critical aspect of a team's work, but this is easier said than done. The working definition of building consensus is twofold (DuFour et al., 2024).

1. When all viewpoints have been heard (even, and especially, for those against a particular action).

2. The will of the majority is evident.

That's it. Two parts. Get everyone's voices in the room and then have 51 percent or more ready to move forward. It's worth highlighting that the notion that we should make sure that those opposed have been heard is a significant shift from how teams typically operate. Most often, we function from the perspective of trying to convince those opposed of the error of their ways. Instead, this definition of consensus seeks for us to understand the reasoning behind their opposition. This is a big difference in approach and leads to greater understanding for all involved.

Fist to Five Tool

Once all voices have been heard, even (and especially) those most opposed, then the fist to five strategy is one effective way to see if the will of the majority is evident while also allowing for a gradation of enthusiasm behind any given proposal. Use the following script to introduce the use of the fist to five strategy when a decision needs to be made.

[Say]: "Before we make a decision on this particular issue, does everyone feel that they have been able to fully express their perspective—not just that you've been able to express your view, but that you've been heard and understood?"

[If the answer is no (or a version of no like "never mind" or "it doesn't matter") from anyone, say]: "Tell us more so we can fully understand." [Be sure to paraphrase (chapter 4, page 88) so that you can be sure that you understand and that they feel heard.]

[If the answer is yes, say]: "Before we move forward, let's be sure we have consensus. Please individually and silently think about where you stand on this issue." [Restate the issue and proposal.] "Use the following scale, but don't show us where you fall just yet:

"5 is that I support this to the extent that I'll be on the front lines to lead it.

"4 is that I support it fully, but don't ask me to lead it.

"3 is that you support it, but have some reservations.

"2 is that you have significant reservations and are not in favor.

"1 is that you are fully against this proposal, but you won't sabotage it." [Consider laughing when you make this statement so that folks don't interpret your statement as meaning that you assume that someone might sabotage it.]

"And 0 means [Chuckle with a pause] that you will sabotage it."

[Pause]

"On the count of three, show us your thoughts."

The key number on the fist to five scale signifying support is a 3. If you have at least half of respondents with a 3, 4, or 5, move forward.

Once you see the results, if there is a majority in support, say, "It looks like we have _____ out of _____ in support of this proposal, so let's move forward."

If there is not majority support, then say, "So, we do not have a consensus. How should we move forward?"

Reflection Questions

When you have finished using the fist to five tool, use a journal or notebook to reflect on the following questions.

- At what point did you know that you had everyone's voices in the room without proverbially beating a dead horse?

- What steps might you take to ensure that everyone's perspective is shared in the most efficient manner possible?

- When are times that it will be helpful to use this strategy?

Next-Level Tips

Many times, if a person doesn't feel that they've been heard, they will not outright respond, "No," to the question about being heard. Instead, they might hem and haw, move their head side to side, squirm in their chair, and so on. Remember that nonverbal cues don't lie. Watch for them, as these are what will communicate to you whether or not colleagues *really* feel heard. In other words, don't just listen to the words; also be sure to listen to the nonverbals.

Be sure to listen to the nonverbals.

Additionally, sometimes inadvertent peer pressure on the display of numbers can come into play. Combine this with the move to anonymize it (page 134) to be sure that you're getting an honest assessment of the perceptions in the room. In short, have colleagues write their number on a sticky note or small piece of paper, place everyone's paper in a container, and then pull them out one at a time to see the results.

Forced Choice

If we want to get the most done in the least amount of time with the greatest joy, we often need to limit our options. This is where forced choice comes in. Forced choice is simply providing a limited menu from which we select our choice. As teachers, we do it all the time without realizing it. For example, we might ask students who are working independently or in groups on a task, "About how much more time do you need? One, two, or three more minutes?" In this way, you "forced" three choices on students: one minute, two minutes, or three minutes. No more.

In team meetings, forced choice can be used with time allocations ("Should we devote five or seven minutes to this task next time?"), and also with tasks. For example, for an elementary team, "Should we focus on mathematics or reading as part of our next learning cycle?" For a secondary team, an option might be, "Should our CFA be at the end of this week or the start of the next week?" Of course, as adult learners, the team may decide that the choices you have provided are not adequate. Don't be offended. This is fine. Your work to provide choices prompted movement forward, and that's the point.

Forced Choice Tool

As you prepare for upcoming meetings, consider the tasks that the team needs to accomplish, what decisions need to be made based on the task, and what options might be considered. Note the empty boxes for you to identify additional tasks that may need to be considered. See figure 5.9 for examples of tasks and their accompanying possible forced choice outcomes.

Task	Decision to Be Made	Example Options for Forced Choice
Learning cycle focus	Content area	• Reading • Mathematics • Science • Social studies • Other
Learning cycle focus	Essential standards	Which standards from a list of prioritized standards will be the focus
CFA administration	Timeline	• End of this week, OR • Start of next week OR • This day • This day, OR • This day
Data analysis and usage	Timeline	• End of this week, OR • Start of next week OR • This day • This day, OR • This day

Figure 5.9: Forced choice scenarios.

Reflection Questions

When you have finished considering the forced choice scenarios tool, including adding your own considerations, use a journal or notebook to reflect on the following questions.

- When will it be important to offer forced choice to your colleagues?
- How did using this strategy help with the team's functioning?
- What changes might you make when you use this at a future meeting?

Next-Level Tips

As noted with a few other strategies, the use of an approachable and credible voice (chapter 4, page 96) can make all the difference in how the use of many actions are perceived by colleagues. Try practicing the following statement using a purely approachable voice, coupled with the pause (chapter 3, page 54)—be sure to use the approachable voice all the way through to the end (so "And Option C" will sound more like a question than a statement). Exaggerate your approachable voice to get the full effect. And be sure to include pauses after each punctuation mark.

> So it seems that we have three options before us. Option A. Option B. And option C. Which route should we pursue?

Now try saying the statement again using a purely credible voice and minimal head tilt and movement. Exaggerate. Include the pauses.

Once you regain composure from your laughter at the extreme-sounding nature of each of these, read the statement again. This time, combine an approachable and credible voice to make it be both the most accessible to your colleagues as well as signal (through your nonverbals) that this is a decision to be made and not a continuation of conversation. It might go something like this.

> [Highly approachable] "So it seems that we have three options before us."
>
> [Still approachable] "Option A." [Pause] "Option B." [Pause]
>
> [Now credible] "And option C." [Pause]
>
> [Back to approachable] "Which route should we pursue?"

No doubt you can clearly hear the impact of choosing an approachable voice and a credible voice has on what is communicated. Be sure to choose and implement the voices that will have the greatest impact.

Putting It All Together

Use the tools in figures 5.10 and 5.11 (page 152) to reflect on your work. Following is a story of a teacher team leader and a description of the team and its members that will assist you in pulling together your learning from this chapter. Consider what content from this chapter might best assist her in leading the team.

> Maria is a middle school teacher team leader who has been in this role for just a few years. As a middle school immersed in the middle level philosophy, teams meet daily for about forty-five minutes. Two of those meetings per week are for "student concerns," which largely involves student behaviors and does not address the four critical questions of a PLC. One meeting per week is allocated for departments to

meet across teams, and then one to two meetings per week are for the grade-level team to focus on the development of IDUs, or interdisciplinary units. Maria serves as a team lead for both her grade-level team and her department.

Each of the teams on which Maria serves might be described as "good teams" by outsiders. They get along with each other, and minimal adult drama comes from them. Administrators point to the teams that Maria leads as examples for others to look toward, and occasionally, visitors from both within the school and outside of the school come and observe how their meetings proceed.

However, while considered exemplars for team functioning, when it comes to getting improved results for students, this is an area that is lacking. Fortunately, Maria recognizes this, knows that the purpose of a team is to improve team practice and results for students, and has decided to take some steps to make this happen. She knows that bumps will likely ensue as she pursues this course of action.

Based on this scenario, circle the responsibilities, assumptions, and mindsets that you believe will be most critical for Maria to keep at the forefront of her mind. How might you suggest she does this? Use figure 5.10 (page 152) to complete this activity.

Having considered the responsibilities, assumptions, and mindsets, which of the moves, techniques, and strategies would you suggest for Maria as most useful at the team's first (and subsequent) meetings? How would you suggest she go about using them? Use figure 5.11 (page 152) to complete this activity.

Possible Next Steps

Because Maria knows that she can only control herself, she begins by considering the responsibilities, assumptions, and mindsets. Being mindful of the need to keep (or make) it safe as they move forward with challenging their current practices, she decides that the second responsibility of building capacity needs to be her focus. She also realizes that conflict will likely ensue, and since she has a personal aversion to conflict, she wants to regularly remind herself that conflict is actually good (assumption number five). She explicitly shares with her colleagues the notion that if three people are in a room, and if all of them agree, then two of them are unnecessary. Finally, she decides that, while meetings are not currently drudgery, she wants to spread the contagion of joy with her words and deeds.

The work of the team, in the past, has not been dysfunctional. It just hasn't achieved results. So, keeping this in mind, Maria will be sure to attribute excellence, both explicitly and implicitly, whenever possible. She wants team members to be honored for their past contributions while ensuring that future practices can lead to improved student learning outcomes. Also, to help with this, Maria decides to intentionally use fourth point to reference past practices that may not have been helpful in improving the function of the team.

Responsibilities, Assumptions, and Mindsets	Notes for How to Keep This in Mind
Responsibilities: 1. Make it safe. 2. Build capacity. 3. Do the work.	
Assumptions: 1. People do the best that they can. 2. You can only control you. 3. Behavior communicates. 4. People want to get stuff done. 5. Conflict is good.	
Mindsets: 1. To see what others don't (yet) see in themselves. 2. To be humble with a posture of learning. 3. To spread the contagion of joy.	

Figure 5.10: Pulling together your learning reflection chart.

You Do It Yourself	
Moves and Techniques	**How and When Might Maria Use It?**
Specificity	
Decontaminate space	
Attribution	
Individual rapport	
Anonymize it	
Fourth point	
Mode of communication	
We Do It Together	
Strategies	**How and When Might Maria Use It?**
Data usage	
Self-assessment	
Fist to five	
Forced choice	

Figure 5.11: You do it yourself and we do it together vignette chart.

The team has previously used email for most communications, so she decides to explicitly suggest to the team a new norm, which is that email will be used for information only. Team meetings are for dialogue and understanding, followed by decision making. This is met with enthusiasm, as folks want to get stuff done in meetings while simultaneously not being offended by emails that should be conversations.

Maria knows that, should one person become offended at the direction the team is starting to take, her role in gaining rapport with that person will be critical in overcoming that potential roadblock. She decides that she will practice this skill regularly—both having and not having rapport with friends, family, neighbors, and colleagues. She knows that if this skill does not become second nature, then she will struggle to effectively use it when conflicts emerge.

In terms of strategies, Maria decides to start with having the team regularly use a self-assessment to reflect on their practices and identify next steps. She identifies several of the tools noted in that section that will prove useful for this purpose, and the third point that these data provide will be helpful for making it safe while also building capacity.

As she considers the use of these self-assessments, she thinks about what data will be helpful to overcome any potential obstacles. Maria realizes that the data from the self-assessments themselves will prove useful, particularly from the critical issues survey that highlights the specific actions that the team must take to get better results for themselves and students. She also knows that the best data will be student performance data, and she considers what student data, CFAs, in particular, will be most helpful to the team as she seeks specificity to improve practices.

Maria also thinks to herself about how the meeting space that they have previously used is associated with feeling good but not with changes to practice. Because of this, she approaches the administration about having their meetings in a conference room, in this way decontaminating space (even though, in this case, the contamination isn't necessarily negative; it's just not productive).

Maria works with the administration and other teacher team leaders to create, as a draft, a potential productive timeline for the work of the team, and this timeline is based on the critical issues survey self-assessment. In taking the anonymized results of that self-assessment to the team, she decides to use a combination of forced choice and fist to five to engage the team in using the draft timeline to create their own priorities for the work of the team.

While changing the trajectory of the work of the team from one where members are comfortable to one where improvements are happening will be a challenge, Maria is committed. The responsibilities, assumptions, and mindsets are front of mind, and on her calendar, she schedules to review these once every two weeks, reflect on her application of them, and consider a personal focus for the next two weeks. Once a month, she reviews the list of moves, techniques, and strategies to identify where she wants to continue to grow. She also uses the results of the team self-assessments not only to guide the work of the team but also to reflect on her own leadership skills and development.

Summary Reflective Questions

When you have finished completing the pulling together your learning reflection activity, use a journal or notebook to reflect on the following questions.

- What lessons might you take from Maria's experience and plan?

- What will you apply to your setting?

- What next steps do you see yourself taking?

- What criteria will you use to determine whether or not you are being successful in that implementation, and what course corrections might you need to make?

Conclusion

Roadblocks will inevitably appear as your team works to improve their practice and results for students. This chapter detailed a number of actions that you yourself might take to help the team transform collaboration: avoiding generalizations and getting into specificity, decontaminating space as appropriate, attributing virtues to your colleagues, and ensuring individual rapport when conflict emerges. Further, employing the techniques of anonymizing the work, using fourth point, and considering the mode of communication will all help move the team forward. The four strategies that the team might take together to overcome obstacles include the use of data, regular self-assessment, decision making using a fist to five scale, and limiting options through forced choice.

Chapter 5: You Do It Yourself Planning and Reflection Tool

Now that we have explored these moves and techniques for overcoming obstacles, consider your own situation and reflect on what you will begin to use immediately. Which moves and techniques will you need to practice before using? What sort of systematic schedule might you create for implementing? And which ones will you reserve for later on in your leadership journey?

You Do It Yourself				
Move or Technique	To Start Immediately	Needs Some Practice	When and How Will I Practice?	Save for Later
Specificity				
Decontaminate space				
Attribution				
Individual rapport				
Anonymize it				
Fourth point				
Mode of communication				

The Teacher Team Leader Handbook © 2025 Chad M. V. Dumas • SolutionTree.com
Visit **go.SolutionTree.com/PLCbooks** to download this free reproducible.

Chapter 5: We Do It Together
Planning and Reflection Tool

Now that we have explored these strategies for overcoming obstacles, consider your own situation and reflect on what you will begin to use immediately. Which strategies will you need to practice before using? What sort of systematic schedule might you create for implementing? And which ones will you reserve for later on in your leadership journey?

We Do It Together				
Strategy	To Start Immediately	Needs Some Practice	When and How Will I Practice?	Save for Later
Data usage				
Self-assessment				
Fist to five				
Forced choice				

The Teacher Team Leader Handbook © 2025 Chad M. V. Dumas • SolutionTree.com
Visit **go.SolutionTree.com/PLCbooks** to download this free reproducible.

What we learn today doesn't make yesterday wrong, it makes tomorrow better.

—*Unknown*

CHAPTER 6

Refining Your Skills

This chapter is all techniques—specific moves that you can take to increase your influence and improve the team's effectiveness, efficiency, and joy. Each of these is subtle, and people will likely not even consciously know that you are doing them. However, they *will* have a positive impact as you subconsciously influence others through the nonverbals that alter perception, helping to transform collaboration in your team!

You'll notice that this chapter doesn't have any strategies that the team pursues together. That's because, at this point, the refinements will come in your individual leadership and interpersonal skills. Which means that . . .

You Do It Yourself

We will begin our exploration of specific techniques with the frozen gesture, a great technique that helps to make pauses impactful (Grinder, 2018; Zoller, 2024). We will then move to the beat gesture, to help you to emphasize what you want to be sure is emphasized (Grinder, 2018; Zoller, 2024). The way you hold your hands, and where you hold them, communicates to others (Grinder, n.d.b). A whisper, counterintuitively, communicates intensity (Grinder, 2018), while interrupting yourself captures attention (Zoller, 2024). All of these subtle techniques will be important refinements to your ability to communicate to your colleagues while influencing the work. In total, these techniques will greatly assist you, personally, in influencing your team as you work to become a more effective teacher team leader.

This section will cover the following techniques.

- Frozen gesture
- Beat gesture
- Hand position

- Whisper
- I interrupt myself

159

160 THE TEACHER TEAM LEADER HANDBOOK

After learning about and exploring these techniques, consider your own situation and reflect on what you will begin to use immediately, what you will need to practice before using, what sort of systematic schedule you might create for implementing, and which ones you will reserve for later on in your leadership journey. Please use the blank reproducible tool at the end of this chapter (page 169) to complete this activity after reading You Do It Yourself (page 159).

Frozen Gesture

When you speak with someone, you are likely using gestures. Some people use gestures to the point where folks know that they "talk with their hands." A frozen gesture is a specific type of gesture that enables you to add emphasis by freezing it (Grinder, 2018; Zoller, 2024). Coupled with a pause (chapter 3, page 54), the frozen gesture builds space into a conversation for thinking and emphasis. It communicates to others that you are not finished with your thoughts. A frozen gesture is just what it sounds like: It's a hand gesture that you simply stop moving. Any gesture will do, and it's simply frozen. Only move the gesture when you are speaking. And freeze the gesture when you pause.

Finally, be sure to *actually* freeze the gesture. It can be tempting to keep moving your hand, head, or body. Be still. Freeze that gesture and stop talking.

> **The frozen gesture builds space into a conversation for thinking and emphasis.**

Frozen Gesture Reflective Tool

Set up your phone to record yourself practicing using a frozen gesture, then use the frozen gesture and pause to say the following:

"There are three things on our agenda for today." [Break eye contact, look at the agenda, and pause with a gesture toward the agenda as a third point]. *"What else needs to be added?"* [Continue looking at the third point with a frozen gesture toward it.]

After recording yourself, watch it to see what changes you need to make to combine elements of an approachable and credible voice (chapter 4, page 96) with your pause and frozen gesture. Try using the frozen gesture with other statements and reflect on the impact. Use figure 6.1 to complete the activity. A sample is provided here, while a blank version is available online.

Reflective Questions	Your Responses
How did using the frozen gesture feel to you when you did it?	It felt really weird. I definitely need to practice to make it natural, because when I see other people use it, it's really impactful, and I want to have a similar impact.

Reflective Questions	Your Responses
What did the use of the frozen gesture look like when watching it?	*Oddly enough, it looked natural. It just felt unnatural when doing it.*
When would be good times to be sure to use the frozen gesture?	*I think it will be important to use the frozen gesture when I want to make an important point. I could also use it while using a third point to direct people's attention to the agenda, our data, or our work on the whiteboard.*
A tendency is to keep moving (or talking) through the frozen gesture. What steps might you take to ensure that you don't do this?	*I will remember to breathe when I freeze, and as part of breaking eye contact, I will think about ensuring that my gesture remains frozen.*

Figure 6.1: Frozen gesture reflective tool.

Visit **go.SolutionTree.com/PLCbooks** *for a free reproducible version of this figure.*

Reflection Questions

When you have finished recording yourself and using the frozen gesture reflective tool, use a journal or notebook to reflect on the following questions.

- What impact do you notice the frozen gesture having on team meetings?

- When do you see yourself using the frozen gesture in order to improve team functioning?

Next-Level Tips

The frozen gesture works particularly well when you pause to give folks an opportunity to think. If you have a member of the team who is a verbal processor and doesn't allow others that time to think, the frozen gesture can be helpful in creating that space without calling that person out. As part of the pause, your hand may come up and out, with fingers slightly rounded, palm up, and combined with a breath and breaking of eye contact. This frozen gesture typically will also "freeze" any response from others, as they can see you thinking. If it doesn't, then they clearly have more on the topic that needs to be said, or you have continued to move and have not actually frozen your gesture. To assist with giving that time to think, be sure to break eye contact with your colleagues. If you maintain eye contact, one of two things will likely happen: The person you are looking at will (1) start to respond to your question or statement or (2) perceive that you are trying to manage their behavior. Neither of these outcomes is helpful.

Beat Gesture

The beat gesture is an effective nonverbal tool, used with your hands, to emphasize a point (Grinder, 2018; Zoller, 2024). Think of a conductor who is marking out the "beat" for the band, choir, or orchestra. And the beat happens at the *ictus*—a fancy Italian word for the bottom "bounce" that happens when making the beat.

So the beat gesture refers to the ictus that you will create to emphasize, in a regular beat, the words that you want to be emphasized. For example, suppose you were to say, "This is a really important point." To emphasize that it really *is* an important point, you would drop your hand and arm at several different points: first, on the word "this," then again on the first syllable of "really," a third time on the second syllable of "important," and a fourth ictus on "point." Of course, you would also pause slightly after each of those words and beat gestures.

Potential Phrases for Using a Beat Gesture Tool

Use figure 6.2 to practice using the beat gesture on some sample phrases. Watch yourself in the mirror or video record yourself and watch it. Reflect on the effectiveness of your use of this action, and consider when and how you might use it. A few sample reflections are provided, a blank version is available online, and additional rows are provided for you to add your own examples.

Reflection Questions

When you have finished completing the potential phrases for using a beat gesture tool and using the beat gesture in both practice and with colleagues, use a journal or notebook to reflect on the following questions.

- When do you notice other people using a beat gesture? How does it help them emphasize key points?

- What steps might you take to remember this action to emphasize key parts of the work?

Next-Level Tips

When you are using the beat gesture, as noted in the description, be sure to briefly pause after each gesture. This pause is not long, but for added emphasis, inhale (breathing, chapter 3, page 50) prior to the next word and beat (without making you hyperventilate, of course!). Depending on the phrase, that inhale might be audible. Further, you might consider adding the whisper (page 165) if you're intending for this important message to be inspirational.

Phrase	Words to Emphasize on the Beat	Reflection on Your Use	When and How You Might Use It
This is really important.	• This • Really • Important	*Make sure my hands look natural and not contrived. I tend to have a very stiff hand position, and this looks awkward.*	*Use when highlighting potential next steps for the team.*
Who will do what by when.	• Who • What • When	*It looks weird if I do the frozen gesture all in the same physical space. So I want to move where the ictus is— moving from left to right for others looking at me (but right to left from my perspective).*	*Use when the team makes a decision, but not every time (I don't want to overuse the beat gesture). Use only when it feels like we definitely need to have action taken and it might not be clear that we need to take action.*
Let's be really clear.	• Really • Clear		
What standards will we determine to be absolutely essential?	• Ab- • -Solutely • Essential		
Let's look at our data together, student by student and skill by skill.	• Student • Student • Skill • Skill		
How will we know that students know it?	• Know • Know		

Figure 6.2: Potential phrases for using a beat gesture tool.

*Visit **go.SolutionTree.com/PLCbooks** for a free reproducible version of this figure.*

Hand Position

Interestingly, our hands communicate a lot about who we are, how we are feeling, and our intended message (Grinder, n.d.b). Going back to the days when we might have to fend off someone, quite literally, with our hands, the act of seeing someone's hands helps us to subconsciously trust them. Conversely, someone who keeps their hands under the table or behind their back (when standing) will have a harder time engendering trust from others

(Coleman, 2021). So, without doing anything with your hands, simply make them available to be seen. We trust people more when we can see their hands.

Now that your hands are visible, how you position them makes a difference in what others perceive you are intending to communicate. Straight fingers, coupled with a rigid elbow position at or close to 90 degrees, and your forearm perpendicular to the ground, communicates intensity and directiveness. Figure 6.3 provides a visual example of this. When you are telling someone what to do, and there's no question about your directive, straighten your fingers and make that elbow a rigid 90 degrees. This is more of a credible position for directing work, and, of course, you will rarely use this positioning as a teacher team leader with your colleagues—this is simply so you can be aware of how you might position your hands as a default.

On the other hand (yes, that pun was definitely intended), take those straight fingers, gently curve them, roll your wrist so that the palm is up, and soften the angle at your elbow. Now you are communicating openness and approachability. Try it now, and you will feel a significant difference between these two subtle hand positions. See figure 6.4 for a visual reference.

> We trust people more when we can see their hands.

Figure 6.3: Hand communicating instruction or direction.

Figure 6.4: Hand communicating approachability.

	Hand Position Considerations
Credible	• Straightened fingers • Forearm perpendicular to the ground • Stiff elbow approaching 90 degree angle
Approachable	• Curve fingers • Palm up • Elbow more relaxed

Source: Zoller, 2019. Used with permission.

Figure 6.5: Hand gesture tool.

Understand how these different positions communicate to others. Be sure that your intended meaning is being communicated. Generally, as a teacher team leader facilitating the work of the team, you will likely be using more open hand gestures to elicit the thinking and feeling of your colleagues.

Considerations for Hand Position

Use figure 6.5 to assist you in preparing for and reflecting on your use of hand position, depending on the situation. As a reminder, you'll want to regularly ensure that your hands are visible to your colleagues to subconsciously communicate that you are trustworthy.

Reflection Questions

When you have finished considering the hand gestures tool, use a journal or notebook to reflect on the following questions.

- What do you notice about other people's use of their hands to communicate?
- What is your default hand position when engaging with colleagues? Students? Family?
- When will it be important for you to be mindful of your hand positions while working to increase the effectiveness of your team?

Next-Level Tips

Combine your hand position with the beat gesture (page 162) to be sure that you are emphasizing what you want to be emphasized. A beat gesture with a more credible hand position and the use of a credible voice (chapter 4, page 96) will drive a point home. However, it can also come across as aggressive or angry if you are not careful. A beat gesture with an approachable hand position will be perceived as emphatic but softer. Try out different combinations while watching yourself in the mirror or by video recording yourself and then viewing it. You'll find what works for you to be able to assist your team in increasing effectiveness.

Whisper

This particular technique is counterintuitive, but it's quite impactful: When you want to deliver inspiration, whisper it (Grinder, 2018; Zoller, 2024). Many times folks will become more animated when they try to deliver an important or inspiring message. But this gets old quickly. Instead, deliver inspiration with a whisper, though your voice doesn't necessarily have to be quiet—it becomes breathy, and the intonation drops.

Pay attention to how politicians, comedians, actors, and others use this technique. Notice that when it comes time to deliver a message that is inspirational, many times they will choose (with coaching from nonverbal experts) to make their voice get airy, and they almost whisper the words. They drop the volume and pitch of their voice, and then the breathiness of the tone comes through. Deliver inspiration with a whisper. It really works (Grinder, 2018; Zoller, 2024).

166 THE TEACHER TEAM LEADER HANDBOOK

Phrases for Using Whisper Tool

Use figure 6.6 to identify phrases for which you might use a whisper, and then practice it prior to actually using it. Video record yourself and watch it. Reflect on the effectiveness of your use of this action and consider when and how you might use it. Some potential phrases are provided for you, and additional rows are provided to add your own examples. As with other reproducibles, a completely blank version is provided online.

Phrase	Reflection on Your Use	When and How You Might Use It
"This is really important."	It feels more natural for me to only whisper "really important." Adding a pause before "really" also seems to add emphasis, as well as a beat gesture on "rea-" and "-por."	Use when confirming with the team that the essential standard that the team has identified for the next unit is really important.
"We nailed it."	I should emphasize "nailed" with the whisper, not necessarily the entire phrase.	Use after reflecting on the implementation of CFAs, or looking at the data, or after making instructional decisions.
"Let's get really clear."	I need to be careful that this doesn't come off as patronizing. I need to practice this more so it isn't interpreted as being dictatorial.	Use prior to identifying essential standards, or creating a timeline, or developing CFAs. In all of these cases, "Let's get really clear . . ." is the stem leading to the next phrase of what we will get clear about.
"How can we stretch ourselves?"		
"We could not have done this alone."		
"Think of the difference we're making in students' lives."		

Figure 6.6: Phrases for using whisper.

*Visit **go.SolutionTree.com/PLCbooks** for a free reproducible version of this figure.*

Reflection Questions

When you have finished utilizing the phrases for using whisper tool to prepare for, practice, and implement phrases to whisper, use a journal or notebook to reflect on the following questions.

- When do you notice others delivering inspiration with a whisper?

- When do you see yourself using this technique?

Next-Level Tips

When you deliver inspiration with a whisper, consider combining it with the beat gesture (page 162), or at least with pauses (chapter 3, page 54), as appropriate. Pauses, of course, are also typically accompanied by an audible in breath (chapter 3, page 50), so consider where an audible inhale may be helpful to amplify your message and impact.

I Interrupt Myself

Our brains are hardwired to notice when something different happens. When you're in a room with lots of sound, a sudden lull in the volume will catch your attention. Same thing with a sharp or loud outburst of some sort. The brain notices changes, and it's biologically built in. The technique of interrupting yourself leverages this built-in tendency (Zoller, 2024) when needing to capture the attention of your colleagues, without saying something like, "Hey, colleagues, I need your attention!"

For example, you might say, "So, as we think . . ." [Interrupt yourself by pausing for a second or two, possibly inhaling to accompany that pause, and include a frozen gesture if you so desire while simultaneously breaking eye contact with the group]. Then resume, starting the phrase over: "So, as we think about . . ." What you did was start to say something, then interrupt yourself, and then simply restart and continue on. The interruption will catch the attention of your colleague's brains, enabling them to home in on what you're about to say as you move forward.

When you interrupt yourself, be sure to breathe. This looks and feels natural and will add a silent pause to the room, allowing the brains of your colleagues an additional clue to pay attention to what is coming next. Additionally, interrupting yourself needs to be done while you break eye contact. As noted in chapter 4 (page 102), eye contact can be perceived as a tool to manage others' behavior. Adults don't like to have their behavior managed, so it's important not to give this perception. When you interrupt yourself, as part of the pause, be sure to break eye contact with folks. Look up. Look down. Look out a window. It doesn't matter. Just don't look folks in the eye during the silence of your own interruption. Finally, maximize this technique with a frozen gesture (see page 160). The frozen gesture, coupled with the silence and broken eye contact in the midst of your interruption of yourself, will most certainly get people's attention.

The "I Interrupt Myself" Checklist Tool

Practice interrupting yourself, and as you do so, use the items in figure 6.7 (page 168) to assess yourself. Be sure to also video record yourself and watch that video to get the maximum impact of your self-assessment.

- Seamless interruption of yourself
- Pause
- Breathe
- Break eye contact
- Frozen gesture

For further refinement of this technique, consider:

- Interrupting yourself in the middle of a multisyllabic word
- When restarting, lower your
  - Speed
  - Volume
  - Pitch
  - Intensity

Figure 6.7: I interrupt myself tool.

Reflection Questions

When you have finished using the I interrupt myself checklist tool, use a journal or notebook to reflect on the following questions.

- Did your interruption cause others to also pause? If so, what made it effective? If not, what might you do differently next time?
- What refinements might you consider for your use of this technique to increase your effectiveness?

Next-Level Tips

Two tips will take this technique to the next level. First, interrupt yourself in the middle of a multisyllabic word. For me, this requires forethought to think through what word I might interrupt myself in the middle of in order to maximize my impact. A go-to word that I use for this is "thinking" in the phrase, "One of the things I'm thinking . . ." I interrupt myself in the middle of the word "thinking," and then when I restart, I will continue with, "One of the things I'm thinking about is . . ."

Second, when you resume speaking, do so at a lowered speed, volume, and pitch. This will also likely lead to a lower level of intensity of speaking, and this shift will be noticed by your colleagues as you work to increase the effectiveness of the team.

Conclusion

In your work as a teacher team leader, you have laid the groundwork for the effective functioning of your team. This chapter detailed specific techniques that you might find helpful to advance the team's work even further by increasing the impact that you, personally, have on the actions of the team. The frozen and beat gestures assist with emphasizing key points, and your hand position helps to create an open environment. Using a whisper allows you to make sure that the points you want emphasized are highlighted, and interrupting yourself helps to gain attention when needed. Taken together, these actions will significantly increase your impact on the team, and thereby transform collaboration by increasing the team's ability to get more done, in less time, and with greater joy.

REPRODUCIBLE · 169

Chapter 6: You Do It Yourself Planning and Reflection Tool

Now that we have explored these techniques for refining your skills, consider your own situation and reflect on what you will begin to use immediately. Which techniques will you need to practice before using? What sort of systematic schedule might you create for implementing? And which ones will you reserve for later on in your leadership journey?

You Do It Yourself				
Technique	To Start Immediately	Needs Some Practice	When and How Will I Practice?	Save for Later
Frozen gesture				
Beat gesture				
Hand position				
Whisper				
I interrupt myself				

The Teacher Team Leader Handbook © 2025 Chad M. V. Dumas • SolutionTree.com
Visit **go.SolutionTree.com/PLCbooks** to download this free reproducible.

Accept the challenges so that you can feel the exhilaration of victory.

—George S. Patton

CHAPTER 7

Addressing Challenges
From the Field

Some readers may just skip to this portion of the book to see how to apply the moves, techniques, and strategies shared throughout the rest of this text. If you're one of those people, welcome! Glad to have you aboard. I have no doubt that, as you read these real life stories and considerations for how to both proactively and reactively respond to the challenges presented, you will then go back into the book and read up on the specifics. However, if you started reading from this point: Please go back and read the introduction and chapters 1 and 2 first. These portions provide an important foundation for the application of these skills and will help to ensure that your implementation of this learning will become productive habits. Without the foundation of the identified responsibilities, mindsets, and assumptions of a teacher team leader, the application of these skills could very well become manipulative. And manipulation is not conducive to transformed collaboration.

Please know that the example solutions shared next are not exhaustive. As you know, human beings are complex. There is no one "right" way to engage with colleagues. As such, what I present are simply *some* ways that a teacher team leader might consider using to approach those challenges. No doubt you will modify what I present to fit your own personality, style, and the needs of the team. And no doubt you will identify additional ways to approach these challenges to improve the team's effectiveness and infuse greater joy in the work. Let's begin!

Challenge: The Team Is Too Large or Too Small

Let's start our exploration of challenges with a fairly simple (though not easy) physical problem that teams may have: the size of a team. The number of people on a team, does not, by itself, determine what the effectiveness of the team will be. And yet, the larger the group becomes, the more skillful the members need to be in order to be effective (Garmston & Wellman, 2016). A skilled facilitator can help a team become more effective for short bursts of time. But in order for the team to become a team and become effective over time, it is the members themselves who have to become more skillful. Hence, your second responsibility: build capacity.

> The larger the group becomes, the more skillful the members need to be in order to be effective.

Let's deal with two extremes of team size: too large and too small. My own observation is that six members or larger is the tipping point, if you will, for when struggles can start to emerge due to the sheer number of people and opinions. The solution is really quite simple: divide the team into smaller groups for large portions of the work. For example, the team might get together at the beginning of a meeting to ground themselves and gain clarity on the outcomes, and then they move into groups of three to five to do the work of a team. There might be a check in at some point in the middle of the meeting with members of each subgroup sharing updates, questions, insights, and so on. Finally, at the end of the meeting, an opportunity to come back together to share, celebrate, and set the agenda for next time might be appropriate. This splitting up will likely not necessarily include moving to a different room, as the physical movement takes time. Rather, simply separating to different ends of a table or part of the room may be the most efficient way to make this happen.

Of course, when the full team is together (as with smaller groups, as well), it's even more important to use protocols (chapter 1, page 22) to ensure that you maintain psychological safety with equity of voice. The larger the group, the more dominating certain folks may become, and the more docile others will be. Don't assume that just because you're coming back from small groups that the large group will be highly functioning. Processes like designating who will share out from each group will be important (and rotated on a regular basis—whether formally or informally).

While, observationally, the ideal size of a team seems to be three to five people, there are many occasions when a team is two people—the other extreme that's part of this challenge. This can go one of three ways: (1) incredible synergy where each member pushes each other to be better than they can be by themselves, (2) the two people become so close that they start *groupthink*, where they fail to challenge each other to get better, or (3) the two so strongly despise each other that the tension in the air is thick enough to cut with a knife. The first option is ideal, and this is what we want.

The second option, where groupthink becomes the norm, is a challenge that will involve lots of others as expert (chapter 4, page 111) to push each other's thinking. It will also involve questions (chapter 4, page 92) and sentence stems (chapter 4, page 113) to help each other consider new perspectives. Finally, self-assessment (chapter 5, page 143), particularly if each person does it individually and then shares with the other, can be a catalyst to break free from such a rut.

The third possibility, members who despise each other, is likely the most challenging scenario. Your first responsibility is psychological safety, and this becomes more challenging when two people have strong animosity toward each other. In this case, all the actions in chapter 3 (page 45) will be crucial to create that psychological safety, particularly the use of inclusion, third point, pausing, group rapport, breathing, and laughter and humor.

Challenge: Members Fail to Follow Norms

Having addressed a potential physical concern for the size of the team, let's now move into more complex challenges of teams, challenges involving social and emotional dimensions to the work. While having norms is an important prerequisite to being able to follow them, having norms doesn't mean that the team will automatically follow them. And this is often the case in many teams that are struggling. Before sharing some thoughts about how to possibly remedy this challenge, let's consider some potential root causes of this challenge. I believe it's important to consider these root causes, because the solutions will be different depending on the root cause. Possible root causes for the failure of members to follow established norms include the following (DuFour et al., 2024).

1. Team members didn't develop them or have voice in norm creation, so they don't actually reflect team members' needs.

2. The team does not regularly revisit and revise norms.

3. Individuals do not hold each other accountable to the norms.

Let's take time to explore each of these in the upcoming sections.

1. Team Members Didn't Develop or Have Voice in Norm Creation, So They Don't Actually Reflect Team Members' Needs

Team norms need to be formally reestablished every year. This process doesn't take very long, twenty minutes on the high end (see norms, chapter 3, page 60, for a great protocol), and it is worth every minute it takes. You see, norms are not just rules to follow. My view on norms has been enhanced thanks to Ferriter (2020), because he argues that norms are an expression of your needs. Think about that for a moment; norms are an expression of our needs. So, if the norms do not meet the needs, change the norms.

Before school starts every year, your team will likely convene for the first time. Even if all the people are the same as last year when you established your norms, those people have changed. They have grown, learned, and developed new knowledge, skills, and insights. The same norms that were created a year ago may or may not meet their needs now, so toss out those old norms. Don't even look at them. Don't "contaminate" your thinking with those norms of last year's you. Start from scratch. Create norms based on the needs of the team at this time using the protocol detailed in chapter 3 (page 60).

2. The Team Does Not Regularly Revisit and Revise Norms

Sometimes, when we establish our norms, we put them down on paper, laminate them, and don't revisit them over the course of the year. This is a mistake. Norms need to be living guidelines to meet your needs. Allow for the ability to make revisions based on how things are going.

Your team will want to reflect on its adherence to the norms, probably at the end of meetings on a regularly periodic basis (the first few meetings of the year, for sure, and then maybe monthly or quarterly after that). This is a great time to raise certain norms that may not be meeting everyone's needs. For example, if you reflect at the end of the meeting and find that for a few weeks, one or more members have been arriving late, consider asking the team, "Given that our norms include starting and ending on time, what might we do, collectively, to ensure that we start on time?" Be sure to use an approachable voice (chapter 4, page 96), combined with a third point (chapter 3, page 57) of the norms posted on a chart paper or screen. You may want to consider an option of going later (if that truly is an option), or maybe having a different time to meet (again, if that's an option). Opening the dialogue will go a long way in trying to solve this problem without creating defensiveness.

If the norm being broken is about staying on task, raise this as part of the reflection. Better yet, one of your colleagues may raise it if it's a problem. In this case, as is likely with other norms being violated, the team may consider having a norm watcher (some teams call them a traffic controller). Or, even better yet, brainstorm ways that the team can hold each other accountable for the norms in simple, low-risk ways for adhering to the norms (see the next root cause for more of a discussion on this).

3. Individuals Do Not Hold Each Other Accountable to the Norms

Sometimes, even with everyone having a voice in the norms, as well as regular reflection, members will still avoid holding each other accountable. In this case, you have to make the accountability to the norms less of a hammer and more of a gentle nudge. Make accountability a reminder rather than punishment.

It may be helpful to recognize, from the start, that because we are all human beings, we are all imperfect. This means that every single one of us will, at some point (or many points), violate a norm. And this is OK. What is *not* OK is violating norms without being called out on them (in a kind, loving, and respectful way, of course). Most people appreciate being reminded of norms. Remember assumption number four: "People want to get stuff done."

Holding each other accountable doesn't have to be a big and scary deal. Here are a few ideas I've seen from teams that have proven effective.

> **Every single one of us will, at some point (or many points), violate a norm.**

- Revisit the norms at every meeting (beginning and end) until they become a habit. When you do this, it will probably be likely that the team will need to do more than just read the norms (silently or out loud). Boredom will seep in quite rapidly if you do this. Instead, engage in meaningful repetition. You can sometimes have colleagues share their responses, but other times, this can just be a silent reflection. You might consider using one of the following prompts, like "Given our norms, which ones . . ."

  - "Might you particularly struggle with today?"

  - "Might you focus on?"

  - "Might the team potentially struggle with today?"

  - "Should the team focus on?"

- Use a signal of some sort when colleagues are violating a norm. Some teams might download images of "Norm" from the television series, *Cheers*, because he was intended by the writers to be someone who represented "normal" people, and we want our norms to become part of our normal operations. They then put his image on popsicle sticks and have those around the table for meetings. Whenever someone violates a norm, they simply raise a picture of Norm, and everyone laughs and gets back to work. Other teams, on the other hand, might have a different image on a popsicle stick for celebrating when the team follows norms. You might consider having both.

- Some teams will have a safe word that is used when a norm is being violated. This typically involves something that causes everyone to laugh because it's an inside story, such as an event (like in Vegas?) that you all went to where it was a good time but wouldn't necessarily be appropriate to delve into details in a professional setting. It could also be a local establishment that brings a level of joy to some folks or another kind of fun way to remind people to come on back and focus on the work at hand.

- Sometimes teams like to go beyond a little signal of a safe word or gesture and actually have something on the table to toss at others (lovingly, of course). One team I worked with had the words "toss something not sharp and gently at them" at the bottom of their agendas. Another had little plush toys to toss. Yet another had Nerf guns. Find a way to hold each other accountable, and make it fun. It doesn't have to be, nor should it be, a harsh calling on the carpet.

- Every single one of us will break a norm at some point. One team I worked with decided to recognize this from the get-go and randomly assigned norms to break on specific meeting dates by each person to see if the team would hold them accountable. It was as simple as little slips of paper with a norm on each in one basket, and then upcoming meeting dates on slips of paper in another basket. Each person draws out a norm and a date, and, without others knowing which norm or date, they will break the given norm at the given meeting. They had fun with it, and it was a nice chance to see if everyone really meant it that they would follow their norms, and, more importantly, hold each other accountable to those norms so the team could get more done, in less time, and with greater joy.

Challenge: The Team Isn't Following the Agenda

Let's say your team created their agenda (at the end of the last meeting), you have reviewed it at the beginning of the meeting, and everyone agrees to it, and yet folks don't follow the agenda. If the team doesn't follow the agenda, it's important to have a few foundational elements in place. These foundational elements include the following.

1. Having and following norms

2. Identifying roles for different people to fulfill during meetings

3. Ensuring that there is clarity of why the time of the team is important

4. Ensuring clarity on what the work is that needs to be accomplished

1. Not Following Norms

If members are not following norms, then this is an issue that needs to be addressed. First, ensure that everyone's voice is accessed in developing those norms. Second, be sure that all members commit to the norms, either formally or informally. If they do not commit, then ask what needs to be added, changed, or deleted to meet their needs. Finally, set up systems for team members to hold each other accountable to the norms. It is not your job, as the teacher team leader, to perform the job of officer on duty, ensuring that all comply. Rather, it is your job to ensure psychological safety, build capacity, and help the team to do the work. Part of building capacity is helping the team to identify roles (chapter 3, page 62), one of which is to monitor team members' adherence to norms. See the challenge on team members not following norms (page 173) for a more detailed explanation of ways to address this challenge.

2. Roles and Timekeeping to Keep Everyone on Task

As noted in chapter 3 (page 62), it may be necessary to identify roles for team members to take on as part of running meetings. A few roles that many teams find helpful include norm monitor, facilitator, taskmaster, and notetaker. These different roles can greatly facilitate helping the team accomplish what it says it wants to accomplish at each meeting.

Finally, it may be helpful, when setting the agenda for each meeting, to identify how long each item on the agenda should take. This process will make sure that the team identifies how much time they want to spend on different tasks as well as guide the taskmaster in ensuring that those times are monitored and adhered to based on the desires of the team.

3. Clarity of Why the Time as a Team Is Important

If people are not utilizing the time of the team well, as evidenced by a failure to stay aligned with the agenda, they may not understand why collaborative time is so important. If this is the case, it may be helpful to access others as expert (chapter 4, page 111) and read about the importance of collaboration for improving adult learning and, thereby, student learning (DuFour et al., 2024).

To avoid the perception of lecturing your colleagues, you might consider selecting one quote per meeting and having it at the top of the agenda. This quote, then, could be the basis of the inclusion activity (chapter 3, page 65) to focus everyone's mental energy in the room, get everybody's voices in the room, and build community as colleagues connect with each other and the content. Using a third point (chapter 3, page 57) may also be helpful, in addition to the use of a protocol (chapter 1, page 22) for examining such quotes.

> **If people are not utilizing the time of the team well, they may not understand why collaborative time is so important.**

4. Clarity of the Work That Needs to Be Done

It may be that people understand why it's important to work together, and yet they may not be clear on what work needs to be done. If this is the case, it may be helpful to use a self-assessment (chapter 5, page 143) for colleagues to reflect on their use of meeting times. As part of such a self-assessment, use questions (chapter 4, page 92) to help probe what can be done to improve team functioning. Of course, as part of your questioning, be sure to use an approachable and credible voice (chapter 4, page 96).

Challenge: The Team Fails to Follow Through on Decisions

Maybe you've been part of a team that makes decisions but doesn't follow through on them. On one team that I was part of, I tallied the number of decisions we made in a given year. Of the eighty-one decisions made, more than a third were *not accomplished*, and (more than) another third had not been reported back on, so it was unknown if those decisions had been implemented or not. This left roughly a quarter of the decisions made by the team actually implemented. As you can imagine, this level of dysfunction leads to frustration. Why even meet?

A number of root causes could be at play for this particular challenge. Here are a few for consideration.

1. Clarity of what the decision is
2. Clarity of who is responsible for implementation
3. Timelines for implementation
4. Processes for reporting back
5. Memory
6. Lack of trust in the team

In my experience, this challenge is the result of several of the preceding potential root causes. We'll take time to explore each of these in the upcoming sections.

> **Failure to be clear about what decisions have been made can lead to a failure to implement those decisions.**

1. Clarity of What the Decision Is

No doubt you've left meetings where you were unclear what decisions were made. If this is a feeling you have had, then others have likely had the same feeling. At the risk of stating the obvious, failure to be clear about what decisions have been made can lead to a failure to implement those decisions.

To address this challenge, first be clear about what outcomes are being pursued for the meeting (chapter 3, page 69). Further, consider using paraphrasing (chapter 4, page 88) to summarize for the entire team what decisions have been made. For example, "So, it sounds like we're in agreement that we will be giving this CFA on X date and bringing the data to our next meeting. The data will be compiled in tool Y so we can spend our time analyzing it and making next step decisions. Is that right?"

Finally, at the end of the meeting, clarify what decisions have been made. Use the strategy of who will do what by when (chapter 4, page 114) to assist with this by once again reaffirming decisions that were made throughout the meeting.

2. Clarity of Who Is Responsible for Implementation

If it's clear what the decisions are, then the next consideration is to be sure that everyone knows who is responsible for implementation. Like with the previous potential root cause, consider using the strategy of who will do what by when. Sometimes, when it comes time to decide who is responsible for what, there are blank stares and folks awkwardly avoiding eye contact. This might mean that you need to ask for specific volunteers for specific tasks or even volunteer individuals to take on certain responsibilities. Of course, as a team, it will be important to informally, or even formally, track who is doing what so that capacity can be built among all members and that the workload is spread across the team.

3. Timelines for Implementation

If everyone is clear on what decision was made and who is responsible, folks may be unclear about the timelines for implementation. As with the other root causes, paraphrase first (chapter 4, page 88). Use who will do what by when (chapter 4, page 114), write it down (chapter 4, page 110), and ensure that the timelines are crystal clear. Consider also using questions (chapter 4, page 92) to facilitate a clear understanding of the expectations for implementation. For example, "We said we were going to do X. What might be a reasonable timeline to accomplish this task?"

4. Processes for Reporting Back

If, even after the use of actions suggested to this point, members of the team are still failing to implement the decisions of the team, set up a system for staff reporting back the results of the implementation of team decisions. When the team is setting their agenda for the next meeting at the end of the previous meeting (see chapter 3, page 76), include in that next agenda what products need to be brought back for the team to review. Then, be sure that at the next meeting those products are reviewed—few things are as frustrating to team members as doing work outside of meetings in preparation for the meeting that is then not needed or even acknowledged in the meeting.

5. Memory

Sometimes decisions aren't implemented because we leave the meeting and get bombarded with a zillion other things. When this happens, how easy is it to simply forget what decisions were made and what each of us needs to do?

Be sure to have decisions written down (chapter 4, page 110). Use a landing page (chapter 3, page 66) to have one place for people to go for agendas, resources, notes, decisions, and more. Finally, write down those decisions and timelines.

6. Lack of Trust in the Team

Of course, the ultimate root cause of a failure to implement decisions of teams can be a lack of trust in the team. This lack of trust is many times manifested in a failure of team members to share their opinions during the meeting. Then, because individuals don't agree with the decisions made, they sabotage those decisions when the meeting is over. This is a significant problem and will not resolve itself quickly.

Remember how your number one responsibility is to make it safe? The way that you make it safe is through social sensitivity and equity of turn taking (chapter 1, page 22). Inclusion (chapter 3, page 65) will be important to start to build community while connecting with the content and each other. Further, the use of protocols (chapter 1, page 22) will be critical in ensuring equity of turn taking. Over time, with the implementation of the many actions suggested as part of this challenge, trust will build, and team effectiveness will increase.

Challenge: One Member Dominates the Conversation

One of my administrator colleagues would readily admit that they have the "gift of gab." You no doubt know folks who also have this skillset, and you might have this skillset yourself. While the expertise that these individuals share is most definitely appreciated, it can lead to that person dominating the conversation and reducing opportunities for others to share their expertise. Over time, this can lead to friction within the team, including but not limited to others disengaging from the team.

Like other challenges presented here, let's examine some potential root causes (Team Rallybright, 2023) of why one member of your team might dominate the conversation, and then let's identify potential solutions based on those root causes.

1. They are a verbal processor.

2. They are unsure of their own knowledge or skills.

3. They aren't self-aware of their own domination of the conversation.

4. They don't feel heard (or even valued).

Before jumping into each of these potential root causes, let us assume three things: (1) norms have been established by the team, (2) there are methods of accountability for holding each other accountable to those norms, and (3) roles for members of the team include one person who serves as a "norm monitor" (chapter 3, page 60). If none of these are present, start here. Establish norms, have methods to hold each other accountable, and consider having one member who is a norm monitor who safely, and without offense, is in charge of calling folks to account (and celebrating!) for abiding by the norms. If you have all these preconditions met, go on to the following potential root causes.

1. They Are a Verbal Processor

Many of us think by talking, and as we talk through something, we become clearer about the issue. We don't necessarily intend to dominate the conversation—we just end up dominating because we need to process out loud.

If you have a verbal processor on your team who dominates the conversation, they simply need to be provided opportunities to do their processing. In this case, one of the best sets of tools at your disposal are protocols (chapter 1, page 22). Specifically, protocols to get everyone's voices in the room will be really important. Consider those that provide for pairs to talk to each other, then have pairs report out to the rest of the team. As a facilitator of learning, don't just ask for volunteers to report out from the pairs; be sure to have ways to have different people report out to the larger team. As you know, if you simply have volunteers report out, the verbal processors will jump right in, and those more reserved will remain silent.

You no doubt have lots of tools in your toolbox to help a variety of people report out, things like the person with the largest or smallest watch face, whoever has the longest or shortest hair, the person who woke up earliest or latest that day, or whoever had the most or least vegetables the day before. You get the picture. Anything random like this, or something that appears random, is sure to get other voices present in the room.

2. They Are Unsure of Their Own Knowledge or Skills

Oddly enough, I've experienced one or more people who dominate a conversation being someone who is surprisingly unsure of their own knowledge or skills. Their coping mechanism to cover up this shortcoming is to talk—a lot. If this is the case, two particular actions will be paramount: (1) pausing and (2) paraphrasing. Because they are unsure, they need to be reassured for what they know. The pause and the paraphrase (see chapter 3, page 54, and chapter 4, page 88) will be particularly helpful with this, as will attribution (chapter 5, page 129) to attribute skills and expertise to them, specifically.

3. They Aren't Self-Aware of Their Own Domination of the Conversation

Some folks don't even know that they are dominating the conversation. If this is potentially the case, engage your team in a self-assessment (see chapter 5, page 143). To guarantee the safety of the group, couple that self-assessment with the move to anonymize it (chapter 5, page 134). Several of the self-assessment tools could be useful, including reflecting on the adherence to norms (chapter 3, page 60) on a weekly basis and the quarterly self-assessment tool for a more in-depth reflection on a quarterly basis (Ferriter, 2020).

4. They Don't Feel Heard (or Even Valued)

Sometimes, in our profession, or maybe just in life, we don't get the appreciation that we deserve. We may not feel heard or valued. I'm talking about appreciation not just as educators, but as human beings: simple, small recognitions of the work and contributions that we are making to the lives of young people and each other. Sometimes, those colleagues are on our teams. When we don't feel heard, we may compensate by dominating conversations. This is because if we don't feel heard, we feel like we need to say what we have to say again. And again. And again.

As before, the most powerful tools in your toolbox are the pause and paraphrase (chapter 3, page 54, and chapter 4, page 88). While you may feel exasperated by the repetition and domination by one person, take a deep breath (but do not sigh). Pause. And then paraphrase. You may be surprised to find that your dear friend just wants to know and feel that they have been heard and valued. If it feels helpful, write down the key points of the paraphrase as a third point and to be sure their thinking does not get lost.

Challenge: One Member Doesn't Engage in the Conversation

Interestingly enough, the root causes and solutions for this challenge are very similar to those for colleagues who dominate the conversation but with small differences (Busch, 2022). Those differences from the previous challenge are in italics.

1. They are an *internal* processor.
2. They are unsure of their own knowledge or skills.
3. They aren't self-aware of their own *silence*.
4. They don't feel heard or even valued *anyway*.

> **Internal processors need time to think.**

1. They Are an Internal Processor

Internal processors need time to think. Unfortunately, in the hustle and pressures of our daily lives, we don't get or take much time to just think. In the case of internal processors, give them and yourself space to do this. As with the previous challenges, protocols (chapter 1, page 22) will help.

Before having folks share their thoughts verbally, have them write their thoughts down first. This can be on a sticky note, 3×5 note card, a handout, or any other document. Just create some silence to write down thoughts or at least think to themselves. I usually provide a prompt like, "Let's take ninety seconds to silently and individually jot down your thoughts on topic Y." The phrase "silently and individually" is important to say; otherwise, your verbal processors will jump in to verbally process, and this will drive your internal processors crazy. So be sure you emphasize the words *silently* and *individually* without finding fault or blame by simply pausing before and after those words. Once everyone has had a chance to jot down their thoughts, use protocols to get everyone's voice in the room. See the previous challenge for tips on how to do this.

2. They Are Unsure of Their Own Knowledge or Skills

While this root cause is counterintuitive to the previous challenge (for people who dominate conversations), this root cause makes sense for this challenge: People who are unsure of their own knowledge or skills may tend to keep their thoughts to themselves because they are intimidated and fear embarrassing themselves. Again, protocols are important to get their voices in the room, especially when combined with anonymizing it (chapter 5, page 134).

You may also consider the move of attribution (chapter 5, page 129). This move can start to build confidence in folks who lack this confidence. And finally, the use of self-assessments (chapter 5, page 143) can also start to build confidence where it is lacking, because confidence comes from competence. As a team and individuals become more competent in their work, both individually and as a team, the confidence will come along, but developing that competence and confidence comes through explicit self-assessments that enable the individual and team to identify, build on, and celebrate strengths.

3. They Aren't Self-Aware of Their Own Silence

While some are not aware of their dominance of conversations, others aren't aware that they are largely silent. Simple self-assessments (chapter 5, page 143) of the work of the team may prove particularly helpful. Additionally, consider anonymizing it (chapter 5, page 134). Sharing the results of those self-assessments with a specific protocol to access everyone's expertise will be important. Finally, don't underestimate the power of a simple, "Hey, colleague X, what are your thoughts on this matter?" to get their voice in the room.

4. They Don't Feel Heard or Even Valued Anyway

This is, unfortunately, a sad reality for some of our colleagues. Since they don't feel heard or valued, they simply disengage and don't speak up. Three actions will be particularly important for you to address this root cause: (1) protocols, (2) pausing, and (3) paraphrasing (chapter 1, page 22; chapter 3, page 54; and chapter 4, page 88, respectively), and including some attribution (chapter 5, page 129) along the way will also prove beneficial.

> **Confidence comes from competence.**

Challenge: The Work Meanders and Doesn't Gain Momentum

When teams are getting started with doing the right work of ensuring that every student masters grade-level essential learning outcomes, they can struggle. They can get caught in minutia and fail to gain momentum; it is simply easier to focus on tasks like managing paperwork, coordinating logistics, and other tasks that do not improve our practice or student results. As a teacher team leader, you want to be aware of this and help the team to keep moving the work forward. A few considerations may help.

1. Clarify the importance of the team in improving each other's practice and student results.
2. Clarify what the work of the team is (four critical questions).
3. Establish an overall timeline for the year.
4. Align agendas with the overall plan.
5. Set deadlines for accomplishing the work (who will do what by when).

Let's take a look at each of these separately.

1. Clarify the Importance of the Team in Improving Each Other's Practice and Results for Students

Two of the most influential educational leaders of our time, DuFour and Marzano (2011), state that no matter how much any of us know, none of us, by ourselves, can know enough to meet the needs of every student. They go even further to say that no matter how good we are at our craft, none of us, by ourselves, is skilled enough to get every student to high levels of learning. And, even further, no matter how talented any of us may be, our talents, by themselves, pale in comparison to what is needed to reach every student. But just telling people this may or may not have an impact. Consider accessing others as experts to read and talk about the importance of collaboration and each aspect of the work around the four critical questions. *Learning by Doing, Fourth Edition* (DuFour et al., 2024) has handy one page downloadable reproducibles for the "why" behind each part of the collaborative process.

2. Clarify What the Work of the Team Is

I have met very few people who categorically disagree with that first consideration: that it takes a village. However, teams too often fail to meet their intended promise, partially because they are not focused on work that will actually improve our practice and results for students. This is where the work of the four critical questions comes into play. In a nutshell, these four critical questions are: (1) What do we want students to know and be able to do? (2) How will we know when they have learned it? (3) What will we do when they don't learn it? and (4) What will we do when they do learn it? (DuFour et al., 2024). Effective teams use these questions to drive their work. Almost everything the team does revolves around these four critical questions. Not field trips. Not coordinating bus schedules. Not planning for parent-teacher conferences. Not a whole host of other adminis-trivia that gets in the way of the real, important, and impactful work of the team: the four critical questions. The critical issues survey (the first column in the tool for outcomes, chapter 3, page 69) as a self-assessment (chapter 5, page 143) and guide for creating a timeline (chapter 4, page 107) can assist with identifying the specifics of the work of a team around the critical questions.

3. Establish an Overall Timeline for the Year

One reason that teams get stuck in the muck and fail to gain momentum is because they are too concerned about doing things right the first time and therefore spend too much time on any one of the four critical questions. Keep it moving. Use the timeline in chapter 4 (page 107) as a possible starting point for the team to develop their own timeline based on units, priority standards, amount of time for meetings, and more. Alternatively, use the resource at www.tinyurl.com/DumasTimeline as another option (chapter 4, page 107) to determine the team's own timeline.

4. Align Agenda With the Overall Plan

First of all, remember that your timeline is a draft timeline that you create before starting in on the work. Be prepared to make revisions as needed, as obstacles will no doubt crop up along the way. However, once you have created your timeline for the year, it's important to be sure that you follow it to the greatest extent possible. Use it to guide the creation of agendas (chapter 3, page 76) and remember to actually create those agendas at the end of the previous meeting.

5. Set Deadlines for Accomplishing the Work

As part of your timeline that was created above, consider putting into place the strategy of who will do what by when (chapter 4, page 114). These deadlines, together with holding each other mutually accountable for the work, will greatly assist in gaining momentum for the team.

Challenge: Colleagues Listen to Ideas, But Don't Change

We'll close out this examination of challenges and potential solutions with quite possibly the ultimate challenge and purpose of a team: making change happen. Changing practice is hard. Many of us have habits in our classrooms, born sometimes from decades of experience—both as students who experienced a K–12 education and as professionals leading our own classrooms. Some of these practices are beneficial for students; others are simply the result of personal tendencies and unexamined actions. Regardless of where they came from, changing behavior is hard work, and those changes are even harder to make when they are ingrained in our habits or even grounded in deeply held beliefs and identity (Dilts, 1990).

In other words, the challenge of going from (1) listening in a meeting; to (2) knowing or really understanding the concepts, task, or skill; to (3) changing one's practice, is a significant one. You're probably familiar with the notion of a knowing-doing gap (Dumas, 2020), and that success in any field depends on *implementing* what is known or learned. This is the basic challenge: overcoming the knowing-doing gap.

> The knowing-doing gap plagues just about every aspect of our lives.

The knowing-doing gap plagues just about every aspect of our lives, from diet and exercise to spending and saving, from marital relationships to child-rearing techniques. I know I should avoid that sweet dessert or soda and exercise thirty minutes a day, but I eat what I shouldn't and fail to get to the gym

(Or, in my case, I don't even have a gym membership). I know that I should "pay myself first" and put money toward savings and retirement, but I don't do it consistently (or at all). I know I should not yell at my partner or students and instead speak with patience and love, but I don't always do it. I know, but I don't do; hence, I have a knowing-doing gap. I would venture to guess that all of us have this challenge with some aspect of our lives, and so it is with our professional lives. Bridging knowledge of best practice with the actual implementation of best practice is a great challenge. And the team can support each other in the process.

Having put this challenge into perspective—that it is a challenge for everyone, in many aspects of our lives—let's talk about how to support your colleagues in moving from knowing to doing. Remember that you are not a mini administrator, but instead are focused on (1) creating a psychologically safe space, (2) building capacity for doing the work, and (3) doing the work. Finally, it may be helpful to review the assumptions and mindsets (chapters 1 and 2, page 29 and page 34, respectively) to help frame your perspective on this challenge as well. As a reminder, see the following list.

- Responsibilities:
    1. Make it safe.
    2. Build capacity.
    3. Do the work.
- Assumptions:
    1. People do the best that they can.
    2. You can only control you.
    3. Behavior communicates.
    4. People want to get stuff done.
    5. Conflict is good.
- Mindsets:
    1. To see what others don't (yet) see in themselves.
    2. To be humble with a posture of learning.
    3. To spread the contagion of joy.

With this foundation of understanding the challenge of changing one's practice, paired with the clarity of your responsibilities and certain assumptions and mindsets, being clear on outcomes (chapter 3, page 69) aligned with the agenda (chapter 3, page 76) is a great place to start. This ensures that everyone is clear about the intended targets for us, as adults. If this is solidly in place, then be sure that the team is clear on who will do what by when (chapter 4, page 114) at the end of each meeting. From here, please consider taking a look at the challenge of tasks not being completed between meetings as the potential solutions for this challenge are similar to that one.

If Issues Persist After Attempts to Solve Them

The challenges and potential solutions that I have offered here are not a panacea. It is quite possible that, after all of your work to implement new habits, there are still team members who are unable or unwilling to try to overcome a teamwork challenge. At some point, this becomes an administrative issue. Remember that you are not a mini administrator. It is not your responsibility to force people to do their job. It is your responsibility to create the conditions for the team to flourish. You do this through (1) creating psychological safety, (2) building capacity, and (3) helping the team to do the work. Don't get caught in a situation where someone might expect you to be an enforcer of your colleagues. That is not your role or responsibility.

If, after multiple attempts at multiple moves, techniques, and strategies (within the context of the responsibilities, assumptions, and mindsets), the problem still persists, the first step is to mention to your administrative superior to please take a look at your team's notes. While your supervisors may not always read notes of every single meeting, every time, in detail (they have many teams to support, so my experience is that they look at notes with more of a cursory glance than a detailed examination), alerting them to please go in and take a closer look for certain elements will nudge them to do this. If the supervisor doesn't act based on this, or if the challenge continues to persist, I might suggest that you then ask your administrative superior to please stop in on your meetings periodically and watch for the issue. However, because this is something that is persisting beyond all of the interventions you previously took, it is likely that the administrator will need to attend every meeting for a period of time. My suggestion is that they outright say to the team that they understand that there has been a challenge in certain aspects of collaboration, and that they are there to support the team. Of course, the administrator may need to have one-on-one conversations with members who repeatedly pose challenges to the team, but remember, this is not your responsibility.

Conclusion

The challenges of being a team leader are many. A few scenarios are shared here, together with some potential applications of the habits shared throughout this book. While neither the challenges nor the solutions are exhaustive, my hope is that you gained some ideas and perspectives to tackle your challenges with renewed focus, determination, and energy in the pursuit of getting more done, in less time, and with greater joy. At the foundation of each challenge, always remember the responsibilities, assumptions, and mindsets that frame your work in the pursuit of ensuring team effectiveness in getting every student to team-identified, grade-level essential outcomes.

Act as if what you do makes a difference. It does.

—*William James*

Epilogue

As educators, we are the foundation of an ever-advancing civilization. Without us, there are no arborists, sheetrockers, phlebotomists, barbers, statisticians . . . and there are no other educators. If we are to meet the needs of every student in moving our civilization forward, we *must* work together. We simply cannot do it alone. Thus, your role, as a leader of a team of people who are working to impact generations to come, cannot be overstated.

PLCs work. Teaming works. And the role that you play in ensuring the effectiveness of your team is unmatched. The responsibilities that you have, in their barest form, are quite simple. You have to make the space for the work of the team safe. You have to build the capacity of your colleagues to get better at their craft and engage with each other. And you have to make sure that the work gets done.

At the foundation of the moves, techniques, and strategies shared in this book are fundamental assumptions and mindsets that drive all interactions. Further, clarity around your intentions will ensure that you align your behaviors to those intentions and increase the likelihood that you will achieve the desired results.

Remember that many of the moves, techniques, and strategies shared in this text may feel unnatural and even contrived at first. Most anything new will feel that way; you have to learn how to do it. Just like when you learned how to teach, write down what you intend to do, practice with others observing and giving feedback, implement in low-pressure and low-risk scenarios, and, when the time comes, unleash your newly refined prowess on your colleagues. And, of course, don't forget to continue to learn in your daily practice.

This text gives you a framework for implementation and learning, and, quite frankly, without implementation, the time you spent on this text is sadly a waste. Adapt the approaches shared to your experience and needs. Practice, and it will become natural to you.

By implementing the habits delineated in this book, you will, without a doubt, improve your own effectiveness and the effectiveness of your team. You and your colleagues will get more done. You will do it in less time. And you will experience greater joy as part of the sense of accomplishment and satisfaction that come from doing meaningful work together. You will not only transform collaboration, but you will, most importantly, transform the educational experience of the students in your trust.

References and Resources

allthingsplc. (n.d.a). *History of PLC.* Accessed at https://allthingsplc.info/about/history-of -plc on March 31, 2024.

allthingsplc. (n.d.b). *The origins of professional learning communities* [Video file]. Accessed at https://allthingsplc.info/about/origins-of-plcs on March 31, 2024.

Bailey, K., & Jakicic, C. (2018). *Make it happen: Coaching with the four critical questions of PLCs at Work.* Bloomington, IN: Solution Tree Press.

Barth, R. S. (2001). *Learning by heart.* San Francisco: Jossey-Bass.

Bayewitz, M. D., Cunningham, S. A., Ianora, J. A., Jones, B., Nielsen, M., Remmert, W., et al. (2020). *Help your team: Overcoming common collaborative challenges in a PLC.* Bloomington, IN: Solution Tree Press.

Black, J. S., & Bright, D. S. (2019a). *Organizational behavior.* OpenStax. Accessed at https://openstax.org/books/organizational-behavior/pages/14-1-conflict-in-organizations -basic-considerations on April 2, 2024.

Black, J. S., & Bright, D. S. (2019b). *Organizational behavior.* OpenStax. Accessed at https://openstax.org/books/organizational-behavior/pages/6-2-how-the-brain-processes -information-to-make-decisions-reflective-and-reactive-systems on April 4, 2024.

Block, P. (2008). *Community: The structure of belonging.* San Fransisco: Berrett-Koehler.

Bill & Melinda Gates Foundation. (2014, December). *Teachers know best: Teachers' views on professional development.* Accessed at https://usprogram.gatesfoundation.org/-/media/ dataimport /resources/pdf/2016/11/gates-pdmarketresearch-dec5.pdf on May 1, 2023.

Busch, M. (2022, February 21). *Why your team isn't speaking up in meetings (and what to do about it)* [Blog post]. Accessed at www.linkedin.com/pulse/why-your-team-isnt -speaking-up-meetings-what-do-may-busch on April 7, 2024.

Chadwick, B. (n.d.). *Beyond conflict to consensus: An introductory learning manual.* Accessed at https://managingwholes.com/chadwick.htm on April 11, 2024.

Cherry, K. (2023, November 13). *What is the negativity bias?* Accessed at www.verywellmind .com/negative-bias-4589618 on December 29, 2023.

Clarabut, J. (2023, November 20). *Why celebrating is good for you* [Blog post]. Accessed at https://wellbeingpeople.com/christmas/why-celebrating-is-good-for-you/2023 on December 26, 2023.

Coleman, K. (2021, March 31). *Doing this with your hands makes people not trust you, experts say* [Blog post]. Accessed at https://bestlifeonline.com/hands-trust-news on April 6, 2024.

Continental Press. (2023, January 31). *Stress less, focus more: Tips for reducing teacher decision fatigue* [Blog post]. Accessed at www.continentalpress.com/blog/tips-for-reducing-teacher-decision-fatigue on December 20, 2023.

Covey, F. (2021). *Leading at the speed of trust.* Accessed at www.franklincovey.com/courses/leading-at-the-speed-of-trust on June 15, 2021.

Coyle, D. (2018, February 20). *How showing vulnerability helps build a stronger team.* Accessed at https://ideas.ted.com/how-showing-vulnerability-helps-build-a-stronger-team on April 27, 2023.

Davenport, T. H. (2005). *Thinking for a living: How to get better performance and results from knowledge workers.* Boston: Harvard Business School Press.

Davies, M. (2021, October 6). *Can you have trust without being vulnerable?* [Blog post]. Wise Ways Consulting. Accessed at www.wisewaysconsulting.com/can-you-have-trust-without-being-vulnerable on June 23, 2021.

Deming, W. E. (1986). *Out of the crisis.* Cambridge, MA: The MIT Press.

DiGangi, J. (2023, September-October). The anxious micromanager: Why some leaders become too controlling and how they find the right balance. *Harvard Business Review.* Accessed at https://hbr.org/2023/09/the-anxious-micromanager on December 9, 2023.

Dilts, R. (1990). *Changing belief systems with NLP.* Capitola, CA: Meta.

Drucker, P. F. (1959). *Landmarks of tomorrow.* New York: Harper.

DuFour, R. (2016). *Advocates for professional learning communities: Finding common ground in education reform.* Accessed at https://allthingsplc.info/wp-content/uploads/2023/10/AdvocatesforPLCs-Updated11-9-15-1.pdf on March 31, 2024.

DuFour, R., & DuFour, R. (2005). Whatever it takes: How professional learning communities respond when kids don't learn. [Conference presentation]. Educational Service Unit #3, Omaha, NE.

DuFour, R., & DuFour, R. (2008, March 11). *Who should decide the agenda for collaborative team meetings?* [Blog post]. Accessed at www.allthingsplc.info/blog/view/27/who-should-decide-the-agenda-for-collaborative-team-meetings on January 2, 2024.

DuFour, R., DuFour, R., Eaker, R., Many, T. W., & Mattos, M. (2021). *Revisiting Professional Learning Communities at Work®: Proven insights for sustained, substantive school improvement* (2nd ed.). Bloomington, IN: Solution Tree Press.

DuFour, R., DuFour, R., Eaker, R., Many, T. W., Mattos, M., & Muhammad, A. (2024). *Learning by doing: A handbook for Professional Learning Communities at Work®* (4th ed.). Bloomington, IN: Solution Tree Press.

DuFour, R., Eaker, R. E., & DuFour, R. B. (2005). *On common ground: The power of professional learning communities.* Bloomington, IN: National Educational Service.

DuFour, R., & Marzano, R. (2011). *Leaders of learning: How district, school, and classroom leaders improve student achievement.* Bloomington, IN: Solution Tree Press.

Duhigg, C. (2016, February 28). *What Google learned from its quest to build the perfect team.* Accessed at www.nytimes.com/2016/02/28/magazine/what-google-learned-from-its-quest-to-build-the-perfect-team.html on May 1, 2023.

Dumas, C. (2020). *Let's put the C in PLC: A practical guide for school leaders.* Ames, IA: Next Learning Solutions Press.

Dumas, C., & Kautz, C. (2014). Wisdom from the factory floor: For best results, limit initiatives, build capacity, and monitor progress. *Journal of Staff Development, 35*(5), 26–34.

Edmondson, A. C. (2023). *Psychological safety*. Accessed at https://amycedmondson.com/psychological-safety on December 20, 2023.

Faunalytics. (2012). *The better listener, your husband or the dog?* Accessed at https://faunalytics.org/whos-the-better-listener-your-husband-or-the-dog on May 1, 2023.

Ferrari, P. F., & Rizzolatti, G. (2014). Mirror neuron research: The past and the future. *Philosophical Transactions of the Royal Society, 369*(1644). http://doi.org/10.1098/rstb.2013.0169

Ferriter, W. M. (2020). *The big book of tools for collaborative teams in a PLC at Work*. Bloomington, IN: Solution Tree Press.

Fisher, R., Ury, W., & Patton, B. (2006). *Getting to yes* (2nd ed.). New York: Penguin.

Freire, P. (1970). Pedagogy of the oppressed: Chapter 3. Accessed at http://www.historyisaweapon.com/defcon2/pedagogy/pedagogychapter3.html on April 1, 2024.

Fullan, M. (1993). *Change forces: Probing the depths of educational reform*. Levittown, PA: The Falmer Press.

Gallo, A. (2023, February 15). *What is psychological safety?* Harvard Business Review. Accessed at https://hbr.org/2023/02/what-is-psychological-safety on December 20, 2023.

Garmston, R., & McKanders, C. (2022). *It's your turn: Teachers as facilitators—A handbook*. Burlington, VT: MiraVia.

Garmston, R. J., & Wellman, B. M. (2016). *The adaptive school: A sourcebook for developing collaborative groups* (3rd ed.). Lanham, MD: Rowman & Littlefield.

Ginnot, H. (1972). *Teacher and child: A Book for parents and teachers*. New York: Macmillan

Godat, D., & Czerny, E. J. (2021). The big misunderstanding: Not everything is communication! *Journal of Solution Focused Practices, 5*(2).

Goel, A. (2023, December 19). *How to start an email: 16 proven openings to boost your success rate* [Blog post]. Accessed at www.gmass.co/blog/how-to-start-an-email on December 29, 2023.

Goleman, D., Boyatzis, R., Davidson, R. J., Kohlrieser, G., & Druskat, V. U. (2017). *Building blocks of emotional intelligence: Emotional self-awareness: A primer*. Florence, MA: More Than Sound.

Greer, L. (2019, July 24). *Why teams still need leaders*. Accessed at https://sloanreview.mit.edu/article/why-teams-still-need-leaders on May 25, 2023.

Greer, L. L., de Jong, B. A., Schouten, M. E., & Dannals, J. E. (2018). Why and when hierarchy impacts team effectiveness: A meta-analytic integration. *Journal of Applied Psychology, 103*(6), 591–613. https://doi.org/10.1037/apl0000291.

Grinder, M. (2018). *The elusive obvious: The science of non-verbal communication, third edition*. Michael Grinder & Associates.

Grinder, M. (n.d.a). *2-point vs 3-point communication*. Accessed at https://michaelgrinder.com/2-point-vs-3-point-communication on December 2, 2023.

Grinder, M. (n.d.b). *Boost your charisma with nonverbal communication: How hand placement boosts your charisma–even when you don't speak*. Accessed at https://michaelgrinder.com/boost-charisma-hand-placement on December 29, 2023.

Grinder, M. (2007). *The elusive obvious: The science of non-verbal communication.* Michael Grinder & Associates.

Hall, B. (2021). *Powerful guiding coalitions: How to build and sustain the leadership team in your PLC at Work.* Bloomington, IN: Solution Tree Press.

Hattie, J. (2023). *Visible learning: The sequel: A synthesis of over 2,100 meta-analyses relating to achievement.* Abingdon-on-Thames, England: Routledge.

Intention. (n.d.). In *Merriam-Webster's collegiate dictionary.* Accessed at http://www.merriam -webster.com/dictionary/intention on May 28, 2024.

Johnson, W. (2022, January 26). *Celebrate to win.* Harvard Business Review. Accessed at https://hbr.org/2022/01/celebrate-to-win on January 2, 2023.

Kahneman, D. (2011). *Thinking, fast and slow.* New York: Farrar, Straus and Giroux.

Knight, J. (2023, December). *Can administrators be coaches? It's complicated.* [Conference presentation]. Learning Forward Annual Conference, Washington, DC.

Kramer, S. V. (n.d.). *What's a PLC meeting, anyway?* Accessed at www.solutiontree.com /blog/what-is-a-plc-meeting on March 31, 2024

Lambert, L. (1998). *Building leadership capacity in schools.* Arlington, VA: ASCD.

Learning Forward. (2023). *Culture of collaborative inquiry.* Accessed at https://standards .learningforward.org/standards-for-professional-learning/conditions-for-success/culture-of -collaborative-inquiry on May 22, 2023.

Lencioni, P. M. (2002). *The five dysfunctions of a team: A leadership fable.* San Francisco: Jossey-Bass.

MacDonald, E. B. (2023). *Intentional moves: How skillful team leaders impact learning.* Thousand Oaks, CA: Corwin Press.

Many, T. W., Maffoni, M. J., Sparks, S. K., & Thomas, T. F. (2018). *Amplify your impact: Coaching collaborative teams in PLCs.* Bloomington, IN: Solution Tree Press.

Mayo Clinic Staff. (2021). *Stress relief from laughter? It's no joke.* Accessed at https://www .mayoclinic.org/healthy-lifestyle/stress-management/in-depth/stress-relief/art-20044456 on June 11, 2023.

Mehrabian, A. (1972). *Nonverbal communication.* Piscataway, NJ: Aldine Transaction.

Michigan Alliance for Families. (n.d.). *Behavior is communication.* Accessed at https://www .michiganallianceforfamilies.org/behavior-is-communication on April 2, 2024.

Mindset Works. (n.d.). *Decades of scientific research that started a growth mindset revolution.* Accessed at www.mindsetworks.com/science on April 3, 2024.

MindTools. (n.d.). *Building rapport: Establishing strong two-way connections.* [Blog post] Accessed at www.mindtools.com/a9f9kqi/building-rapport on April 5, 2024

Muhammad, A., & Cruz, L. F. (2019). *Time for change: 4 essential skills for transformational school and district leaders.* Bloomington, IN: Solution Tree Press.

National School Reform Faculty. (2023). *NSRF Protocols and activities...from A to Z.* Accessed at https://nsrfharmony.org/protocols on May 24, 2023.

New Jersey Department of Education. (2015). *Collaborative teams toolkit: Tools to support collaborative team structures and evidence-based conversations in schools.* Accessed at www.state .nj.us/education/AchieveNJ/teams/Toolkit.pdf on June 28, 2021.

Nielsen, M. (2024). *The 15-day challenge: Simplify and energize your PLC at Work process.* Bloomington, IN: Solution Tree Press.

Owens, R. (2023, June). *Transformed people transform people* [Conference presentation]. PLC at Work Institute, St. Charles, MO.

Parker, W. (2017, June 14). *Entanglement and why messaging matters.* Accessed at https://williamdparker.com/2017/06/14/pmp069-entanglement-why-messaging-matters on June 3, 2024.

Paul, A. M. (2023, April 15). *Use "creative abrasion" as a source of energy.* Accessed at https://anniemurphypaul.substack.com/p/use-creative-abrasion-as-a-source on May 22, 2023.

Rensch, T. (2020, May 28). *The power of a highly skilled facilitative leader.* Accessed at https://thecorecollaborative.com/the-power-of-a-highly-skilled-facilitative-leader on April 27, 2023.

Research for Better Teaching. (2023, January 18). *Part 5: Garmston/McKanders—Polarity management* [Video file]. Accessed at www.rbteach.com/videos/collection/12?video=153 on June 5, 2023.

Riess, H. (2018). *The empathy effect: Seven neuroscience-based keys for transforming the way we live, love, work, and connect across differences.* Boulder, CO: Sounds True.

School Reform Initiative. (2023). *Protocols.* Accessed at www.schoolreforminitiative.org/protocols on May 24, 2023.

Senge, P. M. (1990). *The fifth discipline. The art and practice of the learning organization.* London: Random House.

Shappell, J. (2020). *Want to influence others in 2020? Listen to them* [Blog post]. Accessed at www.navalent.com/resources/blog/want-to-influence-others-in-2020-listen-to-them on June 29, 2021.

Sonju, B., Powers, M., & Miller, S. (2024). *Simplifying the journey: Six steps to schoolwide collaboration, consistency, and clarity in a PLC at work.* Bloomington, IN: Solution Tree Press.

Sparks, D. (2007). *Leading for results: Transforming teaching, learning, and relationships in schools* (2nd ed.). Thousand Oaks, CA: Corwin Press.

Stillman, J. (2024). *57 years ago, a legendary psychologist discovered the 7-38-55 rule. It's still the secret to exceptional emotional intelligence.* Accessed at www.inc.com/jessica-stillman/7-38-55-rule-57-years-old-secret-exceptional-emotional-intelligence.html on March 29, 2024.

Team Rallybright. (2023, February 16). *How to manage a dominating personality on your team* [Blog post]. Accessed at www.rallybright.com/how-to-manage-a-dominating-personality-on-your-team on April 7, 2024.

Tickle-Degnen, L., & Rosenthal, R. (1990). The nature of rapport and its nonverbal correlates, *Psychological Inquiry, 1*(4), 285–293.

Van Soelen, T. M. (2021). *Meeting goals: Protocols for leading effective, purpose-driven discussions in schools.* Bloomington, IN: Solution Tree Press.

Williams, K. (2023, December). *Ruthless equity: Disrupt the status quo and ensure learning for all* [Conference presentation]. Learning Forward Annual Conference, Washington, DC.

Wiseman, L., & McKeown, G. (2010). *Multipliers: How the best leaders make everyone smarter.* New York: Harper Business.

Wood, A. (2023, July 31). *New psychology research indicates laughter can communicate a lot more than good humor.* Accessed at www.psypost.org/2023/07/new-psychology-research-indicates-laughter-can-communicate-a-lot-more-than-good-humor-167342 on August 24, 2023.

Zoller, K. (2019, December). *The choreography of presenting* [Conference presentation]. Learning Forward Annual Conference. St. Louis, MO.

Zoller, K. (2022, December). *Re-imagining resistance* [Conference presentation]. Learning Forward Annual Conference. Nashville, TN.

Zoller, K. (2024). The choreography of presenting: The 7 essential abilities of effective presenters. Thousand Oaks, CA: Corwin Press.

Zoller, K. & Lahera, A. I. (2021). *HeartSpace: Practices and rituals to awaken, emerge, evolve, and flourish at work and in life*. Burlington, Ontario, Canada: Word & Deed.

Index

A

abstracting paraphrase, 88–89, 91

accountability

    avoidance of, 19

    lack of, 174–175

    mutual, 16

acknowledging paraphrase, 88–89, 91

adaptability, 130

addressing challenges from the field, 8, 171, 188–189

    colleagues listen to ideas but don't change, 186–188

    if issues persist, 188

members fail to follow norms, 173–176

    one member doesn't engage in the conversation, 183–184

    one member dominates the conversation, 180–182

    team fails to follow through on decisions, 178–180

    team is not following the agenda, 176–178

    team is too large or too small, 172–173

    work meanders and doesn't gain momentum, 184–186

affective vs. creative conflict, 32

aligning agendas with the overall plan, 184, 186

Amplify Your Impact (Many et al.), 26

and (not but), 87, 100–101, 117, 120

    "and" tool, 101

    reflection questions, 101

Angelou, M., 126

anonymizing it, 124, 134–135

    next level tips, 137

    reflection questions, 137

    tool, 135–136, 152, 156

approachable and credible voice

    addressing challenges, 174

    approachable vs. credible voice, 98

    gaining momentum, 87, 96–97, 117, 120

    refining your skills, 164–165

    reflection questions, 98

    tool, 97–98

    voice continuum tool, 97

assumptions, 29–30, 38, 191

    addressing challenges, 187

    behavior communicates, 30–31

    conflict is good, 30, 32

    defined, 29

    necessary, 171

    overcoming obstacles, 152

    people do the best they can, 30–31

    people want to get stuff done, 30–32

    you can only control you, 30–31

attribution, 124, 129

    addressing challenges, 183–184

    next level tips, 131

    reflection questions, 131

    tool, 130, 152, 156

B

Bailey, K., 26

beat gesture, 99, 159, 162, 169

    next level tips, 162

    potential phrases, 162–163

    reflection questions, 162

behavior communicates

    addressing challenges, 187

199

overcoming obstacles, 131–134, 148, 152

    understanding your approach, 30–31, 38, 41

being and doing with social sensitivity, 20–22

being humble with a posture of learning

    addressing challenges, 187

    overcoming obstacles, 152

    understanding your approach, 35–36, 38, 41

Big Book of Tools for Collaborative Teams in a PLC at Work

    (Ferriter), 26

Bill & Melinda Gates Foundation, xiv, 4

Block, P., 3, 20

body language. *See* behavior communicates

boredom, 175

breaking eye contact

    frozen gesture, 160–161

    gaining momentum, 87, 102, 117, 120

    I interrupt myself, 168

    next level tips, 104

    reflection questions, 104

    tool, 102–104

breathing, 50–51

    next level tips, 51–52

    reflection questions, 51

    tool, 51

brilliance, 130

Bronte, C., xvi

building capacity, 23, 27, 191

    addressing challenges, 172, 187, 188

    how knowledge workers build capacity, 23–25

    identifying look-fors in, 24

    overcoming obstacles, 152

    relationship with efficacy, 25–26

    understanding your approach, 37–38, 87

Building Leadership Capacity in Schools (Lambert), 24

C

category labels, 40

    types of actions you and the team can take, 40

celebrations

    gaining momentum, 105, 107–108, 117, 121

    next level tips, 110

    reflection questions, 108

    tool, 108–109

changing behaviors, 186–187

clarity

    about your intensions, 191

    of importance of the team, 184–185

    of the work that needs to be done, 178

    of what the decision is, 178–179

    of what the work of the team is, 184–185

    of who is responsible for implementing a decision,
179

    of why time as a team is important, 177

    around content, 4–5

collaborating, 5, 13, 15–16

    addressing challenges, 177

    breaking eye contact, 102

    overcoming obstacles, 130–131

    understanding your approach, 32–34

colleagues listen to ideas but don't change, 186–188

collective commitments, 110

common formative assessments (CFAs), 63, 105–106, 108,
111

common goals, 16

Community (Block), 3

conflict is good, 30, 32, 38, 41

    addressing challenges, 187

    overcoming obstacles, 152

considerations for hand position, 164–165

Costa, A., 6

COVID-19, xv

creating community, 19–20

creativity, 130

D

Dannals, J. E., 14

data usage, 141–142, 152

    evidence tracking tool, 142

    next level tips, 143

    reflection questions, 143

Davenport, T. H., 23

de Jong, B. A., 14

decontaminating space

    next level tips, 127

    overcoming obstacles, 124, 126–127, 152, 156

    reflection questions, 127

    sample form, 128

    tool, 237

dedication, 130

defining your role, 7, 13–14, 27

    major characteristics of a team, 16–17

    what your role is not, 15–16

    why your role is importance, 14–15

    your responsibilities, 17–26

DiGangi, J., 2

directive vs. collaborative scale, 60

do it yourself and we do it together vignette chart, 82

doing the work, 26–27, 37–38

    addressing challenges, 187

    overcoming obstacles, 152

Dolcemascolo, M., 6

Drucker, P., 23

DuFour, Rebecca, xiv, 3–4, 6, 61–62

DuFour, Rick, xiv, 2–4, 6, 13, 26, 16, 61–62, 71, 185

Duhigg, C., 22

Dumas, C., xiii–xvi

dysfunction. *See* identifying dysfunction

E

Eaker, R., xiv, 3–4, 62

Edmonson, A., 17–18

    website, 18

email vs. fact to face, 140–141

energy, 130

establishing an overall timeline for the year, 184–186

examples and samples

    decontaminating space form, 128

    decontaminating space, 128

    hand position, 164

    reflections on intentions, 34

    running agenda template, 77, 80

    work timeline, 107, 110

F

fear of conflict, 18

fear of embarrassment, 183

fear of failure, 36

Ferrari, P. F., 37

Ferriter, W. M., 62, 173–174

The 15-Day Challenge (Nielsen), xvi

The Fifth Dimension (Senge), 3

fist to five, 136, 141, 146, 152

    next level tips, 148

    reflection questions, 148

    tool, 146

focus, 130

forced choice, 141, 148, 152

    next level tips, 150

    reflection questions, 149

    tool, 149

fourth point, 99

    overcoming obstacles, 124, 137–138, 152, 156

    reflection questions, 138

    tool, 138–139

    when to use, 139

Freire, P., 18, 30–32

frozen gesture, 159–160

    I interrupt myself, 168–169

    next level tips, 161

    reflection questions, 161

    reflective tool, 160–161

Fullan, M., 13

G

gaining momentum, 8, 87

    putting it all together, 115–119

    we do it together, 104–115

    we do it together planning and reflection tool, 121

    you do it yourself, 87–104

    you do it yourself planning and reflection tool, 120

Garmston, R., 6, 88

gestures and words of inclusion, 87, 98–99, 117, 120

    next level tips, 99

    reflection questions, 99

    tool, 99

    words of inclusion, 100

getting started, 8, 45–46

    putting it all together, 79–83

    theory in action, 46, 60

    we do it together, 58–79

    we do it together planning and reflection tool, 84

    you do it yourself, 46–58

    you do it yourself planning and reflection tool, 83

getting work done, 87

Ginnot, H., 33

giraffe conversations, 36

Goleman, D., 20–21

Google, 17

Google Docs, 111

Greer, L. L., 14

Grinder, M., 6, 50

group rapport, 47

    next level tips, 50

    reflection questions, 49

    think-do-say-feel tool, 48

    tips for group synchronicity tool, 48–49

"group-think," 172–173

H

hand position, 159, 163–164, 169

    considerations for, 164–165

    hand gesture tool, 164

    next level tips, 165

    reflection questions, 165

Hattie, J., 26

Help Your Team (Sonju et al.), 26

how knowledge workers build capacity, 23–25

humor in specific situations, 53

I

I interrupt myself, 99

checklist tool, 167–168

next level tips, 168

refining your skills, 159, 167, 169

reflection questions, 168

icebreakers vs. inclusion, 65–66

Ictus, 162

identifying dysfunction, 18–19

identifying essential standards, 136

if issues persist after attempts to solve them, 188

inattention to results, 19

inclusion, 59, 65–66

activity ideas too, 66–67

next level tips, 66

reflection questions, 66

individual rapport, 124, 131–134

building tool, 134

overcoming obstacles, 152, 156

reflection questions, 134

individuals do not hold each other accountable, 174–176

instructional and assessment strategies, 4–5

intentions, 32–34

example reflections on, 34

interdependence, 16

internal processors, 183

J

Jackson, M., 16

Jakicic, C., 26

Jane Eyre (Bronte), xvi

Jones, J. E., 96

K

Kahneman, D., 55

knowing-doing gap, 186–187

knowledge workers

defined, 23

how they build capacity, 23–25

L

lack of commitment, 19

lack of trust in the team, 180

Lambert, L., 24

landing page, 59, 66–68

next level tips, 68

reflection questions, 68

Landmarks of Tomorrow (Drucker), 23

laughter and humor, 52–53

humor in specific situations, 53

reflection questions, 53

tool, 53

types of humor, 54

leadership, 24, 130

Learning by Doing (DuFour et al.), 26, 185

Let's Put the C in PLC (Dumas), xiii

M

MacDonald, E. B., 6

Maffoni, M. J., 26

maintaining equity of voice, 22

major characteristics of a team, 16–17

Make It Happen (Bailey & Jakicic), 26

making a decision, 136

making it safe, 17–18, 27, 37–38, 191

addressing challenges, 187–188

being and doing with social sensitivity, 20–22

creating community, 19–20

gaining momentum, 87

identifying dysfunction, 18–19

maintaining equity of voice, 22

overcoming obstacles, 152

Man in the Mirror (Jackson), 16

Many, T. W., 26, 52

Marzano, R., 13, 185

Mattos, M., 62

maximizing effectiveness, 6

McKanders, C., 6

Meeting Goals (Van Soelen), 22

Mehrabian, A., 38

members fail to follow norms, 173, 178

individuals do not hold each other accountable, 174–176

members don't have voice so they don't reflect members' needs, 173–174

team does not regularly revisit or revise norms, 174

memory, 180

Michael Grinder website, 50

Michigan Alliance for Families, 31

mindsets, 34–35, 38, 41, 191

addressing challenges, 187

defined, 34

necessary, 171

overcoming obstacles, 152

to be humble with a posture of learning, 35–36

to see what others don't (yet) see in themselves, 35

to spread the contagion of joy, 35, 37

mirror neurons, 37

mirroring technique, 131–133

mode of communication

next level tips, 140–141

overcoming obstacles, 124, 138–139, 152, 156

reflection questions, 140

tool, 140

modeling, 113–114

moves and techniques, 38–39, 41

overcoming obstacles, 152

mutual accountability, 16

N

National School Reform Faculty (NSRF) website, 22

next level tips. *See also* tips

anonymizing it, 137

attribution, 131

beat gesture, 162

breaking eye contact, 104

breathing, 51–52

celebrations, 110

data usage, 143

decontaminating space, 127

fist to five, 148

force choice, 150

frozen gesture, 161

gestures and words of inclusion, 99

group rapport, 50

hand position, 165

I interrupt myself, 168

inclusion, 66

individual rapport, 134

landing page, 68

mode of communication, 140–141

norms, 62

others as experts, 113

outcome, 76

paraphrasing, 90–92

pause, 56–57

physical arrangement, 60

planning the work, then working the plan, 106

questioning, 94–96

roles, 65

running agenda, 79

self-assessment, 146

sentence stems, 114

specificity, 126

third point, 58

whisper, 166

who will do what by when, 115

writing it down, 111

Nielsen, M., xvi

nonverbal cues. *See* behavior communicates

norms, 59–61

addressing challenges, 176–177

creation tool, 61

importance of establishing, 173–174

next level tips, 62

reflection questions, 62

regularly revisiting and revising, 174

tips for following, 61–62

O

one member does not engage in the conversation, 183

they are an internal processor, 183

they are not self-aware, 183

they are unsure of their own knowledge or skills, 183

they don't feel heard or valued, 183

one member dominates the conversation, 180–181

they are a verbal processor, 181

they are not self-aware, 181–182

they are unsure of their own knowledge or skills, 181–182

they don't feel heard, 181–182

open-ended questions, 93–94

organizing paraphrase, 88–89, 91

others as experts

gaining momentum, 105, 111–112, 117, 121

next level tips, 113

reflection questions, 112–113

tool, 112

outcomes, 59, 69–71

critical issues and their outcomes tool, 71–75

next level tips, 76

outcome tracking tool, 72

reflection questions, 72

template, 69–70

overcoming obstacles, 123

putting it all together, 150–154

theory in action, 127, 129, 133

we do it together, 141–150

you do it yourself, 123–143

you do it yourself planning and reflection tool, 155–156

P

paraphrasing

addressing challenges, 182, 184

gaining momentum, 87–90, 106, 117, 120

next level tips, 90–92

reflection questions, 90

three types, 88–89, 91

tool, 90

passion, 130

pause, 54–55

addressing challenges, 182, 184

frozen gesture, 159–161

gaining momentum, 88–89, 99, 102, 106

I interrupt myself, 167–168

next level tips, 56–57

reflection questions, 56

types of pausing tool, 55–56

whisper, 167

Pedagogy of the Oppressed (Freire), 30

pendulum effect, 71

people do the best they can, 30–31, 38, 41

addressing challenges, 187

overcoming obstacles, 152

people want to get stuff done, 30–32, 38, 41

addressing challenges, 187

overcoming obstacles, 152

physical arrangement, 59

directive vs. collaborative scale, 60

next level tips, 60

reflection questions, 59

planning the work, then working the plan, 105–106, 117, 121

next level tips, 106

potential work timeline tool, 106

reflection questions, 106

work timeline sample, 107

PLC at Work® process, xiii–xiv, 4

first critical question, xvi, 95

four critical questions, 26, 71, 185

work, 191

about, 2–3

plurals, 93–94

possible roles, tasks, and reflection tools, 63–65

praising, 35

Presler, S., 6

Prickett, T., 6

problem solving, 130

processes for reporting back, 179–180

prompts, 144–145

protocols, 22

addressing challenges, 184

psychological safety. *See* making it safe

pulling together your learning reflection chart, 81

putting it all together

gaining momentum, 115–116

getting started, 79–81

overcoming obstacles, 150–154

pulling together your learning reflection chart, 116–117

pulling together your learning reflection chart, 81, 152

summary reflective questions, 83, 119, 154

you do it yourself and we do it together vignette chart, 81, 117, 152

Q

quantitative vs. qualitative data, 141–142

questioning, 87, 92–94, 117, 120 (*see also* open–ended questions; reflection questions)

considerations and potential stems, 94

next level tips, 94–96

R

refining your skills, 8

refining your skills, 159

you do it yourself, 159–167

you do it yourself planning and reflection tool, 169

reflecting on norms, 136

reflecting on team functioning, 136

reflection questions. *See also* summary reflective questions

anatomizing it, 137

and (not but), 101

approachable and credible voice, 98

attribution, 131

beat gesture, 162

breaking eye contact, 104

breathing, 51

celebrations, 108

data usage, 143

decontaminating space, 127

fist to five, 148

forced choice, 149

fourth point, 138

frozen gesture, 161

gestures and words of inclusion, 99

getting started, 83

group rapport, 49

hand position, 165

I interrupt myself, 168

inclusion, 66

landing page, 68

laughter and humor, 54

mode of communication, 140

norms, 62

others as experts, 112–113

outcome, 72

paraphrasing, 90

pause, 56

physical arrangement, 59

planning the work, then working the plan, 106
    questioning, 94
    roles, 65
    running agenda, 77
    self-assessment, 146
    sentence stems, 114
    specificity, 126
    third point, 58
    whisper, 166
    who will do what by when, 115
    writing it down, 111
reframing, 35
relationship between building capacity and efficacy, 25–26
    potential symptoms of lack of efficacy, 25
relationship building, 4–5
relationship management, 20–21
Rensch, T., 14
reproducibles
    addressing challenges, 187
    building capacity, 23–27, 37–38, 87, 152
    doing the work, 26–27, 37–38, 152
    making it safe, 17–22, 152
    necessary, 171
    overcoming obstacles, 152
    we do it together planning and reflection tool, 84, 121, 156
    you do it yourself planning and reflection tool, 83, 120, 155, 169
Riess, H., 37
Rizzolatti, G., 37
role and approach, 37–38
    category labels, 40
    moves and techniques, 38–39
    strategies, 39
    what we do together, 39
roles, 59, 62–63
    next level tips, 65
    possible roles, tasks, and reflection tool, 63–65
    reflection questions, 65
roles and timekeeping to keep everyone on track, 177
roles, tasks, and reflections chart, 64
running agenda template, 59, 76–77
    agenda template, 77–78
    next level tips, 79
    reflection questions, 77
    template option 2 sample, 77, 80
Ruthless Equity (Williams), xiii

S

safe word, 175–176

School Reform Initiatives website, 22
Schouten, M. E., 14
seeing what others don't (yet) see in themselves, 35, 38, 41
    addressing challenges, 187
    overcoming obstacles, 152
self-assessment, 141–143, 152
    addressing challenges, 184–185
    more done in less time with greater joy, 144–145
    next level tips, 146
    reflection questions, 146
    tools, 144–145
self-awareness, 20–21
self-management, 20–21
Senge, P., 3
sentence stems, 105, 113, 117, 121
    next level tips, 114
    reflection questions, 114
    tool, 113–114
setting deadlines for accomplishing the work, 184, 186
setting norms, 136
the shift from teacher to teacher team leader, 4–5
skills needed to collaborate and inquire, 5–6
SMART goals, 16, 68, 95, 106
social awareness, 20–21
Sonju, B., 26
Sparks, S. K., 26
specificity, 124, 152, 156
    generalization to specificity tool, 124–125
    next level tips, 126
    reflection questions, 126
spreading the contagion of joy, 35, 37, 38, 41
    addressing challenges, 187
    overcoming obstacles, 152
strategies, 39, 152
summary reflection questions
    overcoming obstacles, 154
    putting it all together, 83
synchronicity, 47
synergy, 172

T

teacher team leader actions, 7–8, 43–44
    addressing challenges from the field, 8, 171–188
    gaining momentum, 8, 87–121
    getting started, 8, 45–84
    overcoming obstacles, 123, 159–169
    refining your skills, 8
teacher team leader foundations, 7, 11–12
    defining your role, 7, 13–27
    understanding your approach, 7, 29–41

The Teacher Team Leader Handbook (Dumas), xiii, xvi–xvii

teacher teams
- as engines of improvements, 3–4
- the shift from teacher to teacher team leader, 4–5
- skills needed to collaborate and inquire, 5–6

team does not regularly revisit or revise norms, 174

team is not following the agenda, 176
- clarity of the work that needs to be done, 178
- clarity of why time as a team is important, 177
- not following norms, 177
- roles and timekeeping to keep everyone on track, 177

team is too large or too small, 172–173

team members are not self-aware
- of their domination of conversation, 181–182
- of their own silence, 183–184

team members are unsure of their own knowledge or skills, 181–184

team members don't feel heard, 181–184

team members don't have voice so they don't reflect members' needs, 173–174

team members who despise each other, 172–173

teams fails to follow through on decisions, 178
- clarity of what the decision is, 178–179
- clarity of who is responsible for implementation, 179
- lack of trust in the team, 180
- memory, 180
- processes for reporting back, 179–180
- timelines for implementation, 179

tentative language, 92–94

theory in action
- gaining momentum, 93, 97, 109, 115
- getting started, 46, 60
- overcoming obstacles, 127, 129, 133

think-do-say-feel tool, 48

third point, 57
- next level tips, 58
- reflection questions, 58

Thomas, T. F., 26

timelines for implementing a decision, 179

tinyurl.com/DumasTimeline website, 186

tips. *See also* next level tips
- for following norms, 61–62
- for group synchronicity tool, 48–49

tools
- "and," 101
- approachable and credible voice, 98
- beat gesture, 162–163
- breaking eye contact, 102–104
- building individual rapport, 134
- celebrations, 108–109
- decontaminating space, 130
- evidence tracking, 142
- fist to five, 146
- forced choice, 149
- frozen gesture, 160–161
- generalization to specificity, 124–125
- gestures and words of inclusion, 99
- hand position, 162–163
- I interrupt myself, 167–168
- mode of communication, 140
- others as experts, 112
- paraphrasing, 90
- potential work timeline, 106
- pulling together your learning reflection chart, 152
- say something, 112
- self-assessment, 144–145
- sentence stems, 113–114
- voice continuum, 97
- we do it together planning and reflection, 121
- whisper, 165–166
- you do it yourself and we do it together vignette chart, 152
- you do it yourself planning and reflection, 120

triggering defensiveness, 93

trust
- absence of, 18, 178, 180
- fear of failure and, 36
- individual rapport, 131–132

turn taking, 22

types of actions you and the team can take, 40

types of humor, 54

types of paraphrasing, 91

types of pausing tool, 55–56

U

understanding your approach, 39

understanding your approach, 7, 29, 41
- assumptions, 29–32
- intentions, 32–34
- mindsets, 34–37
- role and approach, 37–40

V

Van Soelen, T., 22

verbal processors, 181

Visible Learning (Hattie), 26

voice tone, 132, 134

volume and intensity, 132, 134

W

we do it together strategies, 8, 22
- celebrations, 105, 107–110
- data usage, 141–143, 152, 156
- fist to five, 141, 146–148, 152, 156
- forced choice, 141, 148–150, 152, 156
- gaining momentum, 104–105, 117
- inclusion, 59, 65–67
- landing page, 59, 66–68
- norms, 59–62
- others as experts, 105, 111–113
- outcomes, 59, 69–76
- overcoming obstacles, 141–150
- physical arrangement, 59–60
- planning and reflection tool, 121

planning the work, then working the plan, 105
- roles, 59, 62–65
- running agenda template, 59–79
- self-assessment, 141, 143–146, 152, 156
- sentence stems, 105, 113–114
- team teacher leader actions, 58–59
- theory in action, 109
- who will do what by when, 105, 114–115
- writing it down, 105, 110–111

Wellman, B. M. 6, 88
what your role is not, 15–16
when to use fourth point, 139
whisper, 159, 165, 169
- next level tips, 167
- phrases for using, 165–166
- reflection questions, 166

who will do what by when, 105, 114–115, 117, 121
- next level tips, 115
- reflection questions, 115

why your role is importance, 14–15
Williams, K. C., xiii–xvii, 35
wisdom, 130
words of inclusion, 100
work meanders and doesn't gain momentum, 184
- aligning agendas with the overall plan, 184, 186
- clarity of importance of the team, 184
- clarity of what the work of the team is, 184–185
- establishing an overall timeline for the year, 184–186
- setting deadlines for accomplishing the work, 184, 186

work timeline sample, 110
writing it down, 105, 110–111, 117, 121, 180
- next level tips, 111
- reflection questions, 111

Y

you can only control you, 30–31, 38, 41
- addressing challenges, 187
- overcoming obstacles, 152

you do it yourself strategies, 8
- and (not but), 87, 100–101
- anonymizing it, 124, 134–137, 152
- approachable and credible voice, 87, 96–98
- attribution, 124, 129–131, 152
- beat gesture, 159, 162–163, 169
- breaking eye contact, 87, 101–104
- breathing, 50–52
- decontaminating space, 124–128, 152
- fourth point, 124, 137–139m 152
- frozen gesture, 159–161, 169
- gaining momentum, 87–88
- gestures and words of inclusion, 87, 98–100
- group rapport, 47–50
- hand position, 159, 163–165, 169
- I interrupt myself, 159, 167–168, 169
- individual rapport, 124, 131–134, 152
- laughter and humor, 52–54
- mode of communication 124, 138–140, 152
- moves and techniques, 117
- overcoming obstacles, 123–141
- paraphrasing, 87–92
- pause, 54–57
- planning and reflection tool, 120
- questioning, 87, 92–96
- refining your skills, 159–169
- specificity, 124–126, 152
- teacher team leader actions, 46–47
- theory in action, 93, 97
- third point, 57–58
- whisper, 159, 165–167, 169
- you do it yourself planning and reflection tool, 169

Z

Zoller, K., 6

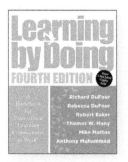

Learning by Doing, Fourth Edition
Richard DuFour, Rebecca DuFour, Robert Eaker, Thomas W. Many, Mike Mattos, and Anthony Muhammad
In this fourth edition of the bestseller *Learning by Doing*, the authors use updated research and time-tested knowledge to address current education challenges, from learning gaps exacerbated by the COVID-19 pandemic to the need to drive a highly effective multitiered system of supports.
BKG169

The 15-Day Challenge
Maria Nielsen
The 15-Day Challenge offers a step-by-step process for collaborative teams that builds on the three big ideas and four critical questions of a PLC at Work®. In each chapter, you'll find practical actions for how to support all students in mastering essential learning standards.
BKF969

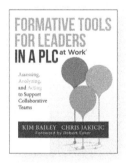

Formative Tools for Leaders in a PLC at Work®
Kim Bailey and Chris Jakicic
Learn, do, and lead with the guidance of *Formative Tools for Leaders in a PLC at Work®*. With this practical resource, you'll discover how to gather evidence from staff, use that evidence to gauge your PLC's effectiveness, and then make targeted decisions about next steps for improvement.
BKF990

How to Coach Leadership in a PLC
Marc Johnson
Through this how-to guide, you'll investigate why strong leadership is a crucial element of successful PLCs. Discover leadership strategies for building a collaborative culture, learn how to build shared values among educators, and explore techniques for monitoring progress on your PLC journey.
BKF667

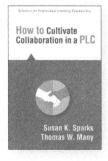

How to Cultivate Collaboration in a PLC
Susan K. Sparks and Thomas W. Many
Establishing a collaborative culture can significantly impact student achievement and professional practice. With this how-to guide, you'll gain clarity on the work of teams in a PLC, uncover the elements of effective team development, and learn to navigate challenges along the way.
BKF678

Visit SolutionTree.com or call 800.733.6786 to order.

Quality team learning **from authors you trust**

Global PD Teams is the first-ever **online professional development resource designed to support your entire faculty on your learning journey.** This convenient tool offers daily access to videos, mini-courses, eBooks, articles, and more packed with insights and research-backed strategies you can use immediately.

GET STARTED
SolutionTree.com/**GlobalPDTeams**
800.733.6786